CORPORATE POWER IN AMERICA

RALPH NADER'S CONFERENCE ON
CORPORATE ACCOUNTABILITY

CORPORATE POWER IN AMERICA

EDITED BY
RALPH NADER
AND MARK J. GREEN

GROSSMAN PUBLISHERS
NEW YORK   1973

Copyright © 1973 by Ralph Nader

First published in 1973 by Grossman Publishers
625 Madison Avenue, New York, N. Y. 10022

Published simultaneously in Canada by
Fitzhenry and Whiteside, Ltd.

SBN 670–24217–9

Library of Congress Catalogue Card Number: 72–80161

Printed in U. S. A.

PREFACE

Corporate Power in America is the product of our "Conference on Corporate Accountability" held in the fall of 1971 in Washington, D.C. The Conference brought together economists, political scientists, and lawyers who had distinguished themselves by their studies and commentary on corporate power. Their assignment: discuss proposals to restrain corporate power. We have long been familiar with the often adverse ways corporations affect people, but specific structural remedies to correct corporate abuses have not been forthcoming. The aim of the conference, and therefore of this book, is to push beyond diagnosis to prescription, to emphasize not merely what is wrong but ways to right it.

As even the table of contents indicates, there are many ways one can go about this. The contributors, as would be expected, often differ in their views and proposals. Some look to the courts, other dismiss the judiciary; some value regulation, others disdain it; some value "corporate democracy," others disparage it; some opt for public enterprise, others for competitive capitalism. Consequently, each writer is responsible for his own essay, as there was no attempt to harmonize the conflicting views. In fact, the hope was that out of the diversity of ideas would emerge proposals appealing both to the public and to policy-makers.

No proposal in this book will leap out as a panacea. Some may be hopeless while others may never have been tried. But some meshing of the best of them can make corporations responsible to more than merely their own self-contained rules and narrow horizons. As law professor Abe Chayes has written, "the modern business corporation emerged as the first successful institutional claimant of significant unregulated power since the nation-state established its title in the sixteenth and seventeenth centuries." Our large corporations are unparalleled as buffers shielding their executive decision-makers from public inquiry and accountability. A supposed democracy should not suffer the exercise of such uncontrolled power.

Ralph Nader
Mark Green

October, 1972
Washington, D.C.

CONTENTS

PART THREE
OTHER RESTRAINTS ON CORPORATE POWER

PART ONE

PROBLEMS OF
CORPORATE POWER

I

ON THE ECONOMIC IMAGE
OF CORPORATE ENTERPRISE

JOHN KENNETH GALBRAITH*

Any discussion of the modern corporation—of the two thousand largest firms that contribute around half of total product in the United States—requires, if it is to be useful, a remarkably basic decision. How, in relation to the state, are these firms to be regarded? Are they to be assimilated to the public sector of the economy? Or do they remain a part of what has always been called the private or market sector of the economy? Is one to have a public or a traditional view of the modern corporation?

In the traditional image of the corporation, a conceptually sharp, even immutable line divides the corporation from the state. There is government; there is private enterprise; the two do not meet. The distinction is deeply cherished by all whose careers and livelihoods are identified with the firms in question. No matter how intricately the firm is involved with the government, it is still private enterprise. This image of the corporation as something separate and wholly distinct from the state is not normally assumed to require any theoretical justification. It is the way things are—the way they were ordained to be. Only someone with an instinct for inconvenience suggests that

* Professor of Economics at Harvard University; director of Price Controls for the Office of Price Administration (1941–43); ambassador to India (1961–63); chairman of the Americans for Democratic Action (1967–69); author of *American Capitalism* (1951), *The Affluent Society* (1958), *The New Industrial State* (1967), and many other books and articles.

firms such as Lockheed or General Dynamics, which do most of their business with the government, make extensive use of plants owned by the government, have their working capital supplied by the government, have their cost overruns socialized by the government, and (as in the case of Lockheed) are rescued from misfortune on their nongovernmental business by the government, are anything but the purest manifestation of private enterprise. And this being so of Lockheed, the question certainly does not arise with American Telephone & Telegraph, General Motors, or General Electric.

But there is, of course, a theoretical justification. The corporation can be private because its operations are subject to the regulation—to the presumptively comprehensive discipline—of the market. The market allows of private purpose because it keeps it aligned with public purpose. The market is an expression of public preference and desire. The firm responds to the market. The firm is thus under public control and the public cannot be in conflict with itself. There are, admittedly, exceptions. Thus, no scholar of independent mind who was unpaid for his opinion would argue that Lockheed or General Dynamics was subordinate to the market. Or (the counterpart case) would it be suggested by many that these firms are subordinate to the political process—that the demand for their products is an expression of public need in which they themselves play a passive role. It is recognized that the Department of Defense persuades the modern weapons firm to produce what it needs. And it is recognized that these firms persuade the Department of Defense to need what they produce. Such firms retain their rationale as private enterprise not because of any conceivable theoretical justification but as a consequence of political inertia and caution. It is politically convenient so to regard them, and also for many politicians a great deal safer.

It is also recognized that the market rationale fails in respect of other large firms. They become large and powerful in their markets. Monopoly or oligopoly replaces competition. So great is their power that the state may be in some measure suborned. But the market in theory remains, though imperfectly, a decisive force. The monopoly pursues profits; what it can make is ultimately subject to the decisions of consumers as to what to buy or not to buy. Though he pays more than he should to the monopolist, the consumer is still presumably sovereign.

And there is a remedy for excessive power by the corporation both in markets and over the government, which is to decentralize the firm, to break it up. Then the original competitive power of the market is restored; the power to suborn the state is reduced or eliminated. The conditions under which private business can be private are thus re-established. But this alternative means recourse to the antitrust laws—laws, it is agreed even by their friends, which have not been effective over the past eighty years of their existence. Big business has indubitably become bigger, more powerful, more monopolistic; still, the antitrust laws are absolutely indispensable to the traditional imagery of the private corporation. Many cannot accept the modern corporation as it is, but they can accept it as it might be if the antitrust laws were enforced. And they can always imagine that some day these laws might be enforced. So with the aid of the antitrust laws they can remain, with no appreciable damage to conscience, with the traditional and essentially conservative position.

The public view of the corporation involves a basic break with the foregoing dialectic. It holds that not only Lockheed and General Dynamics but also A.T.&T., General Motors, Jersey Standard, United States Steel Corporation, and the other great corporations involve a clear break from the economy and polity of the classical market. As they grow and become more powerful, such firms acquire, increasingly, a public character. They become public institutions. The clichés of private enterprise survive but serve primarily to disguise the essentially public character of the great corporation, including its private exercise of what is, in fact, a public power. Such a corporation fixes its prices; it controls its costs; it persuades its consumers; it organizes its supply of raw materials; it has powerful leverage in the community; its needs are, *pro tanto*, sound public policy; it has, on frequent occasion, a hammerlock on the Pentagon.

In this view the large specialized weapons firm is only the extreme case. The line here between public and private enterprise is so exotic as to be impalpable. One can accept it only as a device for diverting the eyes of Congressional committees, the Comptroller General, and the general public away from things like executive compensation, lobbying, political activity by executives and employees, profits, and bureaucratic error or nonfeasance; in the case of an admitted public bureaucracy or a full-fledged public corporation, these items would invite highly unwelcome attention. It is a formula for hiding public business behind the cloak of corporate privacy.

Again, the specialized weapons firm only begins the analysis. General Motors sets the prices for its cars (and, in conjunction with the other automobile companies, for all cars) with public effect. And it negotiates wage contracts with public effect. And it designs cars and incorporates or rejects safety features with public effect. And it decides on engine design and emissions with public effect. And it persuades the public to its designs with public effect. And it power-fully influences highway construction with public effect. The public decisions of General Motors in the course of any year are far more consequential than those of any state legislature. So with other large firms.

The public view of the corporation not only accepts the tendency for it to assimilate itself to the state but regards this tendency as irreversible. It follows that there is no longer a presumption that the corporation has private affairs that are protected from public scrutiny. Nor is there any presumption that it must be free of public regulation or, for that matter, public ownership. On the contrary, the presumption is favorable to public intervention. The great corporation exercises public power, power that affects the health, well-being, and general happiness of those who are subject to it. This power is exercised—as even its possessors concede—in pursuit of the interests of the corporation. Since this power is no longer subject to the discipline of the market—is no longer *aligned* with public purposes by the market—there is no reason to believe that, except by accident, the exercise of public power by the corporation coincides with the public interest. There is, accordingly, a presumption in favor of action that aligns it with the public interest. So it comes about that on matters as diverse as design of products, acceptance or rejection of technical innovation (such as the SST), prohibition of adverse environmental effects both of the production and consumption of products, military policy, control of wages and prices, and control (as in the case of cigarettes) of public persuasion, one finds the legislature intervening to align corporate power with public purpose. In all this effort there must be an acute perception of the danger that the corporation will regulate its regulators. But it is to such regulation and other recognition of the public character of the firm, and not to the rehabilitation of market constraints, that one looks for protection and advance of the public interest.

It will not come to everyone as a shock that I think the public view of the corporation is the right one. The market will not be restored. Great currents of history cannot be reversed by small laws. The technological, capital, and planning requirements of modern economic activity are inconsistent with the classical market. As to the antitrust laws, they are eighty years old and the last really important dissolution occurred sixty years ago. Each new generation of reformers has held that only the feckless ineptitude and cowardice of their predecessors had kept the market from being restored. Then, their bravery notwithstanding, they too have failed. It is sensible to conclude that if these laws were going to work wonders for anyone but the lawyers, they would have worked their wonder by now.

They have become, in fact, a basic support to irresponsible corporate power. For they sustain the hope, and thus perpetuate the myth, of the all-powerful market. Consequently, they keep alive the illusion that business is private. They keep the burden of proof on those who propose regulation, or even disclosure. And they totally suppress the possibility (or specter) of public ownership. No one could do more for General Motors than this.

To recognize that the great corporation is essentially a public entity is to accept that its acts have a profoundly public effect. And that is to accept, as noted, the legitimacy of regulation that aligns its actions with public goals. Autonomy may still be accorded to the corporation. This is necessary for effective administration—for efficiency. But this is a pragmatic decision, and no principle is involved. Where the public interest—in safety of products, effect on environment, effect of price and wage settlements on the economy, the equity of profits and executive compensation—is at issue, there is no natural right to be left alone. Nor is there any natural right to secrecy. Nor is there any barrier in the case of the specialized weapons firms like Lockheed or incompetent ones like Penn Central to stripping away the purely artificial façade of private enterprise and converting the corporation into a fully public enterprise. In recent years church groups and other people of conscience have been agonizing over whether they should invest funds for good works in makers of weapons. It is a ridiculous question. They should be asking whether these firms should exist as private profit-making entities in a civilized state.

Some will say that the public view of the corporation reacts far too lightly to the problem of bureaucracy. At a time when we are learning to appreciate the power of the Pentagon, can we accept the continued existence of industrial bureaucracy? And, in the case of the weapons firms, can we think of adding the industrial to the public bureaucracy? The concern is well grounded. But we have the corporate bureaucracy now, and we have it now in a worse form. For the one thing more inimical than a bureaucracy that we see is a bureaucracy that we pretend not to see. The one thing worse than a General Motors whose public character is recognized is a General Motors whose public character is denied—and whose immunity to public regulation is defended on such grounds. The one thing worse than a General Dynamics or Lockheed that is publicly owned and publicly controlled is a General Dynamics or Lockheed that is publicly owned but privately controlled. There is no magic in stripping away the myth that the market controls the modern corporation or could be made to do so. But it is the first essential for any reform.

It will be suggested that I have not been exactly evenhanded in my judgments between the traditional and the public view of the corporation. And more is involved in the choice than the wholly explicable self-interest of economists in what they teach and write and lawyers in what they believe and practice. The defense of the market and the antitrust laws has never been a strictly secular phenomenon. Profoundly religious attitudes are involved. Neoclassical doctrine which lies back of these attitudes is more than a mere science; it is a highly developed theology. Added to the sense of unfairness will be the sense of outrage that, inevitably, focuses on anyone who appears to ride roughshod over established faith. Yet both truth and great questions are involved. One can sympathize with religious feeling when he cannot bow to it. As to evenhandedness, there is no natural obligation to be neutral between truth and error—between the right path in economic development and the wrong. Economics is not a branch of the television business.

The great issue that is involved is the future structure of the economic system in the most profound sense. Although it is accepted doctrine in Detroit, not many scholars would insist that the modern great corporation is the ultimate achievement of man. The public view of the corporation portends a public development, foreseeing that the great corporations eventually become public enterprises. It invites the use of a word long banned from reputable discussion in the United States, or whispered only among minority cults, which is socialism. The traditional view, as its proponents will be the first to concede, holds up no such prospect—or specter. And that, indeed, is another way of describing its service to the *status quo*. For as long as there is a serious effort to turn back to the eighteenth century, there will assuredly be no advance to the twenty-first or even the twentieth.

II

GOVERNING THE GIANT CORPORATION

ROBERT A. DAHL*

In this essay I propose to focus exclusively on alternative ways of controlling the *large* nonfinancial corporation. By "large" I mean the two hundred to five hundred largest nonfinancial business firms in the United States. Although they are only a tiny proportion of the 1.4 million corporations that file tax returns, they play a role of exceptional importance, present special problems of government and control, and may well require solutions that might be inappropriate for smaller firms.

TWO AXIOMS

It is important to establish at the outset two propositions that seem to me elementary and obvious; these axioms, nonetheless, are in this country widely ignored and even denied:

First axiom: Every large corporation should be thought of as a social enterprise, that is, an entity whose existence and decisions can be justified only insofar as they serve public or social purposes. At one time this axiom was taken for granted. From the outset corporations were (as they still are) not only chartered by the state but they

---

* Professor of Political Science at Yale University; President of the American Political Science Association (1966–67); author of *Congress Foreign Policy* (1940), *Who Governs?* (1961), *After the Revolution?* (1970) and others.

were often, as with the American colonies and the British East India
Company, treated as an arm of the state. Even if the axiom tended
to be lost sight of in the later nineteenth century, and is often forgotten today, it is absurd to regard the corporation simply as an
enterprise established for the sole purpose of allowing profit-making.
One has simply to ask: Why should citizens, through *their* government, grant special rights, powers, privileges, and protections to any
firm except on the understanding that its activities are to fulfill *their*
purposes? Corporations exist because we allow them to do so. Why
should we allow them to exist? Surely only insofar as they benefit us
in some sense.

*Second axiom: Every large corporation should be thought of as a
political system, that is, an entity whose leaders exercise great power,
influence, and control over other human beings.* It would take enormous semantic refinement and an excessive addiction to purely legalistic conceptions to establish that the city of New Haven, for example,
is a political system while General Motors is not. I do not mean to
erase the distinction between political systems that have a legitimate
authority to exercise physical sanctions and political systems that
lack this authority, even if that distinction is slightly blurred. Nevertheless, by its decisions the large corporation may

—cause death, injury, disease, and severe physical pain, *e.g.*,
by decisions resulting in pollution, poor design, inadequate quality
control, plant safety, and working conditions.

—impose severe deprivations of income, well-being, and effective personal freedom, *e.g.*, by decisions on hiring and firing,
employment, discrimination, and plant location.

—exercise influence, power, control, and even coercion over
employees, consumers, suppliers, and others, *e.g.*, by manipulating
expectations of rewards and deprivations, by advertising, propaganda, promotions, and demotions, not to mention possible illegal
practices.

My assumption then is that the large corporation should be considered as both a *political* system and a *social* enterprise. I would not
have labored what seems to me obvious were I not troubled by two
images I retain from the last GM stockholder's meeting. One was a
stockholder rising repeatedly to insist that the sole reason for GM's

existence is to make money for its owners, and the other a remark by
the chairman of the board and presiding officer to the effect that GM
was most definitely *not* a political system. Both my axioms were
denied in the space of a few minutes.

FOUR PROBLEMS

If the large corporation is a social enterprise and a public political
system, the government of the corporation should be very much a
public matter. We not only have a right but an obligation to examine
it critically. Yet it is a curious and somewhat depressing fact that we
know very much less about how large corporations are governed
than we do about such political systems as towns, cities, states, and
the federal government. Why? Largely because the division of labor
among academics and professional observers has made the politics
of business no one's academic business, while ideologues have concentrated on subsidiary questions.

To fill this gap in our understanding, and ultimately in public
polity, I therefore propose that a major investigation be launched by
a committee of the U.S. Senate—either the Antitrust and Monopoly
Subcommittee of the Judiciary Committee, or, because labor is so
deeply involved, the Committee on Labor and Public Welfare, or if
neither of these, a specially constituted committee. It should be
equipped with a substantial professional staff, should plan to hold
hearings over a period of at least a year—for fact-finding, public
education, and examination of alternative solutions—and should
finally formulate legislation dealing with at least four problems: control, ownership, efficiency, and size.

I. *Control: What are the most appropriate ways of governing the large corporation in the United States in the foreseeable future?*

It is useful analytically to distinguish between the internal government of the corporation and external controls over it. There is a
chicken-and-egg problem, however, since what we assume to be possible and desirable at the one level has a crucial bearing on what we
conclude will be possible and desirable at the other.

EXTERNAL CONTROLS. We could rely on the willingness and capacity of self-perpetuating managements, as at present, to fulfill public purposes. This requires a degree of blind faith in leadership that we would surely reject for the government of states; indeed, our whole political heritage requires that we reject it. The problem is exactly equivalent to the ancient problem of classical political philosophy: a system ruled by virtuous and wise philosopher kings might be highly satisfactory, but what guarantees do we have that rulers will be either virtuous or wise? Too much human experience argues against the likelihood of finding a satisfactory solution along these lines, and nothing would run more directly counter to the American political tradition. Are we to have one political philosophy for governing the state and another for governing the economy? I do not think that is, in the long run, desirable.

If large numbers of Americans ever became convinced that they have no control over large corporations, through the market or otherwise, and depend therefore solely on the good will and wisdom of corporate managers, they would rise up at once and insist upon more direct external controls. Doubtless what would then be demanded would be regulatory commissions of some sort, perhaps an ICC for every industry. One has only to mention the ICC to realize why this solution would be unsatisfactory. If Congress and the President have been unable or unwilling to prevent regulatory commissions from becoming captives of their industries, what reason have we to hope for better results simply by increasing the number of regulatory commissions?

One might then opt for some form of direct government operation of industry or at any rate a more direct method of making decisions about goals, priorities, prices, output, and quality. At one time there was among many socialists and planners a faith that direct controls of some sort, uncontaminated by competition, would insure harmony between public purposes and needs on the one hand, and the actions of economic enterprises on the other. Since then a considerable body of experience, not least that of the Soviet Union, has convinced all except a few die-hards that a permanent arrangement of this kind would be unsatisfactory, particularly for a highly advanced economy in a democratic country during peacetime. For the question arises as to how the government managers would have the knowledge and incentives to make publicly desirable decisions. What *is* publicly desirable? The criterion of profit, which the GM stockholder insisted was the only one to be taken into account, at least has the advantage of being concrete and understandable. But argument, debate, and conflict over the most desirable public policies is what politics in a democratic country is all about.

Consequently, either the new philosopher-kings are to be immune from democratic politics or they are not. If they are immune, then everything we know suggests that we shall simply have one small set of people imposing their preferences, values, and priorities on the rest of us. If they are not immune, how—in the total absence of competition and market controls—can the crude output of public opinion, pressure groups, parties, elections, Congressional politics, the White House, and the bureaucracies so shape the millions of concrete decisions made by the five hundred largest firms that they accord with the preferences, goals, and values of the people of the United States? If anyone has ever come up with a clear answer, I am unaware of it.

Thus I am driven to the conclusion that no system of governing the large corporations of this country can be satisfactory unless markets and competition exercise a significant influence over the decisions of economic enterprises. To achieve this external control might well require breaking up giant corporations into smaller units, a step which would not necessarily impair the advantages of scale so often alleged to justify gargantuan enterprises. The conclusion favoring competition stands, I think, no matter how the enterprises are governed internally, or how they are owned; it is a point I shall return to shortly. But first, let me summarize this section by stating two of the questions to which a Senate committee should, I believe, turn its attention:

1. How can controls over large enterprises, exercised by markets and competition, be strengthened to effectuate public purpose?

2. Given the defects and limits of such forms of external control, what additional types are required? In short, what would a full array of appropriate external controls look like, particularly as they might be embodied in a set of concrete institutions that could reasonably be expected to operate successfully in the United States?

INTERNAL GOVERNMENT. Assuming that the corporation's rulers make decisions within some context of external controls, how should the firm be governed internally? The most popular alternative seems to be *control by stockholders*, or what is sometimes called *stockholder democracy*. Yet there are serious difficulties with this solution. The most lethal objection goes to its very premise, that investors, whether individuals or firms, have some special right to govern the firms in which they invest. Beyond the anachronism of viewing stock as a "property right," I can discover absolutely no moral or philosophical basis for such a special right. Why investors and not consumers, workers, or, for that matter, the general public? It would be utterly absurd to argue that investors will suffer more from bad decisions; it is, certainly, a very curious view of suffering, particularly if one thinks of large institutional investors.

Nor can it be argued that investors are particularly interested in running the firm, or especially competent to do so. We can hardly test the matter of competence since, as everyone knows, stockholders simply do not have much to do with governing the large corporations and have never displayed any great desire to do so. If it is difficult to see why stockholders should be granted special rights in the government of the large corporation, it is equally difficult to imagine why they would become sufficiently interested in exercising much real control over the managers. In short, stockholders neither should nor will govern the firm democratically.

Finally, as we have recently been reminded by the Supreme Court, democracy means something like one man, one vote. Certainly it does not mean one share, one vote. Yet either solution seems unsatisfactory. If it is hard to establish the general claim for stockholder control as against control by consumers or workers, it becomes even harder to argue that by acquiring a single share of stock one should acquire a theoretically equal share in decisions, and yet deny any such right to an employee who may have worked the better part of his life for a firm. If, on the other hand, stockholder control is merely intended to insure that the firm's decisions accord with the preferences of investors who own a majority of the stock, the reform seems barely worth the effort.

A second alternative is *control by employees* or, as it is often called, *workers' control*. There the interest of investors, consumers, and the general public would be protected by a greatly strengthened array of external controls, including competition and the administrative and legal enforcement of general standards, while the firm itself would be governed by the employees or their representatives. Perhaps the two major sources of doubt about this solution are whether the external controls can be made sufficiently effective in protecting all the other affected interests, and the effects of such a system of government on incentives and productivity. There are, as we shall see, some reasons for thinking that the impact on incentives could be highly beneficial. The overwhelming advantage of this solution is that it is the only alternative capable of providing for a democratic government within the large enterprise.

A third alternative, *interest group representation*, has been advocated in a great variety of forms, some of them socialist, as with the Guild Socialists, some nonsocialist, as with the variant proposed by the authors of Campaign GM II last year. It rests on the key assumption that external controls cannot provide adequate protection for the various interests affected by a firm's decisions—investors, consumers, employees, dealers, the general public—and that therefore representatives of these interests must participate directly in governing the firm. The great advantage of this solution, then, is that it would, or could, bring to bear on key decisions perspectives and values now generally ignored. It would, I think, represent a marked improvement over what we now have. Unlike employee control, however, it would not represent much in the way of democratization, since decisions would be made mainly through an externally imposed hierarchy.

A fourth alternative is internal governing jointly by representatives elected by workers and stockholders, or, as it is sometimes called, *co-determination*. This solution, a blend of workers' control and interest-group representation, somewhat arbitrarily selects two of the major interests to sit on the governing board, perhaps on the assumption that the other interests can be adequately protected by external controls. Co-determination is prescribed for the German steel and coal industries by a 1951 law, devised under British occupation, and is prescribed in part for the rest of German industry by a 1952 law providing that one-third of the members of the supervisory board (roughly equivalent to our board of directors) must be elected by employees in a secret ballot. Although advocates make only modest claims for the results of co-determination, I notice that a coalition formed by representatives of employees and the state recently evicted the chief executive of Volkswagen.

Three more questions can now be suggested to the proposed Senate committee:

   3. What are the major alternative constitutional forms for the internal government of the large firm?

   4. What are the comparative advantages and disadvantages of each?

   5. What model is most appropriate for maximizing the achievement of American public values, most notably democracy?

II. *Ownership: What is the most appropriate form of ownership to achieve and maintain the kind of government desired?*

I have said that while the analysis of the government of the large enterprise has fallen through the hole in the large, loose mesh created by the intersecting interests of academics, scholars, and the legal profession, it has also suffered from the propensity of ideologues for concentrating on subsidiary questions. The question of ownership is, I believe, an *ignis fatuus* that for well over a century has led ideological searchers into the swamps. The problem of ownership is clearly subordinate to the problem of control. One must first decide how he believes economic enterprises should be *governed;* only then is it productive to ask what forms of *ownership* will best obtain and sustain the desired form of government. To put the matter in somewhat formal language, the form of ownership is clearly not sufficient for determining the form of government of an enterprise. Whether a specific form of ownership is a necessary condition for certain forms of government is less clear.

That the form of ownership does not, per se, determine how an economic enterprise will be governed is confirmed by seeing the similarities resulting from radical variations in the form of ownership. Highly hierarchical, authoritarian government of firms has existed under the extremes of private and public ownership. The old liberal conception of a privately owned enterprise consisting of freely contracting parties operating essentially without hierarchy and power relationships was virtually all myth. The factory was typically a kind of despotism until trade unions began to make inroads on the powers of management. Yet socialists who hoped that hierarchy would vanish if ownership were transferred to the state, or to a disembodied entity called the people, were profoundly disillusioned to discover that, far from ushering in industrial democracy, government ownership merely preserved or even strengthened hierarchical authority. The bosses' names and faces may have changed; their power remained the same, or increased. Probably in no industrial country, it appears, is the domination of management so great and the influence of workers so slight as in the economic enterprises in the Soviet Union.

Although the form of ownership is not then a sufficient condition for any particular form of government, it might be that some ways of governing an enterprise would necessarily require some particular form of ownership. Although I feel some genuine uncertainty on this point, and feel it needs exploration in depth, I am persuaded that pat ideological answers will not do. In at least two respects, the array of alternatives simply cannot be contained within the simple-minded dualisms of the Grand Old Alternatives as conceived in the nineteenth century.

First, ownership is a complex bundle of rights, privileges, and obligations that can be combined or split up in a great variety of ways. It appears to me that when we begin to think concretely about the kinds of structures, behaviors, and processes needed to achieve a particular kind of government, ownership loses concreteness and begins to dissolve like the Cheshire cat. Thus, if stockholders—whether individuals, institutional investors, or government agencies—were denied the right to vote for directors, and if the right were lodged exclusively with employees, what would "ownership" or "property" in the corporation now mean? Possibly a disembodied smile will remain permanently hanging in midair, but I don't see much of the cat.[1]

Second, the Grand Old Alternatives hardly conceived of the richly chaotic reality that has developed over a century in the way that ownership can be distributed. For example, we can imagine a government agency owning anything from zero to 100 percent of the stock of a particular corporation. From all we know of the large corporation, it is safe to predict that the potential power to name the directors and choose the management would pass to the agency long before 50 percent of the stock was obtained, and ordinarily, no doubt, closer to 10 percent. Whether the agency would choose to convert that potential power into actually exercised power, whether it would do so wisely, and whether the agency officials would in time be captured and subverted by the management are all interesting and important questions, but they do not undermine the main point: that there are an indefinite number of possibilities between 100 percent private ownership by individuals and 100 percent government ownership by the federal government.

In view of the complex choice of possibilities by which the bundle of rights and privileges called property can be split up, and also the ways in which particular rights can be distributed among individuals and institutions, a sixth question for a Senate committee to consider can be posed:

6. To achieve and maintain the most desirable form of government of large economic enterprises in the United States, what form or forms of ownership are most appropriate?

Now I realize as well as anyone that even to ask this question will seem to challenge dogmas that corporations are desperately anxious to sustain. Yet the best way to deal with the unthinkable and the unmentionable is to start thinking out loud and making public mention. Americans have too long suffered under the burden of a public ideology that employed defensible ideas of private property to block off attacks on giant and powerful political institutions that were never any part of the American political tradition and which would have left the Founders bleakly pessimistic about the future of their handiwork. A great many ordinary Americans have a strong sense that something is profoundly wrong in conceiving of General Motors as if it were substantially equivalent to a family farm or small business. Yet so long as our public ideology provides no clear grounds for making a distinction, proclaims that General Motors is a "private" business, and fails to insist that it is, rather, a public political system, then we shall continue to find it difficult, even impossible, to approach economic enterprise with the clinical detachment and clear-headedness we need. Needless to say, no group knows this elementary fact better than those who defend the existing government of big business.

III. *Efficiency: What are the comparative efficiencies—economic and otherwise—of different alternatives?*

At least up to this point, I have no doubt betrayed my professional biases as a political scientist by emphasizing the political or constitutional aspects of the large corporation. Admittedly, it would be foolish to argue that the more or less conventional criteria of economic performance are somehow irrelevant in answering the question of what form of government is best. I would, however, advance a few words of caution.

Economic efficiency in its narrower senses is by no means the only relevant criterion for judging the performance of economic enterprises. Fortunately, for most tasks slave labor appears to be much less productive than free labor. But suppose that were not true. Would we advocate the introduction of slavery—in its traditional or more recent forms—because of the gains in output? Although I am very far from an undiluted or uncritical admirer of youth, today's or any other, it is true that young people often see matters with a clarity denied to those of us who, being older, have been more thoroughly brainwashed by our culture. And it is one of the characteristics of many young people today, more than at any other time in my experience, that they sense a hollowness in economic activity that merely satisfies the marginal, material wants of people who, like themselves, have been satiated since infancy. Because we live in a country and a world in which urgent material needs are unmet, it is insensitive, self-indulgent, and dishonest to advocate that the world's poor use holiness to alleviate their poverty. Nonetheless, a change in perspectives is occurring in the highly affluent countries where initially the youth and gradually much of the society—after all, youth does age—will realize that a less historical and culture-bound view of efficiency involves a much broader range of human needs and satisfactions than are usually considered in comparing the performance of economic enterprises. Anxieties over threats to health and environment are already speeding this change in perspectives. But once we begin to think more freely about relevant inputs and outputs, we might have to face such questions as how much we are willing to pay for an increment of self-respect, dignity, and pride.

Still, efficiency and productivity in the narrower sense are important. So far as I have been able to discover, when we ask about the productivity consequences of alternative forms of governing the firm, we enter into a domain occupied mainly by myth, speculation, and fantasy. The point is that despite the prevailing American dogma, the matter seems to be almost completely open. Simply to illustrate how very wrong it would be to jump for the pat answers, let me quote the conclusions of a professor of economics at Cornell, Jaroslav Vanek, arrived at, admittedly, after a purely theoretical analysis:

> Stated very briefly, the conclusion is that the labor-managed productive organization comes the closest to, and may even surpass, a self-employed individual with respect to the attainment of an optimal balance between income on the one hand and effort (*i.e.*, duration, quality, or intensity of work) on the other. Stated in more conventional terminology, it can be said that the labor-managed enterprise appears to be the best form of productive organization (of more than one individual) from the point of view of the incentive it gives to its members.
>
> If we postulate that any firm—whether capitalist, Soviet-type, or labor-managed—must operate with a certain limit of minimum acceptable effort, then normally the labor-managed firm will perform by far the most efficiently—that is, will produce the highest output in quality and volume. Moreover, if such a limit were abolished, it would be only the labor-managed firm that could remain in operation. The capitalist and Soviet-type firms (adhering to a fixed-wage scheme) would be bound to go out of business.[2]

Those theoretical conclusions seem to be supported by the findings of Seymour Melman, a well-known professor of industrial engineering at Columbia, who undertook what must be the only study of its kind—a comparison of carefully matched samples of enterprises under managerial and under cooperative control. After comparing productivity of labor, productivity of capital, efficiency of management, and costs of administration for twelve industrial enterprises in

Israel, six under managerial control and six administered cooperatively, Melman concluded:

1. Industrial enterprises of a modern technical sort can be operated under various modes of decision making. Factory production with powered equipment and division of labor can be efficiently performed without parallel use of managerial decision making. These findings contradict the mystique of technology-determined form in organization of production.

2. Cooperative decision making is a workable method of production decision making in the operation of industrial enterprise.

3. The equal or greater efficiency of operation found in the cooperative, as against the managerially controlled enterprises, is not anticipated from conventional knowledge in economics and industrial management.

4. This investigation does not establish the probability by which cooperative decision making in industrial production may be, systematically, more efficient than managerial control. It is demonstrated that cooperative decision making in modern industry can be as efficient or a more efficient mode of decision making than managerial control. This capability is linked to the pervasive motivational and operational effects of cooperation in decision making and in production, pressing toward stability in operations, and thereby toward optimal use of industrial facilities.

Melman goes on to say:

The findings of this comparative study suggest that social scientists, and others engaged in research on organization, ought to explore the problems of cooperative versus managerial decision making within various economies and cultural contexts, as well as in laboratory and field experiments. Diverse approaches to these problems, exploring the variability of performance of diverse modes of organization, should add to knowledge and have operational importance, insofar as variation in organization can produce meaningful differences in economic efficiency or enlarge the available array of options for viable social organization.[3]

Thus, the seventh question for our Senate committee is:

7. Measured against a variety of costs and benefits, what are likely to be the relative efficiencies of alternative methods of governing the large firm?

IV. *Size: What are the advantages and disadvantages of scale?*

I have throughout been focusing on the very large firm, the giant economic entity. This is because giant firms, like giant states, have and exercise great power and influence, and what they do has a gigantic impact on all of us. An eighth question then is:

8. To what extent are large firms required in order to benefit from the advantages of scale?

The conventional argument that giantism is necessary in order to take advantage of the economies of scale ought to be looked at with very great skepticism. So far as I am able to determine, there is very little in the way of reliable public knowledge on this question, and none that justifies giantism. A good deal of the data needed to settle the question are made inaccessible to the public by secrecy in the firms themselves. Nonetheless, using the best evidence available, a number of analysts have convincingly argued that while economies of scale exist up to a point, many industries have firms which greatly exceed in size what is necessary to secure the advantages of scale.[4] For example, Graham Bannock, an English economist who has worked for Ford and Rover in addition to stints with the Economist Intelligence Unit and OECD, has analyzed the available data in his book *The Juggernauts*. He flatly rejects the popular view that "economies of scale account for most of the increase in output per man in modern industry over, say, fifty years ago."

Even if, as I think is very likely the case, the giant firm is typically beyond the economic optimum, there may nonetheless be advantages to the firm—or rather to its rulers—from its giant size and vast resources. With firms as with states, giantism increases relative power and influence. In a conflict, the giant stands a better chance of surviving, and, in the clinch, neutralizing, defeating, or destroying its enemies. Its capacity for survival results not from efficiencies but simply from access to much greater resources, which the rulers can use to intimidate opponents. Nazi Germany was not a better or more efficient society than the Netherlands, or Belgium, or Denmark, or Norway—but it could overrun them. The USSR, hardly a paragon of efficiency, could defeat Finland. Then, too, just as the status, prestige, income, and wealth of the rulers of a state tend to become bound up with the power and resources of the state, so too the status, prestige, income, and wealth of the rulers of a corporation tend to be greater and more secure the larger the firm. In both cases, society is asked to pay for the psychic and material benefits rulers gain from empire; and ordinary folk are asked by rulers and their ideologues to believe that they also benefit from the grandeur of empire. As it has never been demonstrated that the giant, expansionist state benefits the ordinary people who are regularly called on to sacrifice themselves in its behalf, so too, though in a more subtle way, it appears that business firms have tremendous expansionist drives quite unrelated to the welfare of society in general.

III

THE POLITICS OF
CORPORATE POWER

FRED R. HARRIS*

In the spring of 1971, *Fortune* magazine, that sounding board of populist thought, carried a long and thoughtful article on Ralph Nader. It described his fights to protect the public, it assessed his impact on government and business, and it speculated on his motivations. In the end, *Fortune* came to what it obviously thought was an astounding conclusion about Nader, namely that "Behind all those good works in the name of consumerism . . . his real target is corporate power."[1]

We can be glad at least that *Fortune* has finally gotten the word. Whether the symptom is car bumpers as strong as tissue paper, import quotas that raise the price of gasoline by six cents a gallon, unemployment in the steel industry when it operates at only half of its capacity, or farm subsidies that redistribute income from working people to the rich—the problem is corporate power. This power is not only economic—the ability to set prices without regard to market pressures or to manipulate consumer demand. It is also political—the ability to use the public government to obtain private economic goals. Corporate power means the ability of big corporations to have more than their fair share of influence over the decisions of government.

The fact that special interests are politically powerful is not, of

* United States Senator (D.) from Oklahoma; chairman of the Democratic National Committee (1969–70); author of *Now is the Time* (1971) and the forthcoming *The New Populism*.

course, a new idea. At the turn of the century Senator Boies Penrose (R.–Pa.) candidly told a business group, "I believe in a division of labor. You send us to Congress; we pass laws under . . . which you make money; . . . and out of your profits you further contribute to our campaign fund to send us back again to pass more laws to enable you to make more money."[2] In 1930 political scientist H. L. Childs wrote, "Periodic elections are turning into periodic competitions between personalities, while the day-to-day process of governing a great nation turns into a continuous balancing of pressing interests of more and more highly perfected organized group interests."[3]

This trend has certainly been continued; the evidence is everywhere that concentrated financial interests, somehow, obtain preferential treatment from the government. Lockheed Aircraft gets bailed out of its financial problems, while ten thousand small businesses a year go bankrupt.[4] The big steel, automobile, and insurance companies were allowed to raise prices during Phase I of the wage-price freeze, while auto workers were not permitted to get already negotiated wage increases. Air pollution guidelines proposed by the Environmental Protection Agency were weakened under pressure from big business. Government patent policies were changed quietly one day to allow private companies to profit from publicly financed research. Roughly half of the $3.7 billion of tax money spent per year on agricultural subsidies goes to the top 5 percent of agribusinesses that dominate the production and sales of farm products. ITT seemingly lobbies the federal government into sheer exhaustion, and consequently is permitted to keep the acquisition they wanted most—the Hartford Fire Insurance Company.

All of these are monuments to the political power of big corporations. Corporate power in the political process is a reality. You don't have to believe that, somewhere, there are twelve bankers, politicians, and corporate executives who meet once a week to decide the future of America—there aren't—to see that General Motors has more to say about federal air pollution standards than you or I or even millions like us do. And you don't have to believe that politicians regularly receive bribes—they don't—to see that David Rockefeller gets a better hearing in the Congress than does the average American workingman or woman. Why violate the law by bribing public officials when there are legal and more traditional methods of persuasion that are more effective? Among these methods are campaign contributions, advertising, lobbying, and government-business job exchanges.

Getting elected even to local office today costs thousands of dollars, while running for the nomination and office of President costs millions. Richard Nixon spent about five hundred thousand dollars in 1960 to get his party's nomination for President; in 1968 it cost him more than ten million dollars. Hubert Humphrey, before dropping out after the West Virginia primary, spent about two hundred and fifty thousand dollars in 1960; in 1968, after a late start and without competing with Senators McCarthy and Kennedy in the costly primaries, he still spent about four million dollars prior to the convention. In 1968 all candidates for nomination from both parties spent around forty million dollars prior to the party conventions.[5] Herbert Alexander, director of the Citizens Research Foundation, has estimated that, altogether, it cost about one hundred million dollars to elect the President in 1968, if the costs of the primary campaigns, conventions, and fall campaigns are all included.[6]

Unless he is personally wealthy, a politician has to turn to others to finance a campaign. While labor unions contribute substantial amounts, it is the executives of big corporations who provide the bulk of the money. Senator Russell Long, who as chairman of the Senate Finance Committee is in a position to know, has estimated that 95 percent of campaign contributions at the national level come from businessmen.[7] Mr. Alexander also reports that in 1968 there were quite a few individual contributions in the one hundred thousand dollar and above range. It is unreasonable to expect that this generosity is always forgotten.

While campaign spending is one of the better known expressions of corporate power, it is hardly the only one. Big corporations can use their regular channels of communications—that is, advertising—to translate economic power into political power. What was meant to give consumers a choice in a competitive market can be changed into a tool of political persuasion. A good example is the case of Ford Motor Company and air bags.

At the beginning of 1971, the National Highway Traffic Safety Administration recommended that air bags be required on all cars manufactured after April 1973. This conclusion followed extensive tests showing that thousands of lives are lost in auto accidents where the victim is thrown out of, or against the car; a tested and reliable air bag device has been developed that would inflate in the split second after impact, keeping the driver and passengers effectively in their seats. Air bags are hardly a novel approach to auto safety. The first patent for one was taken out in 1952, and they have been tested on aircraft and surface vehicles for many years. In fact, no less an authority than GM's president, Edward N. Cole, has attributed "extremely good reliability" to air bags.

To Ford, however, along with the rest of the automobile industry, air bags did not make sense for various reasons, one of them being the expense of tooling up for such a lifesaving system. So Ford undertook to "educate" the public. On June 21, 1971, a full-page ad appeared in twenty-seven of the nation's largest circulation newspapers and magazines. Headlined "An up-to-date report on air bags. The good news. The bad news," this huge advertising campaign, paid for as a tax deductible "business expense," purported to give both sides of the issue; in fact, it gave only one side—Ford's. The information given was so biased and so inaccurate that the Department of Transportation (DOT), not otherwise known for courage in the face of Detroit's demands, issued a point-by-point rebuttal of the Ford ads.[8]

This ad campaign, coupled with some high-level lobbying that even the *Wall Street Journal* found excessive, led to a hurried new look by the government. As a result, the date for requiring air bags was moved back more than two years to August 1975. Until then, the automakers will have the option of installing the "buckle starter system," seat belts that are connected with the ignition in such a way that the car won't start without the belt being fastened. This buckle starter system had been considered by the Department of Transportation before, and rejected. In fact, three months before they allowed its use for the next four years, DOT officials had described the system as "not acceptable to the consumer" and said that "most of those who do not presently wear lap and shoulder belts would defeat the system by some means such as buckling the belts behind them, cutting wires, etc." But this buckle starter system had one thing going for it: it was cheaper to install than air bags. So from Ford's point of view, it was a much better idea, and Ford's better ideas are the ones that are listened to in Washington.

Taking a leaf from Ford's book, the Transportation Department announced its cave-in on the air bag question with a press release that began, "Secretary of Transportation, John A. Volpe, said today that he has decided not to delay the requirement that a completely passive restraint system, such as air bags, be installed in all 1976 models."[9] Not until the fourth paragraph did DOT get around to mentioning that the rules had been changed to allow the buckle starter system until 1976 models instead of requiring air bags in 1973, all of which may show that Ford has no monopoly on misleading advertising.

Ford is not the only company using its advertising budget for political purposes. Any big corporation that wants to explain its case to the American people can buy millions of dollars worth of TV, radio, and newspaper advertising at the average taxpayer's expense. According to the tax laws, corporations get a tax deduction for advertising on public issues as "ordinary and necessary business expenses." Within the last year, we have seen the oil companies' tax deductible ads telling how great the fishing is around their offshore rigs, with the clear implication that federal action to prevent pollution from these rigs is unnecessary. The railroads have hired Wally Schirra to point out to the public how vital the railroads are to the American economy, and how vital subsidies are to the railroads' finances. These ads include implied pleas for government subsidies, such as, "Railroads haul more of the things you need than all the trucks, airplanes and barges put together. Quite a performance . . . when you consider they do this job with just about no government aid."[10] Commercial spots also include criticism of railroad regulation that is not quite as subtle. "Well, times have changed, but the great train hold-up still goes on, in a way. Caused by . . . out-of-date regulation. . . . Let's put up-to-date laws in the hands of the men who do the regulating."[11]

In the fall of 1971, a group of President Nixon's big business backers organized to promote the antiworkingman economic policies of the Administration. Hobart Lewis of *The Reader's Digest* and William Marriott, the hotel and restaurant chain owner, set up "Citizens for a New Prosperity" (CNP). It solicited tax deductible contributions from corporations as "ordinary and necessary business expenses" for a propaganda campaign aimed at convincing the American people that the New Economic Policy served more people than just the President's wealthy friends. Their efforts included full-page ads, the distribution of newsletters telling how well the New Economic Policy was working, instructions on how to place ads in local newspapers and how to get a business firm involved in "Citizens for a New Prosperity."

On November 15, 1971, I wrote to Mr. Johnnie Walters, Commissioner of Internal Revenue, urging him to deny corporate tax deductions for this blatantly political project. Mr. Walters replied by saying that "a determination as to the deductibility of amounts contributed must be made on the basis of all the facts and circumstances in each case . . ."[12] In practice, this amounted to a flat rejection of my suggestion. It is interesting to note that one of the facts in all cases will be Section 1.162–20 (c) (4) of IRS regulations, which states that "No deduction shall be allowed under Section 162 (a) for any amount paid or incurred (whether by way of contribution, gift, or otherwise) in connection with any attempt to influence the general public, or segments thereof, with respect to legislative matters, elections, or referendums." This alone should constitute sufficient grounds for denying a tax deduction for contributions, but CNP and its big business supporters, along with the IRS, apparently don't think so. It is of more than passing interest that the cochairmen of The Reader's Digest Association contributed $49,851 to the GOP in 1968, and Lewis himself donated $3,000. In addition, during the 1960s when Nixon was out of office, *The Reader's Digest* printed eleven of his articles and sponsored a number of his foreign travels, thus giving him valuable publicity through those lean years.[13]

Campaign spending and corporate political advertising are two of the legal, widely used, and obviously effective ways of turning concentrated economic power into concentrated political power. Direct lobbying with members of the Congress and industry regulators is another legal technique and, like advertising, is tax deductible. Charles R. Ross, a former member of the Federal Power Commission, knows the many forms, and effects, this lobbying can have:

> Once on the scene, the regulator is confronted by sweet-talking top executivies, tough, hard-hitting lawyers and experts, even including

experts in bugging. The doors of exclusive clubs are opened to the innocent regulators. The lure of life in the lap of luxury with minions to anticipate every desire, and until recently, without any thought as to costs, becomes not just a dream but an actuality if one doesn't get too smart. On the other hand, if one does get too smart, it's back to the farm for our country bumpkin. The flattery, the press releases, the respect afforded an official regardless of performance, the cocktail parties, the utility and regulatory conventions at which comradeship between regulator and regulated is the number one business, all combine to work imperceptively and irresistably towards prolonging "Life on the Potomac," both during and after the period of regulatory appointment. The average intelligent regulator knows only too well how easy life may be, even if he goes home, if he has played ball. The prospect of important legal clients, the thoughts of large political donations and the realization that you can be the Establishment's Number One Boy back home, or a part of the Big Scene here in Washington, insures the "right decision" or, if not, the industry lawyer starts off with the dice loaded in his favor.[14]

Industry lobbying tactics also include the more formal and traditional means of trying to influence Congressional opinion. The case of the El Paso Natural Gas Company provides a good illustration of the appeal of this more conventional approach. In the late 1950s, El Paso bought out its only interstate competitor in California, the Pacific Northwest Pipeline Company, thereby making El Paso the largest single gas pipeline company in America. By 1964 the matter reached the United States Supreme Court, which ruled that the acquisition was in violation of the federal antitrust laws; it ordered El Paso to divest itself of the illegal purchase. Not to be stopped by a minor setback like a Supreme Court decision, El Paso kept the case in the courts, presenting plan after plan to lower courts. But in 1967 and again in 1969, the Supreme Court overturned the plans submitted by El Paso. El Paso seemed to have learned its lesson. The Supreme Court could not be persuaded to approve any of the divestiture plans that had been drawn up. It now occurred to El Paso, however, that the Congress might be convinced to overrule the judicial branch. Therefore, El Paso sought retroactive legislation to make legal for El Paso what was illegal for everyone else.

If a constituent of mine had stolen a car, was caught and convicted but had not yet returned the car, I would be laughed out of Congress if I introduced a bill to exempt him from any penalty. It would not make any difference if I could show that my constituent had made better use of the car than its real owner, or that the real owner was older now and didn't really need a car. The law and order advocates in the Congress would rightly say that "the law is the law" and everyone has to obey it. But when a similar question is raised about the El Paso Natural Gas Company, or other large corporations, suddenly the law is not so religiously obeyed. Senator Philip Hart (D.–Mich.) put the point well:

> When the Poor People's Campaign comes to Washington, disorganized and hesitant, it is regarded as asking for special treatment, for handouts, for subsidies, the Congressional welcome is not enthusiastic.
> But when some large industrial segment loses an antitrust case, there is no hesitancy to ask antitrust amendments to take care of its special problems. The needs of industry—its special treatment— . . . gets general acceptance. It does not have the bad flavor of the poor, noncorporate petitioner.

One reason for this difference in treatment is that El Paso has the resources to sell its case in a way the average person does not. While the interests of consumers were defended by a handful of public-spirited citizens, in the past fourteen years El Paso has paid, for example, the New York public relations firm of Hill and Knowlton over $1.7 million to sell its case.[15] As Professor John Flynn of Utah School of Law, one of the nations' outstanding antitrust experts, has said, "El Paso's ability to do this is derived in part from the ability of a regulated monopoly to charge all company expenditures in the battle off to the rate base. In a very real sense, the public has been bearing the real cost of El Paso's continued attempts to avoid compliance with the law, because the expense of the battle is dropped into the rate base."[16]

Proponents for the bill exempting El Paso from the antitrust law argue that customers of El Paso throughout the Pacific Northwest, ranging from gas distributors to local school systems, have all supported the bill. But as Professor Flynn has pointed out, this is a direct result of the economic power of the company. "El Paso . . . has been diligently lobbying state officials, distributing companies, business groups, and others in the West to support their position for the bill. Consequently, there is an apparent uniformity of support for and no opposition to the El Paso position, and public officials in this part of the country have not had the opportunity of hearing all sides of the case."[17]

Public officials, like everyone else, make their decisions based on the evidence available to them. If, as Professor Flynn indicates, the only evidence available to the Congress traces to the company's lobbying efforts with local groups throughout the Pacific Northwest, then the economic power of El Paso has been effectively translated into political power without direct pressure being brought on a single senator. If, because of its wealth, a company can hire the best lawyers, the best public relations firm, and the best economists, and can invest thousands of dollars in explaining its case to the public, then I think we can fairly say that it has bought political power through lobbying.

A final method for transforming economic power into political power is job interchange between industry and government. Lawyers, economists, specialists in corporate finance, utilities, banking, and all the other fields of government regulation have a limited range of job opportunities. The industry jobs are, of course, the most lucrative. It is obvious that when an individual involved in government regulation starts to look for a job, he will not overlook the positions available in industry. Likewise, industry executives do not overlook government regulators when they seek personnel for vacancies in their corporations. The result is a shift of people between industry and government which is as predictable as the swing of a pendulum.

FCC Commissioner Nicholas Johnson describes this relationship between government regulation and special interests as a

> sub-government [which] is self-perpetuating and endures over a long period of time, unaffected by the tides of opinion and efforts for reform. It is made up of spokesmen for the largest regulated corporations, the specialized law firms and a bar association, the trade press, trade associations, public relations and management consulting firms, and various other hangers-on. . . . It also includes the permanent government staff—regulatory, executive and congressional—which is concerned with day-to-day activities of the

private interests in question. People in this sub-government typically spend their lives moving from one organization to another in
the sub-government. People who pursue the course of protecting
the public interest are rarely admitted to this club.[18]

Such a system is hardly the stuff of which countervailing government
power is made.

But the political impact of job security is not limited to ranks of
the professional staffs. All but one member of the Interstate Commerce Commission who left in the 1960s went to work for the
transportation industry. The "sub-government" based in the Federal
Power Commission, the Interior Department, and the energy industry
certainly rivals the military-industrial complex as the most inbred
group in government. Carl Bagge, former member of the Federal
Power Commission who now heads the National Coal Association,
could tell us something about the problems of dealing with a potential
future employer. Or perhaps we could get the same insights from
Clifford Hardin, who resigned his post as Secretary of Agriculture in
November of 1971 to accept what he himself described as an
"unusually attractive offer" with Ralston-Purina, a major agribusiness
corporation which benefits from numerous federal programs. The
story of Hardin's successor, Dr. Earl Butz, is an especially interesting
one, and warrants examination.

Dr. Butz has spent a professional lifetime traveling between the
Agriculture Department, the board rooms of agribusinesses (including, interestingly enough, Ralston-Purina), and the farm schools of
the land grant colleges. At the time of his nomination as Secretary of
Agriculture in November 1971, Dr. Butz served on the boards of
directors of Ralston-Purina, International Minerals and Chemical
Corporation, and Stokeley-Van Camp, all of which are large agribusiness giants. In addition, he served on the board of J. I. Case, a
leading farm machinery company, until that company was acquired
by Tenneco, the huge conglomerate that dabbles in farming as well
as many other products. As Dr. Butz acknowledged, he was paid
twelve thousand dollars a year by Ralston-Purina; ten thousand dollars by International Minerals and Chemicals; forty-eight hundred
dollars by Stokeley-Van Camp; and three thousand dollars by J. I.
Case. He still owns stock in all these corporations except J. I. Case.[19]

When Dr. Butz was appointed, he promised to disassociate himself from these corporations. But this action did not solve the problem of the new secretary's corporate ties, since he could not so easily disassociate himself from his lifelong attitudes. A good example of how these attitudes were translated into actions can be found in a national symposium on farm policy sponsored by Purdue University, the land grant college where Dr. Butz served for many years as dean of the Agriculture School. Held on April 14–16, 1971, the symposium on "Vertical Coordination in the Pork Industry" was sponsored by Purdue and the U.S. Department of Agriculture, with industry cooperation. It was attended by representatives of feed companies, food chains, economists, and USDA officials. At least nine major executives of the Ralston-Purina Company, of which Dr. Butz was then a director, were on hand, along with twenty-four USDA officials, including two deputy administrators. A part of the program at the symposium was the showing of a Ralston-Purina film depicting the history of the hog industry—an industry fast being taken over by Ralston-Purina. One thing becomes apparent from this story: Ralston-Purina, which was paying Dr. Butz twelve thousand dollars per year, was given a golden opportunity to present its own position in a very forceful manner to top officials of the Agriculture Department. We can only wonder whether small hog farmers were as well represented.

Dr. Butz evidently sees nothing wrong with using the resources of a land grant college, not for the benefit of the small, family farmer, but rather to promote cooperation between agribusiness and agrigovernment. In fact, the variety of conflicts of interest surrounding a man like Secretary Butz are dazzling. Corporate boards and academic administration; government jobs and corporate boards; academic administration and government jobs—no matter which way the areas are combined, they all lead to an overlap which compromises the independence of any of them. No wonder the conglomerates and agribusinesses are driving the family farmer off the land. Who is there to stand up for him when the corporate leaders, academics, and government officials are effectively one and the same?

As I said at the outset, the question is one of institutional structure, not individual morals. The political power of corporations does not depend upon bribes and illegal pressure tactics. It results from the use of legal tools only available to concentrations of financial power.

Corporate power in politics is the use of campaign contributions to elect pro-big business politicians, the use of advertising to sell political views rather than products, the use of tax deductible lobbying to make a case to Congress in ways beyond the reach of the average citizen, and the use of job opportunities to discourage tough regulation. All of these methods are legal but contrary to the public interest.

So what's to be done? Reform of campaign financing is a necessary precondition to reform. In 1971 the Congress passed an amendment to the Revenue Act of that year which provides for a tax credit or deduction for small contributions to political campaigns beginning in 1972. In addition, it authorizes public financing of Presidential campaigns beginning in 1976, through a system in which each taxpayer can check off one dollar of his taxes to be used by the Presidential candidates. While the tax credit section is definitely a step in the right direction, the public financing provision is worthless. Since it authorizes, but does not appropriate, federal funds for Presidential campaigns, the money must be appropriated by Congress separately in each Presidential year. Thus, the issue must be refought every four years. I supported Senator John Pastore's (D–R.I.) original proposal for an automatic appropriation to guarantee federal financing of Presidential campaigns regardless of the veto threats of the incumbent or the filibusters of a Senate minority.

In addition, we should extend the public financing concept to Congressional, state, and local campaigns as well as to primary campaigns. One hopes such a system would allow politicians to rely more on the large number of average voters than on the small number of big contributors often tied to vested financial interests.

Another way to curb the political power of corporations would be to end the business tax deduction for lobbying, which is in no way a cost of producing a product or providing a service. From 1918 until 1962, the tax laws and Internal Revenue Service regulations prohibited businesses from deducting lobbying expenses from their income taxes. The tax "reform" act of 1962 overturned IRS regulations and allowed such deductions. Since the corporate income tax is set at the rate of 48 percent of net earnings, the ability to include lobbying costs as a legitimate business expense means that the average taxpayer is, in effect, forced to pay about half the cost of that lobbying—often against his own interests. Prohibiting business tax deductions for lobbying not only would stop big corporations from using indirectly taxpayers' money to lobby; it would also discourage such lobbying altogether by raising its cost to the individual company.

Rather than permit corporate deductions for lobbying, we should instead consider giving every American a small tax credit or voucher to influence legislation he or she is concerned about. If U.S. Steel and the ordinary citizen were given twenty-five-dollar tax credit for lobbying purposes, U.S. Steel might use the credit and then spend more out of taxable income, and the ordinary citizen might turn his credit over to Common Cause or Ralph Nader, or a big corporation for that matter. At the least, a diversity of inputs into the political process would be encouraged.

Corporate executives and their friends in the Congress will no doubt respond that the unions, the Sierra Club, and the farm organizations, for example, would then gain an unfair advantage. They will contend that Ford Motor Company would get only a twenty-five dollar tax credit for lobbying, while the United Auto Workers, by pooling the credits of all their members, would get millions of dollars. They must be reminded, however, that our democratic form of government is based on the political equality of people, not on economic interests. The individual citizen is the basic unit of our political system. Only he or she can vote, hold public office, or influence legislation—the latter, at least in theory. Unions, farm organizations, and environmental groups are membership organizations, made up of citizens, each of whom have political rights to be exercised separately or jointly. Corporations, on the other hand, are entirely different structures, chartered by the government to serve certain public purposes, and generally organized to make profits for their owners. Only their owners are citizens, with political rights. In his book, *The Corporation Takeover*, Professor Andrew Hacker refers to the familiar pluralist model of democracy, which is a

> society composed of a multiplicity of groups and a citizen body actively engaged in the associational life. . . . Were groups such as the American Medical Association, the United Automobile Workers, the National Association for the Advancement of Colored People, and the American Legion the only participants in the struggle for political and economic preferment then the sociology of democracy

would continue as an effective theory. For in cases like these it may still be assumed, in spite of tendencies toward bureaucratization, that the power of these associations is simply an extension of the individual interests and wills of their constituent members.

But when General Electric, American Telephone and Telegraph, and Standard Oil of New Jersey enter the pluralist arena we have elephants dancing among the chickens. For corporate institutions are not voluntary associations with individuals as members but rather associations of assets, and no theory yet propounded has declared that machines are entitled to a voice in the democratic process. . . . It may profess to speak for its employees, but there is often evidence that not a few on its payroll are quite out of sympathy with the policies advanced by management. It may profess to speak for its stockholders. But . . . many of these are not human beings; and of those who are, votes are cast for each share owned and not by the conventional democratic standard of one ballot per individual.[20]

Repealing the business tax deduction for corporate lobbying would put the cost where it clearly belongs: on the shareholders of the corporations, the ones who profit from it in any case. Just as ordinary citizens could channel their tax credits to consumer, labor, and other groups, the individual shareholders of a corporation could pool their tax credits, if they wished, but the corporations themselves would not receive the massive tax subsidy for lobbying they now enjoy. Until the system is changed, El Paso can deduct the costs from its taxable income, while private groups and citizens contesting the same issue can deduct nothing.

On political advertising, I think the Federal Trade Commission and Federal Communications Commission should look into the possibilities of banning political advertising by corporations. So long as citizen groups are barred from buying air time to express political views on controversial issues, corporations should be barred as well. The FCC and the courts have begun to consider applying the fairness doctrine to controversial corporate ads, as in the case of cigarettes. One form that this can take is "counter advertising," a principle invoked in 1971 against advertisements by Standard Oil of New Jersey which indirectly promoted the construction of the Trans-Alaska pipeline. In this ruling, NBC was required to present views that gave the other side of the pipeline story.[21] The widespread application of this practice, as the FTC has proposed, would help reduce the political power gained by large corporations through the use of political advertising.

Another way to restrain corporate advertising on public issues is to take away the business tax deduction for advertising not related to the distribution of specific goods and services. There is no justification for forcing the average taxpayer to subsidize political propaganda campaigns, such as the Citizens for a New Prosperity's effort on behalf of President Nixon's economic policies. Likewise, if a corporation wants to buy an ad wishing everyone a Merry Christmas or congratulating a class of high school graduates, let them do so out of pretax dollars or out of lobbying funds collected from their stockholders. If I want to discourage pollution or celebrate Christmas, I can think of quite a number of better ways to do it than to turn over my tax money to General Motors.

Reducing economic concentration by breaking up shared monopolies would also help reduce the political power of big business. In any area the size of a big corporation can be translated into political strength. A company with plants in ten congressional districts can expect more congressional champions than a company with plants in only five districts. The economic impact of a single corporation translates into political impact in another way as well. Only companies like Lockheed and ITT can even argue that general rules of competition and antitrust should not apply to them since they are *too big* to tolerate the risk of market failure. Finally, if our giant companies were decentralized, there would be less opportunity for corporations to use their political muscle. We would not be so concerned about big corporations getting special exemptions from the wage-price freeze if we had chosen the course of antitrust enforcement in addition to government regulation to begin with. The same is obviously true of regulated industries. If we replaced the Interstate Commerce Commission with competition in the transportation industry, there would be no worry about the truckers and railroads controlling their regulators.

Many of the same arguments can be made for a federal corporation chartering law. A corporation which grows lettuce in California and makes textiles in North Carolina is in an excellent position to lobby California congressmen for textile quotas, or North Carolina congressmen against including farm workers under the National Labor Relations Board. The dangers are real. And one solution—federal chartering, perhaps including a prohibition against such conglomerates—is real as well. I believe that federal chartering of corporations —embodying public, consumer, and employee safeguards—is one of the new tools the public needs to deal with the immense political power of corporations.

Beyond enacting these institutional reforms, the best way to deal with the political power of corporations is to politicize corporate issues. So long as corporate power is exercised behind closed doors, away from the scrutiny of the people, corporations are likely to win battles by default. The people can win when a private issue becomes a public issue, as was the case with the SST. So long as the people pay little attention to the question, the aircraft firms always won; but once the light of public concern was let in, they were unsuccessful in their lobbyings. The same is true of farm subsidies. So long as the big giveaways to the corporate farms were a "farm issue," the wealthy always won. But when the general public became interested in how their money was being spent, we were able to put a ceiling of fifty-five thousand dollars per crop on the subsidies. That's not low enough and more reform is needed; but with public support, a start was made. When Lockheed requested a federal loan, public outrage brought us within one vote of defeating it. The Penn Central Transportation Company, after a long history of mismanagement that eventually led to bankruptcy, wanted the government to bail them out. The political situation, however, prevented even the introduction of a bill to do so. These and other cases show that when the public gets involved in corporate issues, it is possible to defeat the political power of the giant corporations.

Increasingly, corporate issues are becoming public issues. The real story of the 1971 state and local elections is not the racial one of the Rizzo-Longthreth race in Philadelphia and the Waller-Evers contest in Mississippi. The real story is found in the election of populist Henry Howell as Lieutenant Governor of Virginia, campaigning on a platform of tougher regulation of utilities and insurance, and repeal of the state's sales tax on food and medicine. Howell narrowly lost the Democratic primary for governor in 1969 running on his "Keep the big boys honest" platform. In 1970 he vigorously supported the populist candidacy of George Rawlings, who won the Democratic primary for the U.S. Senate, but lost in the general election. Finally, last fall, Howell was elected lieutenant governor, running as an independent. He is now planning to run for governor again in 1973. There is not a knowledgeable politician in the state who does not think corporate issues are of growing importance in Virginia. Similarly, there was overwhelming approval of Florida Governor Reuben Askew's proposals for a corporate income tax in that state. Even William Waller, the new governor in Mississippi, avoided the politics of race and won the Democratic primary attacking the financial elite which has run that state for years. The growth of the new populist movement in politics in the last three years thus demonstrates the politicization of corporate issues. New populist candidates have by no means always been successful, but in victory and defeat the issues have surfaced.

I do not suggest that the war is won, for it is not. We have won some battles against corporate power; we have lost more of them. But at least they are being increasingly fought on our field. The point is simply this: if we are to deal effectively with corporate power, we must get the issues out into the open, where the public interest can—and does—win. We must insist that every man and woman who runs for President, Senate, or Congress face up to the questions of corporate power in our country.[22] We must demand that they tell us where they stand on decentralization of shared monopolies, federal chartering of corporations, recapturing the regulatory agencies from industry, opening up access to the mass media, no-fault insurance, reforming campaign spending, cutting subsidies to agribusinesses, and all the other corporate issues. These are the kinds of questions that should—and can—decide national elections in the 1970s.

IV

THE CORPORATION
AND THE COMMUNITY

MARK GREEN *

The average American often has great difficulty comprehending the economics of his immediate environment. He knows the air is foul, his job and pension insecure, his taxes up, his political influence marginal. But those who could explain the paradox of a malfunctioning economy with a trillion dollar-plus GNP have been busy elsewhere. Economists pay passionate attention to impersonal formulations of microeconomics (the theory of the firm) and macroeconomics (monetary and fiscal policy); at the same time, they traditionally ignore the multiple and very personal interreactions between the corporation and the community. There is a dearth of economic data and studies on the local effects of corporate enterprise. It has consequently devolved to occasional newspaper stories to describe the blemished reality: what happens when a corporation monopolizes not a product but the work force? What is the effect on a community when it is obliged to "consume" a company's pollution? What recourse does a citizen have when political intimidation and racial discrimination are inspired and promoted by a dominant corporation?

These are telling questions to which the decade of the seventies

---

* Lawyer and director of The Corporate Accountability Research Group in Washington, D.C. He is the co-editor of *With Justice For Some* (1971), co-author of *The Closed Enterprise System* and *Who Runs Congress?* (1972), and editor of the forthcoming volume, *The Monopoly Makers*.

must respond. For the concentration of corporate activity—accelerated by the great merger wave of the late 1960s—intimately affects in two ways communities supporting such economic enterprises. First, local families and owners can become appendages of national and multinational conglomerates. A system of financial, economic, and political cues by absentee owners replaces community self-rule. Justice William Douglas described the pattern:

> [T]here is the effect on the community when independents are swallowed up by the trusts and [when] entrepreneurs become employees of absentee owners. Then there is a serious loss of citizenship. Local leadership is diluted. He who was a leader in the village becomes dependent on outsiders for his action and policy. Clerks responsible to a superior in a distant place take the place of resident proprietors beholden to no one. These are the prices which the nation pays for the almost ceaseless growth in bigness on the part of industry.[1]

Second, rather than absentee-owned firms disregarding a community's welfare, a large local corporation may utterly dominate the town simply by flexing its economic and political muscles. As with absentee ownership, democratic self-determination then becomes more homily than reality. Examples range from state domination, like Anaconda and Montana Power in Montana and DuPont in Delaware, to the company towns which erupted with the sudden expansion of infant industries at the turn of the century. Often in mining, lumber, and textile regions—usually unhealthy, hazardous, grim, and grimy—company towns made their citizens dependent on the company for their work, their homes, and their daily purchases. Employers both underpaid their laborers and then exploited them as consumers. It was a closed circle which inspired the popular lament, "St. Peter don't you call me 'cause I can't go, I owe my soul to the company store."

The impact of a corporation on a community can be reflected by such factors as civic welfare, political sway, industrial pollution, local taxes, corporate philanthropy, local investment and racial discrimination. And whether the source of the impact stems from absentee-run corporations or local dominants, the damage to the community is often quite similar.

CIVIC WELFARE

As conglomerates have burgeoned in the past few years, many local enterprises became branch offices of financial centers in New York City and Chicago. The acquiring corporation has a national if not an international market and perspective. Birmingham, Alabama, or Providence, Rhode Island, is where it manufactures the goods, not where it sells them; hence, the economic committment extends well beyond the community. The branch managers who run the plants understand this point well. "The man who years ago might have been a 'big man in the community' because he headed a large local company," Senator Philip Hart observed, "now finds himself No. 1 in Company Z, which is a subsidiary of Company Y, which is in turn a subsidiary of Company X."[2] For them the town in which they reside may be only a rung on a corporate success ladder. Such managers are transients, staying a few years before being shifted to another corner of the conglomerate's jigsaw puzzle. "[T]heir community roots were the most shallow," said sociologist Robert Schulze, "—if indeed it could be said that they had any community roots at all. The data led us to suspect that perhaps Cibola* . . . was of no great importance to their lives."[3] They are *in* the community, not *of* the community. In fact, the branch manager often views local affairs as something of a risk, more likely to mire his firm in controversial issues than to further his corporate career. One study asked community leaders in three cities whether they thought branch managers were more or less interested in the community than were local businesses; 95 percent, 79 percent, and 57 percent respectively, said "less."[4] One branch manager noted:

> I would try to get into things more if I honestly felt it would help the company, but I honestly don't see how it would. . . . Nobody [here] decides whether or not to use our product. . . . So I've never really tried to get into things here. What we need most—any company does—is business, and this town can't do anything about that.[5]

A manager who *was* interested in some local activities in Worcester, Massachusetts, called his home office to get further cooperation

---

* Cibola, the town's name in this study, as well as those names in studies which follow, are fictitious.

—only to be told by a high-ranking executive, "We couldn't care less what happens in Worcester."[6] Thus, although they occupy positions usually associated with community leadership, these citizens tend to abstain from local activities. This indifference can have a corrosive effect on a community's civic welfare. For power unused is not an open road but an obstacle to citizen action. One empirical study observed that "in the relative power vacuum which exists in Bigtown, community projects are usually doomed if they lack the approval of the industrial, absentee-owned corporations."[7]

Yet even when absentee-run firms *do* become involved in civic affairs, it is often in rearguard actions to protect their own economic interests. They may threaten to leave the town or city, exercising an effective veto over proposals they dislike. Or they support local puppets who utilize power in their behalf—a kind of local imperialism which both paralyzes the civic will and engenders a hostility not unlike that which Chile must feel toward ITT.

As a result of corporate withdrawal or surreptitious control, the independent political infrastructure of a community can collapse, and with it the community's well-being. The seminal study documenting this pattern was conducted for a Congressional committee in 1946 by Professor C. Wright Mills.[8] Noting that by 1944 2 percent of all manufacturing concerns had employed 60 percent of our industrial workers, Mills asked, "How does this concentration of economic power affect the general welfare of our cities and their inhabitants?" To find the answer he studied three pairs of cities. In each pair was a "big-business city," where a few big absentee-owned firms provided most of the industrial employment, and a "small-business city," where many smaller, locally owned firms comprised the community's economic life. His specific conclusions:

—Big-business cities witnessed sudden and explosive jumps in population, leading to real estate booms, speculation, and unplanned suburban sprawl radiating around center city slums; homes were built quickly and poorly. As a result, the operating cost of municipal services was quite high. Growth in the small-business cities was more evolutionary and planned. Homes were better built, the city was better laid out, and municipal costs were lower.

—A quarter of those employed in the small-business city were proprietors or officials of corporations; only 3 percent were self-employed in the big-business city. Plant shutdowns in bad times were obviously more catastrophic in a big-business city, since the local economy was so much more dependent on a few major firms.

—Income was more equitably distributed in small-business cities, as an average of more than twice as many people earned over ten thousand dollars. Thus, while the "independent middle class thrives" in the small-business cities, it does not in the big. There "the independent middle class is . . . being displaced by a middle class consisting largely of the salaried employees of the giant corporations."

Mills attempted to gauge the relative overall welfare in each pair of cities, employing a number of indicators developed by sociologist E. L. Thorndike. They included, among others, measures of general death rates, infant mortality, the number of libraries, museums, recreational facilities, and parks, per capita expenditure for schools and teachers, extent of gas, electrical, and telephone installations, and frequency of home ownership. Of the three pairs of cities, the civic welfare of small-business city substantially exceeded that of the big-business city. Mills concluded that "big business tends to depress while small business tends to raise the level of civic welfare."

These findings were reinforced by another special Congressional study that same year.[9] A group of sociologists compared two California communities which differed in that Arvin was surrounded by large-scale corporate farming, Dinuba by small-scale independent farming. While Dinuba was incorporated in 1906, Arvin had not been by the time of the study. Interviews revealed that the large farmers were satisfied and uninterested in incorporation; one minister said that in fact the large landowners were afraid the laborers "would run the town." Also, the large corporations and absentee landowners could see not benefit to themselves in higher taxes for civic improvements. Arvin residents, therefore, had to approach county officials for any local request, while Dinuba exercised self-rule. By many local standards—high schools, garbage disposal, retail sales, wages and the distribution of income, local clubs, municipal services, and the standard of living—Dinuba was clearly superior. For example, Arvin

lacked a high school, its only playground was on loan from a corporation, and it had a teacher turnover rate five times that of Dinuba.
The report stated that "Large-scale farming does, in fact, bear the
major responsibility for the social differences." This differential, in
turn, can be traced to the lack of self-rule in Arvin, as distant en-
treprenuers and county officials made the decisions which affected
local citizens. The community lacked both the means and the
resolve to redeem the situation, and the large corporations who
could have done something simply didn't care.[10]

In the twenty-five years since these studies were conducted, aggregate economic concentration has significantly increased. Mergers
often aggravate the community cankers discussed previously—which
should hardly be surprising given the buccaneering attitude of merger
managers. While synergistic payoffs are forever cited to justify
conglomerate takeovers, often the motive is pure empire-building.[11]
Edward Krock, the financial wizard of two holding companies (controlling fifteen firms) listed on the American Stock Exchange, can
pick up his telephone, as he reports with some pride, and order a
company president fired in Illinois or a factory closed down in Ohio.
Why do big companies buy small ones, he was asked. "Because of
men's ambitions. They are hungry for money and influence."[12]
While such a consuming drive may get the conglomerateur listed in
Who's Who, it is unlikely to be good news for the community.

In Rochester, New York, for example, employee morale sunk
after local firms were taken over by outsiders between 1950 and
1957; workers both feared plant shutdowns* and felt like small
cogs in a far-flung machine. Employee growth also suffered.
A study of 1963–67 acquisitions of local Wisconsin firms by outside interests found that the premerger growth rate of the acquired
firms was 6.02 percent while the postmerger growth rate was 0.48
percent.[13] Also, employee payrolls of firms taken over by outside
conglomerates increased 15.6 percent premerger but only 2.1 percent

---

* What is known as a "corporate rape" is far from a rare occurrence. In
1967, for example, Teledyne acquired Firth-Sterling, a producer of specialty
steels and tungsten materials. Before 1967 Firth-Sterling had increasing sales
and earnings per share. But after 1967 its steel division was abolished by
Teledyne. Half the work force, or 800 people, were laid off—giving credence
to Isadore Barmash's 1971 title, *Welcome to Our Conglomerate—You're Fired.*

postmerger, a fact which led the author of this study, Jon Udell, to observe that "it appears some conglomerates may have removed a considerable number of higher salaried executives from Wisconsin."

Acquisitions by absentee owners can also reduce the use of local professional services. Udell found that most of the acquired firms shifted away from local accountants and lawyers and toward the accounting and legal services of the parent firm. These findings discredit the argument that such mergers contribute to the growth of local firms and communities due to the financial resources, management skills, and research and development programs of the acquiring corporations.

POLITICAL SWAY

At times company towns have had surface glitter. Pullman, Illinois, created by George M. Pullman of the Pullman Palace Car Company, was built in the 1880s as a model town. Mr. Pullman alone invested eight million dollars in apartment buildings, parks, playgrounds, churches, theaters, arcades, casinos, and more. The town won awards at international expositions for its layout and maintenance. But beneath this classy exterior, there was something rotten in the town of Pullman. It was rife with fear and suspicion, as company spies probed for tips on "union infiltration" or "dangerous" and "disloyal" employees. This company town showed its true constitution during the crunch of the 1893 depression, when it laid off workers, cut wages 25 percent, but did not reduce rents. After investigating Pullman, economist Richard T. Ely concluded that "the idea of Pullman is un-American. It is a benevolent, well-wishing feudalism, which desires the happiness of the people but in such a way as shall please the authorities."[14]

Pullman has its modern parallels, as some five million Americans live in company towns. While *Time* magazine was lauding Kannapolis, North Carolina, because its dominant company, Cannon Mills, "has given money and land for a number of the town's eighty-four churches, built a golf club for its fourteen thousand employees, and contributed most of the cash for a civic auditorium,"[15] local citizens reeled under a barony out of the Middle Ages. Philanthropy here was a small contribution indeed in lieu of greater tax payments. The town of thirty-nine thousand is unincorporated and was subject for decades to the whim of "Mister Cannon," chairman of the board of Cannon Mills, who died in 1971. Until then, he selected and paid the town's twenty-two policemen, he owned the central business district, he controlled the town's only newspaper, his firm dumped four million gallons of industrial waste into the Irish-Buffalo Creek every day, and he opposed incorporation because of the taxes he would have to pay. Did the townspeople want incorporation? Said one, "Nobody with mouths to feed is eager to tangle with the guy who owns the grocery store."[16]

Centralia, Missouri, is an extension of the Chance Electric Company and its former chairman, F. Gano Chance (he retired in 1972), whose authoritarian rule insured that dissidents did not flourish there. One unidentified citizen of Centralia, Missouri, his back to the camera, recently described the political tyranny of his company town to an educational television network:

> *Mr. X:* I realize that any time you have a large factory in a town that the owner of such factory or the one who controls the largest interest in the factory will have great influence, but I am firmly convinced that this is a conspiracy to rule. They control jobs. They control credit. And if they don't control you directly they control your relatives, your son, your daughter. If you're a trustee in a church or have a position of other honor or duty, they will see that you're relieved of it, if you dare to oppose them. You'll also be attacked in such ways as harrassment by phone calls. These calls usually come in the night. When you answer the phone, no one is there. That is the standard form. Although occasionally the caller will abuse you with vicious and vile and profane language. I know of no one employed by the Company who has ever tried to run for public office against one of the Company-sponsored candidates. All of those who have . . . no longer live in Centralia.

Equally feudal is the town of St. Marys, Georgia, nearly all of whose eighteen hundred wage earners are employed by the Gilman Paper Company and its business interests.[17] Gilman interests control the city council, the town's only lawyers, real estate company, bank, and insurance firm. A populist insurgent, Dr. Carl Drury, recently challenged and defeated a Gilman-backed candidate in a countywide election for state representative. An assistant personnel manager at the Gilman mill reported how his superiors "told me to go down to the bag plant, spend all the time and money I needed, and find out who was going to vote for Drury. All of the Drury supporters would be terminated." The personnel manager refused, and was told "Either you get that damned list or that's it." He quit. "It would have been suicide to stay after that," he said.

Another mill worker, however, wouldn't challenge his bosses. "I have a wife, three children, and a mortgage. I am not going to jeopardize them just to give the mill a kick in the ass. The mill knows it and I know it." After the election some people were fired or deprived of business for having supported Drury. And Drury himself was falsely accused of rape by a girl under circumstances strongly suggesting that Drury's campaign opponent, Gilman's attorney, had orchestrated the charges.

Thus, the type of dominance and intimidation represented by a town like Pullman still thrives in company towns throughout America—from paper-pulp towns in Maine, to mining towns in the West, and to textile and paper-mill towns in the South. We realize how one-crop economies in underdeveloped countries can lead to political authoritarianism and economic instability; American analysts often lack the same perception of communities in their own country.

Corporate dominance, however, can occur at the state as well as the local level. DuPont in Delaware is the best (but not the only) example of a "company state." The firm employs 11 percent of the state work force and generates 21 percent of the state's gross product.[18] The DuPont family controls the DuPont company through board membership and the Christiana Securities, the family's holding company, which owns the company that publishes the state's two biggest newspapers, the *Morning News* and the *Evening Journal*. The presence of the family and firm in Wilmington is everywhere— from the DuPont Building, housing the company's huge office complex, to the Playhouse, Wilmington's only legitimate theater and owned by DuPont, to the Wilmington Trust Company, Delaware's largest bank and controlled by the DuPonts. In the city-county complex in Wilmington works the county executive, a former DuPont lawyer, and Wilmington's mayor, whose father was a prominent DuPont executive. The state's one Congressman is Pierre S. DuPont IV; another family member is attorney general; the governor,

Russell Peterson, is a former DuPont research director. DuPont firm or family-connected members comprise a fourth of the state legislature, a third of its committee heads, the president pro tempore of the Senate, and the majority leader of the Delaware House. Twenty-two of the twenty-six Delaware campaign donations of five hundred dollars or more in 1969 were given by DuPont family members or employees, and all the contributions went to Republicans. Finally, DuPont's twelve-million-dollar annual donation to groups around the state gives the family and firm (called "Uncle Dupie" by Delawarians) added political leverage.

The result of this lockhold? The state legislature has failed to reform the tax system, which favors both the DuPont firm and family due to its extremely low property tax assessments and the lack of any tax on either individually owned or business personal property; in fact, a 1970 state law abolished one of the most progressive aspects left in the Delaware tax system—the treatment of capital gains as ordinary taxable income. When the DuPont-connected Wilmington Medical Center wanted to rezone a few hundred acres of county land from industrial to institutional usage in order to move its facilities, it had little trouble convincing the New Castle County Council—although the rezoning, according to professional planners queried, destroyed the land use balance in the county. Five of the seven members of the Council, including the president, were either DuPont employees or family. When the county had to choose between general aviation (business and pleasure flying) or commercial aircraft for the expanded Greater Wilmington Airport, it favored wealthy users by increasing general aviation; no public hearings on the issue were ever held.

The Greater Wilmington Development Council (GWDC) is a nonprofit corporation concerned with urban problems. It is well funded by the DuPont firm and family. Not representative of the whole community, it has historically tilted public bodies toward corporate interests. When a huge downtown shopping center was being planned, the GWDC pushed hard for a connector highway and five thousand-car garage to service suburban commuters, mostly DuPont employees. Many in the community opposed the road, citing air pollution, noise levels, isolation of neighborhoods, and the lack of public input into the plans. Instead, they supported alternate plans for a small downtown shopping area, plus a hospital, public bowling, and a rail and bus transportation center in and out of Wilmington for the 40 percent of city households without a car. Due in large measure to GWDC's urgings, the connector road was approved. The GWDC also promoted an interstate highway in order to accomodate traffic to and from downtown office buildings; as proposed, it would cut through the center of Wilmington and create a severe housing crisis since there was no available housing for low-income relocatees. The highway, opposed by community groups, was built.

INDUSTRIAL POLLUTION

Dominant local corporations often deploy their political power to pollute without challenge. There is little encouragement to stop polluting when a dominant corporation controls the local authorities who supposedly monitor it. Take, for example, Savannah, Georgia, and its mighty Savannah River. They have become garbage dumps for local industry.[19] American Cyanamid, producing, among other materials, the pigment with which to write the m's on M & M's, pours six million gallons of waste water, including over six hundred thousand pounds of sulphuric acid, into the Savannah every day. The Union Camp Corporation, producing paper bags, dumps *thirty-seven million* gallons of waste water daily. According to two scientists at a local pollution conference, Union Camp has so fouled the air with its kraft pulp emissions that the long-range community effects include:

    1. reduced desirability of the community as a place in which to live;

    2. reduced attraction to the community for other new industries and commercial enterprises;

    3. reduced attraction to hotels, motels, and resorts for the traveling business and touring public;

    4. depreciation in property values and rentals in summertime areas;

    5. hazard or inconvenience to travelers because of reduced visability . . .[20]

In addition, of course, there is the damage to the health of local residents, an unquantifiable but palpable penalty for local "progress."

Union Camp's response to such criticism is arrogance, the arrogance of power high in the political saddle. The firm refuses to divulge the extent of air pollution particulates it emits per day. The state's Air Quality Control Branch, whose responsibility includes obtaining just this type of information, is discouraged from doing so due to Union Camp's power. But then Georgia's air pollution law itself was drafted by Glen Kimble, the firm's Director of Air and Water Pollution, who proposed it on "behalf of all Georgia industry." It was Kimble who said of the ecological crisis ". . . it probably won't hurt mankind a whole hell of a lot in the long run if the whooping crane doesn't quite make it." When John Lientz, Union Camp manager, was asked about the likelihood that heavy industrial pumping might dry up the Savannah area's underground water supplies, he answered, "I don't know. I won't be here." A study of Savannah, sponsored by the Center for Study of Responsive Law, asked a Union Camp executive vice president whether there were *any* limitations on their depletion of ground water. "I had my lawyers in Virginia research that," he said, "and they told us that we could suck the state of Virginia out through a hole in the ground, and there was nothing anyone could do about it."[21]

Although Union Camp perpetrates an invisible violence on the city of Savannah daily, it remains largely immune to effective local control. Essentially, the city is hostage to the corporation. Union Camp entered Savannah in 1935 during the Depression, for which the firm has exacted *quid pro quos* ever since. Among other concessions, the following were contained in a 1935 contract between the two sovereigns:

> The parties hereto agree to use their best efforts to secure the necessary action and if possible legislation on the part of the governmental bodies concerned, to protect and save you [Union Camp] harm from any claims, demands, or suits for the pollution of air or water caused by the operation of the plant.
>
> It is agreed in case litigation arises or suits are brought against you on account of odors and/or flowage from the proposed plant that the Industrial Committee of Savannah will pay all expenses of defending such suits up to a total amount of $5,000. . . .

In return for these concessions, the city is being slowly poisoned by its corporate benefactor. And the city's economy is stagnant since new industry hesitates to enter Union Camp's satrapy due to the already polluted environment, the dwindling water supply, and the dominance of the local labor market. Yet Savannah remains in bondage, intimidated by threats that Union Camp will run away to another city if local restrictions become too severe. But it is an unequal contest, for Savannah cannot run away from Union Camp.

Another example of the corporate "donor" poisoning its municipal donee is the Johns-Manville plant in Manville, New Jersey. The plant employs 40 percent of Manville's employees; its payroll accounts for 60 percent of the town's total income. It pays more than half the taxes and has made gifts to hospitals, schools, and recreational facilities. But all is not well in this small industrial town. "People are dying in Manville "of diseases virtually unknown elsewhere" wrote Philip Greer in the *Washington Post*, "and at rates several times the national norms. They are dying, medical experts agree, because they work in the biggest asbestos processing plant in the world."[22] Johns-Manville claims it is doing all it can to reduce the dust levels which lead to disease. Any more costly improvements, the firm warns critics, could lead to plant shutdowns instead.

There are other examples of such Faustian relationships, where a locale looks to a firm or investment to resuscitate its economy—only to find unintended side effects. Union Carbide in Anmoore, West Virginia, U.S. Steel in Gary, Indiana, Anaconda in Butte, Montana— in each place, the town tolerates its own poisoning since it perceives itself to be in hock to the dominant corporation.* But such self-destructing obedience is not inevitable. Between 1968 and 1971, the

---

* There are less obvious variants of the city or town suffering at the hands of its supposed corporate benefactors. Orlando, Florida, was gleeful a few years back when Walt Disney World announced it would build a vast amusement complex there. But today Orlando is glutted with people and cars; it has too few rooms for too many tourists, inflated real estate, high-rises mushrooming everywhere, and overtaxed local services. The World Trade Center in New York City invigorates Wall Street, and also interferes with the television reception of thousands of New Yorkers and creates serious traffic jams. The Chamber of Commerce, bankers, and financiers in San Francisco have been pushing to replace the city's traditional, often elegant architectural standards with intense high-rise development, arguing that it would enhance the city's tax base. But a study initiated by the *San Francisco Bay Guardian,* entitled *The Ultimate High-rise,* concluded that high-rise buildings in San Francisco eat up eleven dollars in services for every ten dollars they contribute in taxes.

American Smelting and Refining Company dumped eleven hundred tons of lead from its towering 828-foot-high smokestack onto neighboring El Paso, Texas. Of 416 children tested by town and firm doctors, 102 had dangerously high lead levels and 25 of the children spent a week or more in hospitals for treatment or observation.[23] El Paso and the Texas Air Quality Board filed suit against ASARCO in early 1972 for its failure to meet air quality standards and its consequent damage to El Paso residents. As a result of a May 1972 judgment, ASARCO agreed to pay fines of $80,500 for eighty-eight specific pollution violations, post $30,000 with the court for any future violations, install $750,000 of additional emission control equipment, and, in a remedy tailored to fit the offense, agreed to pay all the medical expenses for at least thirty months of the 134 children being treated.

LOCAL TAXES

Corporations exact tribute from their neighbors. Instead of demanding coin from each citizen, as imperial governors did in the old days, a more sophisticated legerdemain is employed. Property tax underassessment and special tax zones enable corporate citizens to pay less than their fair share of local taxes, thereby shifting higher tax burdens onto individual citizens. In 1950 Union Camp euchred a law through the Georgia state legislature creating special "industrial zones"— *i.e.*, permanent tax shelters which could never be annexed to the city of Savannah. As a result, Union Camp underpays Chatham County three–four million dollars yearly, or a third of the county's eleven-million-dollar budget.[24] The firm's giant plant complex is assessed at some ninety million dollars for local property tax purposes, not the three hundred–five hundred million dollars that officials of other paper companies estimate would be fair. It now pays 1.4 million dollars in property taxes instead of, assuming a three hundred-million-dollar valuation, 5.1 million dollars.

Again, examples proliferate. U.S. Steel's installation in Gary is underassessed by one hundred and ten million dollars, as reported in the *Wall Street Journal* and confirmed by a study conducted by Senator Edmund Muskie.[25] Refusing to provide information on its capital investments and depreciation schedules, the firm effectively presents its own tax bill to the township assessor. Thus Gary, whose property tax raises 80 percent of its revenue and whose schools suffered a nine-million-dollar deficit in 1971, loses between ten–fifteen million dollars annually. Similarly, in Chicago, U.S. Steel illegally escapes payment of millions of dollars of property taxes every year. A study by a respected citizens group there, Citizens Against Pollution (CAP), estimated that U.S. Steel avoided 16.4 million dollars in taxes in 1970; the combined undertaxation of three other steel companies was eleven million dollars more.[26] Chicago's share of lost taxes alone could triple the city's budget for environmental control. Due in large measure to CAP's campaigns, U.S. Steel's assessment of 45.7 million dollars in 1970 rose to 84.5 million dollars in 1971, still well below the estimated value of 195.2 million dollars.

In the Permian Basin of West Texas, some of the world's largest oil and gas companies own immensely rich properties which are underassessed by more than 50 percent. Since the local county and school district are not receiving fair payments on these properties, small businessmen and homeowners are paying nearly one-third more in taxes to meet local revenue needs.[27] The corporate owners of timberlands in Maine, Georgia, Texas, and the Northwest pay taxes that do not remotely reflect the true values of their properties. The same is true for the coal companies in Appalachia. The ability of local corporations to pressure local governments for preferential rates was openly implied in one businessman's guide. It urged firms to work more with local than state agencies because "they may be able to obtain a 'better break' for you on your property assessment."[28]

CORPORATE PHILANTHROPY

In 1968–69 corporations gave 255 million dollars to higher education, or 15 percent of all voluntary support to schools.[29] Corporate gifts in 1968 totaled 912 million dollars or some 6 percent of all philanthropy in the country.[30] Yet even these gifts amount to only about 1 percent of pretax profits, well below both the Internal Revenue Code's permissible charitable deduction of 5 percent and the average individual taxpayer's contribution of 2.5 percent of adjusted gross income.* [31] But however one views the current level of corporate giving, "the concentration of a large proportion of the wealth of [the] community in the hands of business corporations has made corporate gifts essential if charities are to be privately financed,"[32] according to the basic law text on corporations. For example, DuPont firm and family gifts in Delaware have become "essential" there. As already mentioned in passing, the family's thirty-six foundations in the state, with assets of more than four hundred million dollars, give away over twelve million dollars a year in Delaware; this is almost as much as the city of Wilmington and the county of New Castle each spend for local government functions.

Clearly this infusion of private funds leads to some community benefits. And equally clearly, there are benefits to the donors: gifts can reduce federal, state, and local estate taxes, thereby limiting public revenue; the donor may retain control over the disbursement of funds; the firm reaps invaluable publicity over its community concern; corporate policies can be indirectly promoted.**

But there are costs of dependency, and the more dominant the

* It should also be noted, as the following chart indicates, that the larger a company becomes, the lower its contributions as a percent of net income:

CONTRIBUTIONS AS A PERCENT OF NET INCOME
ACCORDING TO COMPANY SIZE, 1968

Company Size by Number of Employees	Number of Companies	Net Income before Taxes (thousands)	Contributions (thousands)	Contributions as Percent of Net Income
0–249	7	$ 5,276	$ 170	3.22 %
250–499	15	24,926	400	1.60
500–999	24	88,161	992	1.12
1,000–4,999	106	1,914,013	16,404	.85
5,000–9,999	44	2,084,757	16,486	.79
10,000–24,999	66	6,690,541	43,467	.64
25,000 and over	66	23,465,777	156,460	.66
Total	328	34,273,454	234,381	.68

NOTE: Insurance companies are not included.
SOURCE: John H. Watson, III, *Report on Company Contributions for 1968* (New York: National Industrial Conference Board, 1969), p. 2, Table 2.

** In 1967 the Michigan Bell Telephone Company announced it would "adopt" a local high school, "enriching" it by its investment of equipment and instructors. Why this contribution? William M. Day, the firm's president, said it would "help prepare the [potential] shareholders for the business world. We think we can make a real difference in pupil attitudes." *Caveat receptor.*

firm, the more dependent the community. "Dependency on DuPont foundations take two major forms," assert James Phelan and Robert Pozen, authors of *The Company State*; "some private groups change their programs to suit the needs of a DuPont family member and some governmental bodies come to rely on foundations to perform public functions."[33] Private groups can become supplicants to corporate largesse, trying to get a DuPont family member on their boards of Directors, currying favor with foundation decision-makers, fearing the effects of corporate retaliation on controversial programs. Donations are made by a corporate elite without standards or checks or community involvement. With one funding source dominating private donations, citizen initiative is discouraged and the diversity of possible citizen projects limited.

DuPont, therefore, represents the problem of the dominant local firm contributor. Its philanthropic monopoly encourages civic dependence and its donations can be an unspoken *quid pro quo* for property tax and other regulatory leniency. Thus, a firm can take more out of a community through tax underpayment than it returns, although publicity over its generosity convinces communities they are net beneficiaries.

But what about the reverse problem, the paucity of corporate giving? Communities can also suffer if the corporate donations they have come to expect suddenly decline. And corporate giving can in fact decline when a local operation is acquired by an outsider. "Every time a company changes hands, we worry," says Robert F. Cahill, campaign director of the Golden Rule Fund of Worcester, Massachusetts. "Experience has taught us that it wouldn't be surprising if we were to suffer a sharp cut in the company's corporate gift, even if employee giving is not affected."[34] A study of the effect of mergers on Rochester, New York, showed a drop in postmerger corporate contributions; "it was clear that these absentee-owned firms lagged behind the locally owned firms in response to rising community needs."[35]

RACIAL DISCRIMINATION
AND LOCAL INVESTMENT

Professor William Shepherd has shown, contrary to conventional assumptions, that competitive industries are less racialist than non-

competitive ones.[36] When a few large firms have the power to discriminate, they do so; competitive firms, compelled to hire the best
employees, are more colorblind. (For example, until recently
prodded into more affirmative action, General Motors had a dismal
record on black dealerships, managers, or directors.) So too in local
communities. If dominant corporations are hostile or indifferent to
minorities, the law and ethos of the community reflect their attitudes.

—In the early 1960s, New Castle County, Delaware, was not
willing to press for the end of racial discrimination in its real estate
markets. Spurred on by the NAACP, local realtors came close to
imposing this policy on themselves. They needed all realtors and
local firms to agree, however, lest one be tempted to be antiblack
and exploit the racist market. DuPont, after originally promising the
group its support, refused to cooperate. Sources said that company
executives feared repercussions in their Southern plants from such a
stand. The voluntary agreement then collapsed.[37]

—Dearborn, Michigan, is essentially a fiefdom of the Ford Motor
Company. Ford is the city's major employer and pays one-half of its
taxes. Ford's River Rouge plant, the largest factory in the world, is
there; so are the company's headquarters. But while Ford identifies
itself with neighboring Detroit—getting favorable publicity as a
leader of Detroit's renaissance and redevelopment movement—it
underplays its role in Dearborn. There, Mayor Orville Hubbard has
ruled for thirty years as an avowed racist; there are thirteen blacks,
mostly domestics, out of a population of over one hundred thousand.
("Lincoln was ready to ship them back to where they came from.
Now Mrs. Nixon is in Ghana courting them," he complained in
1971.) Recently, Ford built its Fairlane Project in Central Dearborn,
where houses sell for between twenty-eight thousand dollars and
forty thousand dollars. Michigan groups trying to persuade Ford to
include low-income housing in the development were told by a Ford
official of an exchange of letters between Mayor Hubbard and Ford
officials agreeing to keep the price tag high in order to keep out
"undesirables."

—Big local banks can often set a racial investment pattern. When
they show reluctance to advance mortgage money to black areas of a
community, they can initiate that section's physical decline. The same
syndrome occurs when insurance companies "redline" a geographic

area—often black—and then refuse to extend insurance there. In both cases white citizens then realize that the influx of blacks into their neighborhoods would depreciate the value of their homes and property. They behave accordingly.

Control of local banks by corporate cliques has repercussions beyond the racial. The small inventor, the maverick entrepreneur, the politically unpopular enterpriser all would benefit from a diversity of funding sources since it increases the likelihood that someone would risk advancing them money. And the community benefits in turn from the funding of innovative and diverse initiatives. But with centralization comes conservatism, as dominant banks shun risky ventures in favor of servicing their corporate clientele. Wilmington Trust, a DuPont-dominated bank, invests heavily in corporate and government bonds rather than local loans. While the value of these securities was a staggering 60 percent of the loans outstanding for Wilmington Trust in 1969, it was 42 percent for the U.S. Trust Company of New York, 23 percent for the Philadelphia National Bank, and 26 percent at the Girard Trust Company of Philadelphia.[38]

Large corporate interests can tie up local funds in other ways. They often keep large amounts in demand deposits for their special needs; thus, Lammot duPont, Jr. had 2.5 million dollars in his Wilmington Trust checking account and Irenee Du Pont, Sr. had up to eight million dollars deposited in four cash accounts at Wilmington Trust in 1964. Banks must keep much cash on hand to meet big depositor demands for ready access. Wilmington Trust, therefore, retains from 10–15 percent more of its assets in cash and its equivalents than do other Delaware banks.[39] This amounts to some 66.8 million dollars, a huge loss of potential investment for the local economy. Inherited wealth passed on for generations can also freeze large amounts of capital. Frequent turnover and reinvestment of funds, on the other hand, is necessary for a vigorous local economy.

Again, the problems of absentee-controlled firms differ in form, but not effect, from situations of local corporate dominance. The Rochester study previously mentioned concluded that merged companies no longer banked as much locally; big city banks prospered at their expense.[40] The Wisconsin study of outsider acquisitions estimated that 70 percent of the acquired firms shifted to the financial institutions of the parent corporation.[41] The Gulf & Western conglomerate has a specific policy of insisting that local firms it acquires transfer their banking business from local banks to the Chase Manhatten Bank in New York City. Or take Teledyne's acquisition of the Monarch Rubber Company of Hartville, Ohio. An official of the First National City Bank of New York City went to Hartville to make an appeal for the company's deposits. When he later called New York he was told, "Forget it. Teledyne just picked them up and we'll get the deposits."[42] They did—and the First National Bank of Canton lost most of Monarch's deposits, and the Harder Bank and Trust Company lost Monarch's two-and-a-half-million-dollar pension fund. As a top official of one Connecticut bank said, "As soon as a national company picks up some local outfit, the money just shoots down to New York."[43]

But it is cities just like Canton, Ohio (1970 population 108,872, down from 113,631 in 1960) which need local investment from local banks. From community capital investment to the residential home mortgage market, available loan money is like a blood bank to a patient. Without infusions when necessary, it can die. Thus can "banking practices operate like a regressive tax, funneling the money of communities with declining economies to those with brighter economic prospects."[44]

TOWARD REFORM

That communities can be harmed *either* when absentee-owned corporations ignore community interests *or* when local corporations dominate community affairs is not a contradiction. Each damages the polity in its way, albeit in different ways. Common to both, however, is an underlying causation: corporate sway over a community is bad whether exercised or not. Like sleeping with an elephant, every thrashing, grunt, or inaction cannot but have major consequence on its bedmate.

Still, problems of local corporate dominance seem like benefits to many communities: a local hospital is built (which corporate employees use); government contracts for housing or job training are negotiated (permitting diversification and ample profits); a cultural center is constructed (attracting top executives and unbuyable publicity); corporations give money away to local groups and foundations (controlling public policy along the way, and tax deductible as well); research and development centers are promoted (attracting students and contracts). Should corporations police the streets, educate the young, rebuild the slums? Some think that if corporations perform such functions, it is free. But there is no such thing as free corporate benevolence. We gave away the airwaves to corporations expecting free television but paid for it via higher priced advertised products and other costs; towns invite corporations in to enhance their tax base and economy, only to find themselves being taxed by corporate pollution and added service burdens. Our largest cities are collapsing right alongside prosperous corporations, whose officials thrive from the city but live in the suburbs. Ultimately, then, the company's contributions accrue to the company's benefit, often in conflict with community benefit; and ultimately, a community's political, social, and economic structures can wither under the pressure of daily dependency.

Yet the problem of the elephantine corporation in the community remains. While it is conceptually satisfying to urge that corporations concern themselves with economic markets while national, state, and local governments concern themselves with community needs, this conclusion alone will not do. For the market model will not soon work in Kannapolis, St. Marys, Centralia, or Delaware. Many corporations should not have such power over locales, but so long as they do, they must realize their special obligations as leading citizens. They must not abuse their unique sway to exploit the population and to discourage self-rule. Taken alone, this sentiment is inadequate to checkmate corporate depredations. But it does appropriately note that at some basic, noneconomic, nonlegal level, the issue becomes a moral one.

A plant closing is never painless, but its ill effects can be alleviated by an early announcement and vigorous efforts to relocate and retain the laid-off workers—as American Oil did in El Dorado, Arkansas, when it moved away.[45] After a Swedish paper mill reduced the most obnoxious of its kraft mill pollution, its manager inexplicably spent a few hundred thousand dollars more to get rid of the nauseating odor; admitting there were no specific economic returns, he said that "it would attract people to the mill and the community."[46] DuPont refusing to go along with a voluntary open housing ordinance, Ford not building low-income units in its new Dearborn complex, U.S. Steel abstaining on the issue of integration in its Birmingham mills in the early 1960s—in each case seeming neutrality, given the dominant position of the firm involved, had the effect of underwriting antisocial patterns. Yet even within market parameters, it is not impossible to be a good corporate citizen.

But this is more a plea than a proposal. Specific government compulsions, of the kind succeeding chapters focus on, are needed to stop industrial pollution, to assure racial freedom, to encourage local investment, and to reduce corporate economic and political power. As for the corporation-community dilemma, beyond stressing the moral component of a dominant corporation's obligation to the community, a number of external rules could be attempted. If antitrust enforcement were more vigorous against conglomerate mergers—the Nixon Administration settled their anticonglomerate cases before the Supreme Court could set precedent in this area—the extent of absentee control over communities would decline. Rather than wait for some future administration to take the plunge, new legislation should forbid any firm with over two hundred and fifty million dollars in assets from acquiring any other firm unless it spins off an equal amount of assets. This would arrest the trend toward increasing absentee ownership while permitting mergers motivated by real efficiencies rather than stock market manipulation or managerial empire-building. At the same time, state antitrust enforcement should be invigorated to move against local monopolies which federal authorities cannot reach, either due to lack of authority or lack of resources.

In order to make the corporation more responsible to the community, the community should be made more a part of the corporation. One method would require that corporate donations, from firms over a certain asset and employee size, be made to community boards, which in turn would decide where best to allocate the monies. Another alternative would be to require independent public directors elected by the voters in a community to sit on the company board of directors. A variant of this approach envisions a two-tier system of shareholders. *Economic* stock would be held for voting and investment purposes, looking toward the traditional rewards of stock appreciation or dividends; *political* stock would entitle its holder to no economic return but would permit voting on company policy. Political stock would be based on status, not wealth—the status of those very personally affected by a corporation but lacking any say over its actions: *e.g.*, employees and community residents. Clearly such schemes involve a dramatic departure from standard notions of corporate "ownership", but such rethinking and reformulating is precisely what is presently needed. It makes little sense to equate a share of stock in a large corporation with the private property that John Locke had in mind, and it is difficult to argue that a shareholder whose sole involvement in corporate affairs is speaking to his broker once a year is entitled to more of a voice in the corporation than an employee who devotes his or her life to it or a citizen who ingests its contaminating by-products. To better protect community welfare, this lesson must be learned and these proposals, as well as others, must be considered. For the *status quo* can only lead to an accelerating tension and hostility between corporation and community. "It is not creative minds that produce revolutions," wrote H. G. Wells in *The Salvaging of Civilization*, "but the obstinate conservation of established authority. It is the blank refusal to accept the idea of an orderly evolution toward new things that gives a revolutionary quality to every constructive proposal."

PART TWO

THE REMEDY OF
FEDERAL INCORPORATION

V

THE CASE FOR
FEDERAL CHARTERING

RALPH NADER*

Contemporary events reflect a mounting concern over corporate activities. Economic concentration and monopolistic practices, environmental pollution, product safety, occupational health, advertising and deception, employment practices, corporate secrecy, corporate crime, corporate responsibility—the list of inquiry is long, as it should be. But it is important to understand these issues in their historic context, so that in focusing on behavioral effects we do not ignore the institutional causes of corporate depredations. For corporate power and the corporate form did not suddenly erupt full-blown on the American scene in the 1970s. And the causes of, and possible solutions to, problems like corporate power, size, pollution, and secrecy may all be quite related.

THE DEVELOPMENT OF STATE INCORPORATION

It was mid-millennium England when the corporate form first took shape. The Crown vested governmental authority in certain commercial groups to trade in its name. These royal charters regulated the trading company or corporation since only the Crown had the prerog-

---

* Lawyer and lecturer, author of *Unsafe at Any Speed* (1965) and co-author of *What to Do With Your Bad Car* (1971), *Action for a Change: A Student's Manual for Public Interest Organizing* (1971), and *Whistle Blowing* (1972).

ative to govern trade and the right to clothe a private group with public power. This right to control the conditions of the corporation's existence, however, went largely unexercised. Monopoly power without restraint led to numerous abuses. As R. W. Boyden observed of the trading companies, "They tended to be massive, corrupt and inefficient. They grabbed power as an excuse for the failure to do business. . . . They identified themselves with ruling groups to become politically beyond challenge irrespective of their economic services."[1] Many tended to be rapacious and imperialistic, like the East India Trade Company, which even had its own flags, governors, counts, and armies.[2]

This tradition of incorporation as a privilege rather than a right was passed on to the American colonies, which continued it through the Revolution. Special legislative charters permitted some private groups to build bridges, transport water, and undertake commerce. The American Constitution, omitting any references to the power of incorporation, did not change old ways. States continued to charter corporations under special legislative acts, although the frequency of their issuance increased to two hundred in the first decade after the War of Independence.[3] But the process of petition and hearings led to delay, expense, corruption, and favoritism.[4] As a result, and because the pace of economic growth was quickening, a movement began seeking the equal and easy granting of incorporation. North Carolina in 1795, Massachusetts in 1799, New York in 1811, and Connecticut in 1837 led the way by enacting "general incorporation laws," which allowed, without need for legislative approval, the formation of corporations "for any lawful purpose." In the early 1800s most lawyers and judges still viewed corporations as performing public functions in the public interest.[5] But by 1870, according to Professor James Willard Hurst, this notion had all but vanished.[6] Corporations now considered themselves private property owned and controlled by their shareholders.

The power, as distinguished from authority, to form and control corporations had thus passed from the state to the promoters and entrepreneurs of corporate ventures. Instead of granting incorporation after certain legislative minima were met, a new *enabling theory* took shape, giving private groups the flexibility to create their own conditions of existence.[7] These groups were granted more rights than responsibilities. Enabling statutes were premised on the view that free enterprisers acting in their own interest would serve the general social interest as well, or, in the words of John Locke, "private vice makes public virtue."

The state did not entirely abdicate its regulatory role. Charters, though freely available, continued to have size and scope limitations. For example, New York had a capitalization ceiling of one hundred thousand dollars and firms incorporated for one activity, say baking, could not go into another, like gravel mining. Corporations could not own the stock or assets of other corporations and were granted existence only for a specific period of years. Toward the end of the nineteenth century, fourteen states sought to control monopolies by forbidding them in corporate charters. Finally, corporations were prohibited from doing business or owning property outside the state of their existence. These restrictions reflected the historic and prevailing fear of corporate power. One recent writer saw it as the "fear . . . that a corporation was only an artificial personality and therefore did not have a soul or conscience. Lacking a conscience, it had no morals and was prima facie dangerous."[8] So long as corporations remained local, contained by the charter's restrictions, states still maintained the control they considered necessary for the public interest to be served.

But corporations did *not* stay local. What these restrictions tried to avoid is precisely what occurred. In an effort to attract resident corporations into their states, incorporation laws became increasingly liberalized. The winner of the race for corporate citizens went to the state of least restriction. The early victor was undoubtedly New Jersey. In 1866 it permitted the holding of property and doing of business outside of the state. In 1875 it relieved incorporators of their obligation to file their intention to incorporate, and it dispensed with the ceiling on the amount of authorized capital. During the 1880s, in a critical move, it legalized holding companies by allowing corporations to hold and dispose of the stock of other corporations. In the next decade, it removed limitations on the duration of the corporate charter. The result: between 1888 and 1904, 192 of 345 companies with capitalization in excess of one million dollars took out New Jersey charters.[9] New Jersey became the home of the infamous Standard Oil Trust. Trusts and holding companies declared illegal in other states simply transferred their property to corporations organized under the law of New Jersey. Partly as a consequence, the turn of the century merger movement occurred, one which changed the face of industrial America as no merger movement before or since.

But New Jersey's dominance was only temporary, for Delaware was not to be denied. A 1899 law review article notes that:

> Meanwhile the little community of truck-farmers and clam diggers [Delaware] have had their cupidity excited by the spectacle of their northern neighbor, New Jersey, becoming rich and bloated through the granting of franchises to trusts which are to do business everywhere except in New Jersey, and which are to go forth panoplied by the sovereign state of New Jersey to afflict and curse other American communities. . . . In other words, little Delaware . . . is determined to get her little tiny, sweet, round, baby hand into the grab-bag of sweet things before it is too late.[10]

To obtain the business of incorporation, all Delaware did was to be a little worse than New Jersey. Its 1899 business code, drafted by a financial reporter and three corporate lawyers, enacted most of New Jersey's liberalization and then some: any classification of stock could be issued, with or without voting powers; shareholders lost rights to pre-emption; there was no state transfer tax on the resale of securities; annual meetings could be held outside the state; directors need not own company stock to qualify for the directorate; state and tax rates were set slightly below those of New Jersey; and finally, charters permitted directors to issue new stock, change the terms of authorized stock previous to sale, retire preferred stock, and even change the firm's by-laws—all *without* obtaining shareholder consent.[11] Delaware thus took over the lead in the incorporation game, an advantage it has not to this day relinquished. As the local newspapers christened it, Delaware became "The Little Home of Big Business."

Worse than merely win the race, Delaware also set the pace of walking backwards into the future. Other state laws looked to the Delaware code as a model, in the process competing to the lowest common denominator. So long as there was another "Corporate Reno," it was futile for any state to reform its incorporation law. New Jersey Governor Woodrow Wilson, under a challenge from Teddy Roosevelt, did so in 1913 by passing tough, local antitrust measures. The consequence was that chartering business went elsewhere.

In a way, Delaware succeeded too well. Imitative states began to take some of its business away. To meet the competition, liberalizations of Delaware's business code occurred in 1927 and 1929; whereas in 1927, 5,424 charters had been granted generating 824,483 dollars in fees, by 1929 the number had swollen to 7,537 charters and 3,309,698 dollars in fees.[12] But still Delaware wasn't satisfied. Although by 1960 one-third of the top six hundred industrial corporations were headquartered in Delaware, the state decided to further liberalize its business code. A Revision Commission was formed in 1964 which attempted, in its words, "To ascertain what other states have to attract corporations that we do not have." The basic redrafting was done by three private corporate lawyers working on Saturdays in their private offices. The full Commission always anticipated that the state legislature—which of course had to approve the new code since it *was* a public law—would be a rubber stamp; one member of the Commission referred to the legislature as "just a bunch of farmers."[13]

No hearings were held on the final statute and it passed the Delaware legislature unanimously on July 3, 1967. This closed process had its antecedents; a leading member of the Delaware bar assayed the system in 1932:

> Here in Delaware we have an ideal system. Our legislature would never think of passing an amendment to our corporation laws without submitting the matter to the state bar association. Proposals for change are always brought to us first. Our committee considers them, and if we approve them the legislature adopts them as a matter of course. That insures sound laws. Don't you think it is an excellent system?[14]

The new 1967 code contained, among others, these liberalizations: only directors, not shareholders, could propose amendments to the corporate charter; plans for special compensation, stock options, and bonuses were expressly permitted, but without any procedures established either to avoid abuses or to disclose the amounts involved; shareholders were denied appraisal rights; officers and directors could be indemnified by the firm for court costs and settlements of criminal and civil cases without the need for court or shareholder approval.* So that corporate buyers of this product did not miss the point, the statutory preface to it advertised, "New law enabling, not restrictive." These reforms achieved their purpose. While businesses were incorporating at the rate of three hundred a month before the new code's enactment, there were eight hundred registrations a month directly afterwards. By 1969, fifty-six thousand corporations had their birth certificates filed at the Townsend Building in Dover, Delaware, a number including one-third of all the companies on the New York Stock Exchange and one-half of the top one hundred industrial corporations.**

From a time when firms were selectively chartered and controlled by the government, private corporations have grown to huge size and power without commensurate accountability. Promoters and management—not shareholders, not employees, not the community—have nearly unchecked discretion to draft and implement the governance of the corporation. How did this happen? State incorporations laws became a version of Gresham's Law, as the weaker states drove out the stronger ones. Shareholders were too powerless and disinterested, and legislative committees too ignorant and pliable, to challenge this accession of power. The task of drafting state laws remained firmly within the hands of corporate lawyers and businessmen, psychologically identifying with management. A recent *Pennsylvania Law Review* article concludes:

---

* This indemnification provision was "nonexclusive," which meant that any corporation, by its by-laws, could opt for a scheme even more liberal than this one. The code itself permitted indemnification, although the law might have been broken, if the action involved was "not contrary to the best interest of the corporation." The Commission reporter, law professor Ernest Folk, explained that "an act may be contrary to the interests of the state, but it is not for that reason alone a breach of duty to the corporation or even against the best interests of the corporation."[15] So much for the theory that private vice invariably makes public virtue.

** Despite its continued success at enticing incorporators, Delaware's continuing vigilance cannot be underestimated. A headline in the October 14, 1971, *Wilmington Morning News* read "Unit to lure corporate HQs named." The article said, "Formation of a committee designed to attract corporate headquarters and related business facilities to Delaware, was announced by Gov. Russell W. Peterson yesterday." Nor can Delaware be accused of modesty over its preferred position. Before announcing the vote of his state for the Democratic Presidential nomination, the chairman of the Delaware delegation proudly described his state to a nationwide audience as "the home of corporations, chemicals, chickens, and charisma."

> The sovereign state of Delaware is in the business of selling its corporation law. This is profitable business, for corporation law is a good commodity to sell. . . . The consumers of this commodity are corporations and . . . Delaware like any other good business-man, tries to give the consumer what he wants. In fact, those who will buy the product are not only consulted about their prefer-ences, but are also allowed to design the product and run the factory.[16]

And so long as we permit fifty-two different jurisdictions (Puerto Rico and Washington, D.C. included) to compete for corporate char-ters, there can be no improvement. For reform, we must look elsewhere.

A HISTORY OF FEDERAL CHARTERING

The concept of federal chartering has received support throughout our history as the government chartered, owned, or ran a corporate activity. The federal government was a minority stockholder in the first and second banks of the United States. Nationally chartered banks were created by an Act of Congress in 1864. In 1904–5, the American government acquired all the shares of the Panama Railroad Company. World War I "stimulated a wide and rapid extension of the use of the government-owned corporation,"[17] such as the incor-poration and takeover of the United States Shipping Board Emer-gency Fleet. The 1922 China Trade Act, in order to encourage trade with the envisioned, bountiful Chinese market, permits federal char-ters for firms trading with China. In 1924 the federally run Inland Waterways Corporation was formed. In the 1930s the Tennessee Valley Authority, a government authority, performed a function private capital had strongly refused to perform. During the Depres-sion, numerous government-owned corporations arose. Among others, the Federal National Mortgage Association ("Fannie May" in busi-ness parlance) was a government-run corporation formed to buy and sell mortgages to provide a secondary mortgage market. (This federal corporation shifted into private control in the Nixon Admin-istration.) More recently, hydroelectric projects are federally licensed, as are interstate motor carriers (the difference between licensing and chartering will be discussed later). Also, government-business partnerships like Comsat, Amtrak, and the National Corporation for Housing Partnerships are examples of direct involvement by the federal government in the running of a corporation. Thus, there is little doubt the federal government *can* and *has* chartered and created corporations; but at the same time there is little evidence to indicate it has the *resolve* to do so on a major scale.

The idea that the federal government should charter corporations first arose during the Articles of Confederation, when in 1781 Congress granted a national charter to the Bank of North America. During the Constitutional Convention in 1787 James Madison twice proposed, unsuccessfully, that the Constitution expressly empower Congress "To grant charters of corporation in cases where the public good may require them and the authority of a single state may be incompetent."[18] Although no formal vote on it was ever taken, the proposal was rejected by some delegates as unnecessary and by others as leading to monopolies which could dominate the federal government.[19] Thomas Jefferson repeated this anxiety in his arguments with Andrew Hamilton over a United States bank. Such a bank would overawe the states, said Jefferson, permitting vast consolidations of economic power to dominate our economic life. Jefferson lost the battle when Congress and President Washington approved the Bank of the United States in 1791. But Jefferson eventually lost the war as well, since great economic consolidations *did* come to dominate our economy, albeit via state and not federal incorporation.

A century later, in the 1880s, the public became concerned about the economic and political power of the huge trusts. Some reformers called for a form of federal licensing of corporations in order to control their excesses. Instead, the 1890 Sherman Antitrust Act was passed, looking to competition rather than regulation to restrain the trusts. Disillusionment with this solution, however, was nearly immediate. The Supreme Court *Sugar Trust* decision of 1895—holding legal a combination controlling 98 percent of all sugar production since "manufacturing" was not "interstate" commerce—largely emasculated the Act. In addition, Social Darwinists, making a virtue out of reality, approved of the trusts. Presaging today's defenders of corporate giantism, economist E. L. von Halle believed that "they [trusts] come because they must." And another prominent economist, John Bates Clark, reflecting the *laissez-faire* philosophy of his day, said: "Combinations have their roots in the nature of social industry and are normal in their origin, development, and their practical working. . . . To accept the results of this evolution and to meet the demands of the new era is the part of wisdom."[20]

But public and political opinion were turning against the protrust sentiment of the courts and the economics profession. William Jennings Bryan in 1899 went on record as favoring a federal license whenever a corporation wanted to conduct interstate business. Two years later President Theodore Roosevelt had his own idea. In his first message to Congress in 1901, he said, "The first essential in determining how to deal with the great industrial combinations is knowledge of the facts—publicly. . . . The Government should have the right to inspect and examine the workings of the great corporations engaged in interstate commerce." This view took the shape of his proposal for a Bureau of Corporations. At the same time a federal incorporation bill was introduced in 1903. But Congress eventually opted to create Bureau of Corporations as a part of the Department of Commerce, and declined to act on federal chartering legislation.

The Bureau's purpose was exposure of the "bad" trusts. It collected information and conducted investigations into corporate abuses, reporting its findings to the President who could then make them public. There were obvious defeats in this scheme and in its implementation: it was wholly discretionary whether or not the President would use the data collected; it conflicted with antitrust principles by accepting the fact of corporate consolidations; and it had no formal connection to antitrust enforcement by the Justice Department. The *New York Times* charged that the "legislation accomplished nothing. . . . It does not bust the trusts. . . . It will appease the public clamor against trusts and it will do the trusts and combinations no harm. That is to say, it will fool the people, and that is the purpose of the Republican Congress."[21] Roosevelt himself referred to the Bureau's work as "tentative," "advisory," and "experimental." And a recent chronicler of its eleven-year existence concluded that "the essential conservatism of Garfield [the Bureau's first Commissioner] and Roosevelt's unwillingness to antagonize the business community on the eve of a national election . . . combined to make the Bureau take a very narrow view of its authority."[22]

Again opponents of monopolies looked elsewhere for salvation and again federal chartering became a candidate. This time, however, support for the approach seemed overwhelming. Between 1903 and 1914, Presidents Roosevelt, Taft, and Wilson all voiced support for a federal incorporation or licensing scheme in their annual messages to Congress; President Taft had his attorney general, George Wickersham, draft a federal licensing bill and proposed it to Congress in 1911. Mark Hanna, Williams Jennings Bryan, and the U.S. Industrial Commission favored it. Industrialists Judge Gary, James Dill, and John D. Rockefeller all favored versions of the idea (to avoid conflicting state laws); the *Wall Street Journal* and National Association of Manufacturers both supported it in 1908.[23] It was endorsed by the 1904 Democratic Platform, the 1908 Republican Platform, and the 1912 Democratic Platform. Twenty different bills were introduced in one or both Houses of Congress between 1903 and 1914.* Scholars and politicians favored it as a logical way of promoting the public interest.

Despite this array of support, the Clayton and Federal Trade Commission Acts of 1914 became law instead of federal chartering. Support for the latter never coalesced at any one time. Taft had changed his mind about it by 1912, and the Senate Interstate Commerce Committee, after holding lengthy hearings on federal incorporation in 1913, concluded in the final committee report that it was "neither necessary nor desirable at this time."[24] Improving marginally the antitrust laws, and creating a successor agency to the Bureau of Corporations (one with enlarged powers), attracted the most support when the moment of political judgment arrived.[25]

Between 1915 and 1932, eight Congressional bills were introduced relating to federal incorporation or licensing. During the Depression of the early 1930s, however, the National Industrial Recovery Act was passed. In certain respects, Franklin Roosevelt saw the NRA as a form of federalization of corporations, providing "a rigorous licensing power in order to meet rare cases of non-cooperation and abuse."[26] There was brief talk during this time by both labor and

---

* While some bills permitted federal charters or licenses for those who wanted them, others made the federal role compulsory. Nearly all of the versions required annual reports detailing corporate earnings and practices; the public release of some of this information; the end of certain unfair trade practices; and penalties for violation of the reporting or charter provisions.

management of replacing the NRA codes by federal chartering of the large companies and trade associations.[27] Instead, the government opted for the Securities Acts of 1933 and 1934, requiring full and accurate disclosure of material facts in a public offering and regulating the practices of the national exchanges, and other New Deal regulatory schemes—the Federal Communications Commission in 1934, the Public Utility Holding Company Act of 1935, and the Civil Aeronautics Board in 1938.

Nevertheless, the late thirties witnessed the most sustained drive for federal licensing to date. Senator Joseph O'Mahoney, a populist senator from Wyoming, energetically and repeatedly promoted the idea of "National Charters for National Business."[28] By emphasizing that "a corporation has no rights; it has only privileges,"[29] he sought to return to the pre-enabling act days when charters policed as well as permitted. In 1938 his Subcommittee of Federal Licensing of Corporations held four volumes of hearings on S.3072, a bill which he and Senator William Borah cosponsored. Senator O'Mahoney later made it clear that the important choice was between a federal and a state role in the control of the corporate fiction. His proposal, more far-reaching than its predecessors, provided for the following:

> —corporations whose gross assets (including those of subsidiaries) exceeded one hundred thousand dollars were required to obtain a federal license to engage in interstate business;
>
> —detailed information on the financial affaris of the corporation, including dealings with foreign firms, had to be periodically supplied to the FTC;
>
> —diversification "incidental to the business in which it is authorized to engage," as well as ownership of the stock in other companies, was forbidden (but this rule was prospective only, leaving existing relationships unchanged);
>
> —any proposal altering the existing rights of shareholders, as well as any financial dealings between the corporate and the officers and directors, had to be fully disclosed to the shareholders;
>
> —directors could not be employed by or have a financial interest in a competitor, but must have a financial interest in their own corporation;

—any corporation in violation of the antitrust laws, or one which discriminated by sex, employed child labor, or refused to bargain collectively, could lose its federal license and hence its right to do interstate business;

—penalties ranged from nominal fines for a thirty-day period during a violation of the license, to 1 percent of the book value of the capital stock or assets per month, to actual revocation of the license following hearings by the FTC and an action instituted by the Attorney General in any district court.

Although the bill went nowhere—the war effort diffused any momentum the hearings and O'Mahoney's Temporary National Economic Committee (TNEC) had excited—O'Mahoney remained firm in his belief in such legislation. In a statement to the TNEC at its closing session on March 11, 1941, he said:

> It is idle to think that huge collective institutions which carry on our modern business can continue to operate without more definite responsibility toward all the people of the Nation than they now have. To do this it will be necessary, in my judgement, to have a national charter system for all national corporations. . . . One thing is certain: We cannot hope to stop the processes of concentration if we are willing to continue to allow the States to create the agencies through and by which the concentration has been brought about.[30]

In summary, at every point in our history when federal chartering was considered, an alternative remedy was chosen. The outrage against the trusts in the 1880s institutionalized itself in the 1887 Interstate Commerce Commission and the 1890 Sherman Act. Concern during the turn-of-the-century merger wave and depression of 1903 culminated in the Bureau of Corporations, which grew into the 1914 Federal Trade Commission enforcing the Clayton Act. The Depression, demanding urgent reforms, witnessed the creation of the securities laws, industry codes, and additional regulatory agencies. During all these periods, federal chartering was prominent, topical, and finally ignored. Clearly, it is an idea whose time has come and come and come, almost always at moments of economic crisis. Our present economic and social ills—in the midst of corporate abuses and unbridled power—make it topical again.

PROS AND CONS, MOSTLY PROS

Federal incorporation is necessary because state incorporation has failed its past missions and avoided even acknowledging its future responsibilities toward a fast-changing corporate society. And the reason why is clear: what good is it for fifty-one jurisdictions to have tough business codes if one is a coddler? With the states stooping to that lowest common denominator, corporations have conquered. The only remedy for this permissive structure is to have one chartering authority, not fifty-two.

Even *if* state business codes and authorities did not so overwhelmingly reflect management power interests, they would still be significantly incapable of following through to enforcement. Just from their limited geographic jurisdiction over worldwide companies, Delaware cannot restrain General Motors; nor can New Jersey control Standard Oil effectively. Our states are no match for the resources and size of our great corporations; General Motors could *buy* Delaware . . . if DuPont were willing to sell it. A 1968 list of the top 110 corporations, states, and cities by gross revenue found seven of the top ten and forty-one of the top fifty to be corporations (see Appendix to chapter). "The century and a half of state failure," wrote one observer in 1942, "has been the story of a battle between corporate giants and legal pygmies."[31] To control national or multinational power requires, at the least, national authority.

At a time when the federal government becomes increasingly prominent in salvaging our ailing economy, it is an anachronism for the states to create corporations which market nationally and internationally. Quite simply, state borders are not relevant boundaries for corporate commerce. In the context of the evolution of industrial enterprise in the last two centuries, state incorporation makes as much sense as fifty state currencies or fifty state units of measurements. If a criminal crosses state borders, the FBI is called in; if a person crosses a state line with an intent to riot, and does so, the Interstate Riot Act has jurisdiction; if a commodity or a service travels interstate so too should the jurisdiction of the federal government be called into play. In other federal systems—German, Mexican, Brazilian—firms which do business between the states or provinces must be formed under federal law.

While no one solution can cure all the ills of our corporate economy, federal chartering could go far toward an accessible framework for shaping and monitoring corporate power. An array of substantive reforms, discussed subsequently, can be implemented. There are procedural benefits as well. Presently, a charter is a blank check which the corporation signs and then deposits away in ignored files. States do not monitor the firms they have created for violation of their birthright, nor do they impose sanctions for charter violations. Recently in Indiana, AT&T, Penn Central, and De Paul University all lost their corporate licenses to do intrastate business because of their failure to file annual reports. But there were no hearings held and no fines assessed. Until the firms filed their forms, it was business as usual, although they had legally ceased to exist in Indiana. It is quixotic to expect state boards to have either the resources or the will to impose adequate sanctions. An up-to-date federal chartering authority with more comprehensive authority would be far more likely to impose sanctions, or be accessible to citizen power to do so. A federal chartering authority could remind the corporation that the charter is a compact between the government and itself to assure business behavior in the public interest; the authority could also remind the corporation that it holds to charter in trust for public benefit, and if it violates that trust, it can forfeit the charter and right to do business (either *per se* or under existing management).

A federal chartering agency could help equalize the varying burdens and benefits corporations obtain due to the vagueness of different state authorities. Powerful corporations can threaten to run away to a different state if such items as incorporation fees, regulatory laws, and charter provisions are not to their satisfaction. And it is easy to see why a Textron in Rhode Island and a DuPont in Delaware could make its state host anxious. A single federal authority could end this corporate whipsawing of state against state.

There would be those, no doubt, who would disagree both with the need for and efficacy of federal incorporation. But since national chartering as a public issue barely exists, neither do its critics. One can anticipate, however, several likely critical observations. "The government should not manipulate the rights of private property." This historically discredited argument got a good workout recently during civil rights debates over open housing. "A man's home is his castle" was the rallying cry of those who put their private properties on a pedestal in a vacuum. But the 1968 Civil Rights Act, and *Jones v. Mayer* that same year, sharply disagreed. Yes, their property was privately owned, but on the condition, among others, that they not racially discriminate in its resale. Not even the venerable "freedom of contract" is absolute, as the legal qualifiers of duress, coercion, and unconscionability, and minimum wage, maximum hour, and equal employment legislation have long made clear. It must be realized that private property is not a command of the gods but a bundle of rights created by our government*; it hardly seems valid to condemn the government for legally rearranging this bundle of rights when it created them in the first place. As the Supreme Court has said: "[T]he corporation, insofar as it is a legal entity, is a creation of the state. It is presumed to be incorporated for the benefit of the public. . . . Its rights to act as a corporation are only preserved to it as long as it obeys the laws of its creation."[32]

The question of whether the government *should* alter some of the conditions of a corporation's charter leads directly into whether it *can*: "Is it constitutional?" The question breaks down into several. First, can the federal government incorporate at all? Chief Justice Marshall's opinion in *McCulloch v. Maryland*, upholding the constitutionality of the first U.S. Bank, clearly permits the granting of a federal charter. The reasoning was that the bank charter was a legitimate means to effectuate the constitutional end of regulation over interstate commerce.[33] Second, what is commerce and how broad a category is it? This question used to be a red flag to many strict constructionists, but today it is largely moot. It is clear that manufacturing and production are embraced within the concept of "commerce,"[34] and that almost anything affecting interstate commerce can come within the scope of Congressional power. (Here we have the civil rights laws to thank for broadening the constitutional language affecting business[35]; usually, and unfortunately, the reverse is true, as civil rights laws are exploited by corporate defendants,

---

* As a reverse example—for decades one form of private property (*i.e.*, a polluting factory) was permitted by the courts to impair or destroy other property (*e.g.*, crops, homes) under the doctrine of "balancing the equities."

e.g., the 14th Amendment and the fiction that corporations are "people" with personal rights.[36])

Given that the word "commerce" is broadly interpreted, how large a role can the federal government play vis-à-vis the states? The answer is nearly plenary power. The federal government *can* let a state regulate a certain interstate practice, but once it *does* enter the field, its authority is complete and it can pre-empt the state entirely.[37] "Congress alone has the power to occupy by legislation," said the first Justice Harlan, "the whole field of interstate commerce."[38] And this includes prohibition if necessary. Congress has successfully banned from interstate commerce lottery games, diseased cattle, impure food and drugs, prostitutes, and goods produced by substandard labor conditions.[39] Thus, Congress could prohibit absolutely a firm doing interstate business unless it first obtained a federal license or charter.

Finally, "does it unconstitutionally impair prior contracts?" Clearly, the federal government can be guilty of this infringement, as when it tried to change the Dartmouth College charter after the American Revolution. Yet if the government passed legislation affecting equally a type of contract—state charters purporting to permit interstate trade—rather than tried to change a particular charter like Dartmouth's (which would be a bill of corporate attainder), the Dartmouth proscription would not apply. What if a state chartered *in perpetuo* whale killing or strip mining; would that forever tie the hands of national legislation seeking to limit each? A too strict reading of the "impairment of contracts" clause of the Constitution would dwindle to nothingness the "interstate commerce clause."

Going beyond its apparent constitutionality, would federal chartering just increase the power of big government? Would it be socialistic? Since the guiding purpose of federal incorporation is to encourage corporate democracy and competition, it is the precise *opposite* of a centralized, planned economy. To the extent that it attempts to make private firms more accountable to their shareholders and more responsive to competitors, a federal incorporation law is a radically conservative idea. Right now we do have a type of corporate socialism where shared monopolies have freed themselves from the constraints of the competitive market and much law enforcement.

The bureaucracy created would be as trim and nondiscretionary as possible. Only the top one thousand interstate corporations—measured by a combination of sales, asset size, market percentage, and number of employees—would be chartered. Manpower would be scaled to confront the basic problem. The kind of charter provisions being enforced would be as objective as possible: does the firm's market percentage exceed permissible limits? Has the corporation provided profit and cost data per division? Did management double its bonus without notifying the shareholders? Of course, there is no such thing as government without any discretion; if there were, we would have computers as Cabinet officials. Yet excessive discretion must be avoided or else the corporate regulatees would successfully shape their supposed regulators—a situation which now obtains.

What if, because of a federal chartering law, many American firms simply left to incorporate in Bermuda or France? What if they treated us as they treat Canada: a place to do business but not owe allegiance? Or what about companies without countries? Carl A. Gerstacker, chairman of the Dow Chemical Company, told a White House Conference in February 1972 that he looked forward to the day of the "anational corporation," one without any national ties which could, therefore, operate freely and flexibly around the world. Gerstacker revealed how Dow had been studying for a decade the possibility of locating on an island in the Caribbean. The chief obstacle, he said, would be unfavorable tax consequences to investors in the exchange of stock involved in such a corporate emigration.

Any of these business runaways could claim that requirements imposed on them but not required by, say, France would create legal conflicts with their foreign charters. There is only one effective reply: the corporation and foreign government in question either complies with the conditions of the federal chartering law or it cannot trade here. Period. Since the American market is such a large percentage of the world market, we would have the leverage, if we had the will, to make this demand of expatriate firms and foreign authorities. This stance is not wholly theoretical. It is similar to the one the Nixon Administration took with its Western trade partners over international financial and trade markets. With the same conviction, it could be utilized to make a federal incorporation law viable. There are state "foreign incorporation laws" which require out-of-state firms to meet certain local standards (*e.g.*, stringent reporting requirements) in order to do business there. The same principle must apply to firms existing outside our borders who wish to do business here. Another restraint could be an "equalization" tax policy making it difficult for firms to move away and then sell back to the United States.

Finally, one practical problem involves state revenues. Many states have grown fiscally dependent on the income from incorporation fees and corporate taxes. But competition over chartering means that one state's revenue is another state's lost revenue. One critic in 1932 humorously suggested a novel approach to this situation: "It would really pay the other states of the Union, which suffer from Delaware's delinquency, to tax themselves enough to pay the cost of running the Delaware government, absolutely free to that state, if she would just agree to go out of the business of breeding corporations."[40] Federal chartering would not affect state taxation, since a state has the sovereign right to tax land and property within its borders. And to the extent that states would suffer due to the loss of incorporation revenue (such revenues are, in fact, only a tiny part of overall state receipts), the federal government could quite simply increase its state aid accordingly. But mere loss of revenue cannot moot an otherwise beneficial scheme. Again, the ablest retort to this complaint was uttered over half a century ago by an early federal incorporation advocate:

> [T]here is no more reason to object to a Federal incorporation law, because it shifts fees from the states to the Federal government, than there is to object to a National bankruptcy law, because it displaces the fees arising from state insolvency laws. All the fees come from the people, and the essential point is not to which government they go, but which can give the best service for the least money.[41]

THE FEDERAL CHARTERING AGENCY

Assuming that state incorporation laws are the problem—which I do—and that existing antitrust mechanisms, regulatory agencies, and securities laws are inadequate supplements, as many chapters in this book argue, a serious federal chartering law seems the most viable and basic mechanism to achieve corporate accountability, both by its impact and its invigoration of the established regulatory frameworks.

Opting for federal rather than state supervision over national business leaves unanswered whether such a law will be a licensing or an incorporation law. A federal licensing system accepts existing incorporation statutes but requires a national business to obtain a special license with, presumably, higher standards than its state analogue. Federal incorporation for national business supplants rather than complements state incorporation; here the charter creating the corporation would come directly from the federal government.

Federal licensing adds to state remedies without diminishing state powers, and it permits the states to retain their revenues from incorporation fees. Thus, federal licensing goes far to nullify states-rights advocates unhappy with any increase in the federal role. But it is built on a weak foundation. Since state incorporation is the problem, it should not be part of the solution. Further, conflicts between the two authorities at the mutual border of their jurisdictions would inevitably cause confusion. When would the license pre-empt the charter, and when not? Federal incorporation suffers from no such ambiguities. Giant interstate corporations would derive their legal existence from one jurisdiction. Problems of pre-emption and other conflicts between state and federal legislation would be eliminated. It is, in the words of the 1904 Bureau of Corporations annual report, "a clear-cut theory." Finally, a licensing mechanism is far more narrow than a charter's generic comprehensiveness. The analogy is between a regulation and a constitution.

What is needed is a new agency—call it the Federal Chartering Agency (FCA)—to issue federal charters for major corporations engaged in interstate business. The charter would be mandatory not permissive, and it would contain "policing" as well as "enabling" provisions. What is needed now is not a new Corporate Bill of Rights—for rights they amply have—but a Corporate Bill of Obligations. A sketch of some of the possible provisions follow:

1. Corporate democracy would reduce the dominance of the present despotisms commandeering most corporations. The poten-

tial areas of coverage are all those which, unchallenged, have permitted management to rule free of its theoretical electorate. Such areas include the following restrictions: corporate loans to officers and directors should be prohibited, and other "interested" dealings must first be reported to shareholders; all compensation schemes, as well as indemnifications for civil settlements, must be reported to shareholders for their approval; shareholders should be accorded liberalized access to "inspect" corporate records (*e.g.*, profit and loss statements by division, routinely made public; shareholder lists; consumer letters of complaint) and to use the proxy machinery; the largest beneficial owners of the corporation should be without staggered terms for directors, cumulative voting should be mandatory and not just permissive;* shareholders should have the right to amend the by-laws and charter, and to recall directors.[42] These issues, and the topic of public, consumer, and employee directors, are discussed subsequently by Professor John Flynn and Robert Townsend.

2. Strict antitrust standards must be a condition of the charter. Given the abundant evidence favoring competition and condemning monopoly, no corporation would be permitted to retain more than 12 percent of an oligopolistic industry, as President Johnson's antitrust task force recommended. Conglomerates should only be permitted to acquire toe-hold acquisitions in concentrated industries and should spin off an equal amount of assets for any they acquire. Professor Walter Adams elaborates on such possibilities.**

3. Corporate disclosure must replace corporate secrecy to answer such questions as: what are the earnings of hidden subsid-

---

* The National Banking Act requires banks under its jurisdiction to allow shareholders to vote cumulatively. But these banks have effectively repealed this provision by creating their own one-bank holding companies, to whom the cumulative vote rule does not apply. A federal chartering act for nonfinancial corporations could stymie such circumventions.

** The federal statute would have to state emphatically that the new agency and chartering scheme would in no way diminish antitrust enforcement. There would be a tendency on the part of some to assume that the regulatory and oversight functions of a new agency would substitute for competition as a controller of market power. For example, this tacit assumption kept the Justice Department for decades from suing banks under the antitrust laws. Federal incorporation seeks the rejuvenation of antitrust, not its replacement.

iaries and consolidated divisions? Who are the real beneficial owners of a corporation? What is the racial composition of employees and new staff? What product and safety testing have been conducted? What plans exist to meet pollution emissions standards? Since the public is so intimately affected, answers to all these must be made public; shareholders, investors, and government officials need adequate information to act intelligently. If done extensively enough, a corporate information center could be developed, with data by firm, plant, and product available for immediate use on computer tapes to respond to topical questions of significance. Professor Willard Mueller discusses later the problems of corporate data.

4. The corporate charter should "constitutionalize" the corporation, in Professor Arthur Miller's phrase, applying constitutional obligations to this private aggregation of power. What underpins this proposal is what underlies this book: corporations are effectively like states, private governments with vast economic, political, and social impact. A democratic society, even if it encourages such groupings for private economic purposes, should not suffer such public power without public accountability. Again, it is an old, but largely ignored, notion. Thomas Hobbes saw corporations as mere reflections of sovereignty. The British Monarch in the Middle Ages saw them as extensions of royal power. Political scientist Earl Latham calls them a "body politic,"[43] while law professor Walton Hamilton concluded in 1957 that "There has arisen, quite apart from the ordinary operations of state, a government of industry which . . . has its constitution and its statutes, its administration and judicial process, and its own manner of dealing with those who do not abide by the law of the industry."[44] Our large corporations represent just the kind of concentrated power which the Constitution and its succeeding amendments aimed to diffuse. If the constitutional convention were held today it would surely encompass "America, Inc." It makes no public sense to apply the Constitution to Wyoming and West Tisbury, Massachusetts, but not to General Motors and Standard Oil, New Jersey.

Unions too are private groups which have been legislated public power, but on the condition that they behave democratically, with adequate due process safeguards.*[45] The same should hold true for private corporations accorded public power via the chartering compact. Constitutionally it would involve an extension of state action and corporate restraint which is the doctrinal descendant to cases like *Marsh v. Alabama* and *Employees Union v. Logan Valley*,[46] *Shelly v. Kraemer*,[47] and *Griggs v. Duke Power Co.*[48] Very simply, when a corporation deals with its employees, shareholders, and dealers, it must do so in a fair way. For example, First Amendment rights to free speech means that an employee can publish material critical of the firm in a magazine or underground corporate newspaper[49]; Fourteenth Amendment safeguards mean that if an employee refuses to perform an illegal task[50] for a federally chartered firm or blows the whistle on a corporate crime,[51] he or she cannot be fired without a due process hearing with explicit charges and decisive evidence. The Fourth Amendment forbids the firm from searching one's private belongings at work without a warrant. It is inadequate to depend merely on unions to guarantee these rights, since they often ignore them in bargaining sessions. Furthermore, unions account for something under a quarter of all employees; the other 75 percent deserve these protections too. The "Dealers Day in Court" legislation enacted in the fifties focused on arbitrary auto-management policy toward auto dealers which required remedial legislation. Various constitutional norms could have anticipated and made unnecessary such a law. For too long these private governments have enjoyed the private rights of a person (equal protection, search and seizure, denial of property without due process) but have not accepted the governmental obligations of a public body (meting out equal protection, tolerating free speech). A better balance is long overdue.[52]

5. Rules could be devised so that consumers no longer bear the brunt of shoddy or dangerous products. The proper mix of implied warranties, breach of warranty, product liability, class actions, and informational advertising could all either make corpo-

---

* Care must still be taken that such safeguards are not ignored by the authorities and private groups involved, as represented, for example, by the Bureau of Labor and United Mineworkers election imbroglio. The suggested framework is the beginning, not the end, of institutional accountability.

rations pay for their full social cost or provide incentives for the production of better products. At present, due to boiler-plate contracting and legislative and judicial obstacles to class actions, firms can avoid absorbing the cost of the damage they impose.

Hovering over all these provisions would be graduated penalties for violation of the charter. Depending on the nature and frequency of the violations, penalties could run from small absolute fines to fines as a percentage of sales, from management reorganization to executive suspensions, from public trusteeship to the dissolution of the charter. A scale of sanctions must be developed to guarantee compliance with the charter.[53] And to help encourage compliance, a chartering authority would retain the ancient, equitable "visitatorial powers," which, according to Roscoe Pound, was "a power of the state . . . for investigation of the activities of, and correction of the abuses committed or suffered by, the corporate authorities. . . ."[54]

In formulating a federal chartering agency, care must be taken that it does not become as unresponsive and inefficient as some of the present regulatory and enforcement agencies. Lessons should be learned from the past; but at the same time, it would be defeatist and irresponsible to urge no further federal reform measures because some have previously failed. Many corporations go bankrupt, yet the corporation is still a viable legal structure for the production and sale of goods and services. Again it is important to stress the objective nature of the FCA's standards. It would not undertake the imbroglios of rate determinations which naturally invite industry lobbying and a dependence on self-serving corporate data. By dealing with all industries rather than just one (railroads or airlines or the broadcast media) there is less chance of being co-opted by a singularly organized counterattack. To an extent this explains a difference between the SEC and ICC. The FCA should also contain liberal provisions for shareholder and citizen suits—as now institutionalized in the Michigan pollution law—so that agency lethargy or inefficiency could be checked by interested citizen activity. More liberal rights of intervention into government processes could similarly permit public interest lawyers to monitor any misfeasance or nonfeasance. Mechanisms would have to be provided to help insure that a "commissioner" of the FCA be vigorous, nonpartisan, and independent. Furthermore, whatever the chances that the FCA would become as inefficient as an ICC, it would have a great distance to drop before it became as supine and irrelevant as the present state chartering bodies.

While Delaware, for example, cannot dictate terms to GM, the FCA could, but it is not inevitable that it would. Thus, a new federal agency is a necessary but not a sufficient remedy. If it is badly organized with weak powers and no citizen access or participation, it will be ineffective. The form is crucial—but so are its powers.

During a 1968 liberalization of its business code, New Jersey candidly acknowledged that "it is clear that the major protections to investors, creditors, employees, customers and the general public have come, and must continue to come, from federal legislation and not from state corporation acts."[55] Federal incorporation could relieve state chartering agencies of their impossible task of ferreting out antisocial acts committed by corporations; it would, instead, place the burden on corporations, who are granted their status by the society they so affect, to show that they *are* acting in the public interest. This is the essence of corporate accountability.

APPENDIX

SALES OF THE 50 LARGEST UNITED STATES INDUSTRIAL CORPORATIONS AND GENERAL REVENUES OF THE 50 STATES AND THE 10 LARGEST CITIES, 1968; AND THE NUMBER OF EMPLOYEES

	(*$ million*) *1968 sales or general revenues*	*Rank*	*Employees* (*thousands*)*
1. General Motors	20,026	1	728
2. Standard Oil (N.J.)	13,266	2	150
3. Ford Motor Co.	10,515	3	394
4. General Electric Co.	7,741	4	375
5. California	7,525	S1	230
6. New York State	6,462	S2	192
7. New York City	6,221	C1	
8. Chrysler	6,213	5	216
9. Mobil Oil	5,771	6	79
10. International Business Machine	5,345	7	222

SALES OF THE 50 LARGEST UNITED STATES INDUSTRIAL CORPORATIONS AND
GENERAL REVENUES OF THE 50 STATES AND THE 10 LARGEST CITIES, 1968;
AND THE NUMBER OF EMPLOYEES

	($ million) *1968 sales or general revenues*	*Rank*	*Employees (thousands)**
11. Texaco	5,121	8	79
12. Gulf Oil	4,202	9	58
13. U. S. Steel	4,005	10	197
14. Western Electric	3,717	11	169
15. Standard Oil of California	3,297	12	47
16. DuPont de Nemours	3,102	13	112
17. Shell Oil	3,073	14	38
18. Radio Corp. of America	3,014	15	128
19. Pennsylvania	2,970	S3	128
20. McDonnell Douglas	2,933	16	140
21. Standard Oil (Ind.)	2,918	17	45
22. Westinghouse Electric	2,900	18	132
23. Boeing	2,879	19	142
24. Michigan	2,842	S4	115
25. Swift	2,834	20	48
26. International Tel. & Tel.	2,760	21	236
27. Illinois	2,673	S5	122
28. Goodyear Tire & Rubber	2,637	22	113
29. General Telephone & Electronics	2,622	23	151
30. Bethlehem Steel	2,594	24	131
31. Texas	2,590	S6	123
32. Union Carbide	2,545	25	99
33. International Harvester	2,541	26	111
34. Proctor & Gamble	2,438	27	41
35. North American Rockwell	2,438	28	115
36. Eastman Kodak	2,391	29	105
37. Lockheed Aircraft	2,335	30	92
38. National Dairy Products	2,318	31	47
39. General Dynamics	2,253	32	103
40. Ohio	2,251	S7	104
41. United Aircraft	2,212	33	79
42. Armour	2,156	34	38
43. Continental Oil	2,082	35	53
44. Phillips Petroleum	1,981	36	36
45. Firestone Tire & Rubber	1,875	37	95

SALES OF THE 50 LARGEST UNITED STATES INDUSTRIAL CORPORATIONS AND
GENERAL REVENUES OF THE 50 STATES AND THE 10 LARGEST CITIES, 1968;
AND THE NUMBER OF EMPLOYEES

	($ million) 1968 sales or general revenues	Rank	Employees (thousands)*
46. Ling-Temco	1,777	38	40
47. Tenneco	1,777	39	40
48. General Foods	1,651	40	32
49. Monsanto	1,632	41	59
50. Massachusetts	1,608	S8	58
51. Borden	1,588	42	39
52. Grace, W.R.	1,576	43	64
53. Litton Industries	1,561	44	95
54. New Jersey	1,560	S9	60
55. American Can	1,521	44	54
56. Sperry Rand	1,487	46	102
57. Sinclair Oil	1,483	47	19
58. Wisconsin	1,477	S10	64
59. Caterpillar Tractor	1,472	48	59
60. Textron	1,445	49	62
61. Florida	1,443	S11	72
62. International Paper	1,414	50	52
63. Minnesota	1,358	S12	55
64. North Carolina	1,351	S13	65
65. Louisiana	1,349	S14	68
66. Washington	1,339	S15	65
67. Indiana	1,328	S16	67
68. Georgia	1,217	S17	53
69. Virginia	1,171	S18	75
70. Maryland	1,114	S19	47
71. Missouri	1,077	S20	63
72. Tennessee	959	S21	51
73. Alabama	955	S22	44
74. Kentucky	932	S23	42
75. Oklahoma	897	S24	47
76. Iowa	850	S25	41
77. Connecticut	809	S26	41
78. Los Angeles	703	C2	
79. Colorado	658	S27	40
80. South Carolina	653	S28	35

SALES OF THE 50 LARGEST UNITED STATES INDUSTRIAL CORPORATIONS AND
GENERAL REVENUES OF THE 50 STATES AND THE 10 LARGEST CITIES, 1968;
AND THE NUMBER OF EMPLOYEES

	($ million) *1968 sales or general revenues*	*Rank*	*Employees (thousands)**
81. Chicago	634	C3	
82. Oregon	632	S29	40
83. Kansas	607	S30	39
84. Mississippi	599	S31	30
85. West Virginia	582	S32	35
86. Arizona	562	S33	26
87. Washington, D.C.	557	C4	
88. Arkansas	519	S34	28
89. Baltimore	464	C5	
90. New Mexico	458	S35	23
91. Philadelphia	458	C6	
92. San Francisco	415	C7	
93. Hawaii	402	S36	30
94. Detroit	400	C8	
95. Boston	393	C9	
96. Utah	379	S37	23
97. Nebraska	367	S38	25
98. Rhode Island	289	S39	16
99. Maine	250	S40	16
100. North Dakota	250	S41	14
101. Alaska	246	S42	9
102. Delaware	233	S43	11
103. Idaho	230	S44	13
104. Montana	229	S45	16
105. South Dakota	206	S46	13
106. Nevada	175	S47	7
107. Vermont	175	S48	9
108. Wyoming	168	S49	8
109. New Hampshire	155	S50	12
110. St. Louis	138	C10	

* Corporation employment for 1968; state government employment for 1969.
SOURCES: Corporate sales and employees from "The 500 largest industrial corporations," *Fortune,* June 15, 1968, pp. 188–9; state general revenues from Statistical abstract of the United States—1970, Table 620, p. 418; state employment from Statistical abstract of the United States—1970, Table 633, p. 429.

VI

CORPORATE DEMOCRACY: NICE WORK IF YOU CAN GET IT

JOHN J. FLYNN*

Lawyers have long been proud of their profession as the basic tool for ordering rights, liabilities, and individual freedom in a rational and peaceful manner. To achieve this social engineering, they have devoted centuries to categorizing issues into fields of property, fault, willful conduct, consensual relationships, or status.[1] Once the basic theory for analysis is set, legal rules and principles within the broad perimeters of the premise are formulated. Thus, lawyers smugly believe orderly evolution of an institution may take place while the institution is consistently subjected to the "rule of law." Such a conviction is of great importance to a "profession," since it allows the believers to go about their daily tasks in the firm belief that their efforts are meaningful to society, albeit lucrative as well. But often there is a large gap between the solutions of law and those achieved in reality. The gap can be apparent, as in the case of segregation; the gap can be mitigated by enforcement policy, as it generally is with marijuana offenders; or the gap can be wide and largely unnoticed, as it is with shareholder democracy. According to the eminent economist Gardiner Means, corporate democracy is a myth, since the "modern corporation has undermined the preconceptions of classical economic theory as effectively as the quantum under-

* Professor of Law at the University of Utah; Special Counsel to the Senate Antitrust and Monopoly Subcommittee (1970–71); author of *Federalism and State Antitrust Regulation* (1964).

mined classical physics at the beginning of the twentieth century."[2] Largely through the pioneering work of Dr. Means and the late Adolf Berle, the academic world has realized this great gap between corporate law and reality for almost four decades; yet the general public, the business world, and the legislative process have virtually ignored the economic and political implications of this development.

It has never been clear in the field of corporations that the law is the master of the evolutionary process rather than its slave. The latter is perhaps more accurate, as the law of corporations has been an apologist for the economic, social, and political forces which have molded the modern corporation. In part, this failure to subject the evolution of the corporation to the rule of law has been caused by the absence of a clear premise upon which to base the law of corporations.[3] A variety of such premises have been offered in the past. Henry Maine traced the heritage of corporate law to the Roman law of *status*, or the determination of rights and liabilities by attaching legal significance to one's position in society or a unit of society.[4]

Hobbes, hostile to the recognition of artificial legal entities, viewed the corporation as a "chip off the block of sovereignty."[5] The bestowal of the privilege of limited liability, accordingly, was considered a delegation of a portion of the sovereign's authority. Common law practice adhered to this quaint assurance of control by issuing special charters through the sovereign embodied in the monarchy or parliament. In the early history of the United States, the law of corporations also treated the corporation as a privilege granted by the State, a privilege handled gingerly because of the potential abuse of concentrated economic power. This *concession theory* of corporate law formed the basis of Chief Justice Marshall's decision in the Dartmouth College Case.[6]

The advent of general corporation laws created the basic premise that the organizing and governing law of corporations was *property*. The essence of the legal concept of property has been variously defined as the right of possession, the right to exclude others, or as the coalescing of these two. Although sanctified as an end unto itself, at times to the great damage of humanity, the concept of property has served us well for peaceful settlement of disputes and the fundamental protection of human freedom. It has served us especially well in closed corporations and relatively small enterprises where the entreprenurial spirit lives and works because of the continued concurrence of ownership and control. The use of property as the organizing principle for large public issue corporations, however, no longer—and probably never did—offers a workable rule of law. In fact, the precept of property no longer explains what the large corporation is, what it is becoming, and what the rights and liabilities are of those who deal with it. Bayless Manning accurately summed up the absence of a firm theoretical base for corporate law: "We have nothing left but our great empty corporation statutes— towering skyscrapers of rusted girders, internally welded together and containing nothing but wind."[7]

Our corporation statutes assume that shareholders own the corporation, that the powers and rights of shareholders flow from their providing "risk capital," that directors shall manage the business, and that officers are agents of the corporation under the direction and control of the board and with a duty to manage the corporation for the benefit of all the shareholders. None of these claims are true. Shareholders do not provide most of the "risk capital"; directors do not direct; and management has reversed the hierarchy of control. Even corporate management does not believe that a corporation's duty is to its owners and only its owners—the theoretical conclusion of state corporation statutes. Sixty-one percent of the managers surveyed by the *Harvard Business Review* believe that the primary duty of corporate management is to serve, as fairly and equitably as it can, the interests of owners, employees, customers, and the public.[8] Chamber of Commerce advocates should be grievously pained by this recognition by managers that they are more arbitrators of the conflicting interests affected by the corporation than they are exploiters of property for the benefit of the legal owners. Going further, some have said that corporate executives have become agents of the State, bent upon the accomplishment of the welfare objectives of the State.[9] Others have examined the phenomena of the modern corporate state and simply concluded that it is "mindless and irrational, rolling along with a momentum of its own, producing a society that is evermore at war with its own inhabitants."[10]

Whatever the modern corporation is, one thing is clear: the demise of the *status, concession,* and *property* theories in the real world of corporations has not been succeeded by a new legal premise of the corporation. Instead, state corporation laws have been engaged in a century-long race of delegating power to corporate management, all dressed in traditional property concepts. The prizes—franchise, property and other taxes, and business for the local bar—lend weight to the assertion that the states are really in the business of selling their corporate law rather than formulating a coherent legal structure of corporate democracy.[11]

The only modern attempt to equate law with corporate reality has been the federal enactment of the Securities Act of 1933 and the Securities Exchange Act of 1934. But, premised upon a property theory of corporations, this legislation still fails to bridge the span between law and reality. Shareholder democracy is supposedly enhanced and guaranteed by proxy rules, full disclosure requirements in the issuance of new securities, prevention of fraud and manipulation in the sale of securities, prevention of insider trading, and limitations upon the exercise and sale of control. The proxy rules require full disclosure of the purpose for which a proxy is being solicited, information on issues or candidates to be voted upon, an annual report when management solicits proxies at a meeting where directors are elected, and the filing of proxy and solicitation materials with the SEC. If a security holder wishes to communicate with fellow security holders ("owners") and his communication meets the legalistic requirements of the rules, the shareholder's proposal must be sent at company expense along with management's proposals to all the other shareholders so they may exercise control over their "property." Finally, the rules prohibit the solicitation and use of false and misleading proxies, a prescription which may be enforced by private suits for damages and injunctive relief to replace or protect the shareholder's "property."

The theory and structure of the proxy rules read like the magna carta of corporate democracy. But as applied to the large public issue corporation, with thousands of shareholders and a divorce of ownership from control, the proxy rules do not secure corporate democracy. The annual election in large American corporations differs little from elections held in South Vietnam or Poland. Electors are given one slate of candidates, the voting machinery is in the hands of the proponents of one slate of candidates, opposition is easily stifled, and the nominees receive 90 percent or more of the "vote." Thurman Arnold and Franz Kafka, wherever they are, must be watching the annual proxy ritual of large corporations with tears of laughter in their eyes. How can it be otherwise when there are vast numbers of shares outstanding and a huge amorphous electorate with no common bond, interest, or effective procedure for implementing shareholder democracy?[12]

Moreover, the vast majority of shareholders, be they individual or institutional, do not even *deserve* the right to be holders of the franchise. They no longer contribute "risk capital" to the corporation in the traditional sense but rather trade their interests back and forth in that great lottery called the stock market. Their interest is not that of an owner or entrepreneur. Instead, they are investors in a huge crap game, betting upon the ability of the holder of the die (management) to accumulate and expand their holdings and expecting that the liquidity of shares will be maintained by other players of the game. In Berle's words, management has become "the uncontrolled administrator of a kind of trust having the privilege of perpetual accumulation. The stockholder is the passive beneficiary, not only of the original 'trust,' but of the compounded annual accretions to it." Capital for replacement and expansion of assets no longer comes largely from shareholders but is the result of tax gimmicks, debt financing, and retained earnings produced by the enterprise. For example, Ford Motor Company reported net income of $515.7 million in 1970 and paid out $259.2 million in dividends. Between 1961 and 1970, stockholder's equity at Ford rose from $3.128 billion to $5.468 billion, a rise substantially financed by means other than the new investment of risk capital by shareholders.[13] All of which has led Berle to ask, "Why have stockholders? What contribution do they make, entitling them to half of the profits of the industrial system, receivable partly in the form of dividends; and partly in the form of increased market values resulting from undistributed corporate gains? Stockholders toil not, neither do they spin, to earn that reward. They are beneficiaries by position only."[14] In law, one would conclude they no longer have property rights, but enjoy the fruits of the corporate state by virtue of their status as holders of capital to invest in the stock markets.

To all this one might also add: Why have a board of directors? Management control over the proxy machinery, the use of corporate funds for electioneering, and the decline of corporate democracy, as well as the consequent pervasive power of management in our large industrial enterprises, have led to management-dominated boards, with the outside directors selected for their potential for nonaction. At best most boards of directors constitute a bit of mortar in the myth of shareholder democracy, and at worst they constitute a slight drain upon corporate assets to pay for their monthly meetings.[15] There may be much to be learned from Robert Townsend's acid observations about directors in *Up the Organization*:

> While ostensibly the seat of all power and responsibility, directors are usually the friends of the chief executive put there to keep him safely in office; . . . over their doodles around the table, alert directors spend their time in silent worry about their personal obligations and liabilities in a business they can't know enough about to understand. The danger is that their consciences, or fears, may inspire them now and then to dabble, all in the name of responsibility.

Among the remedies Townsend suggests for preventing dabbling, the most effective seems to be to "serve cocktails and a heavy lunch" before the directors' meeting in the fervent hope that directors will fall asleep.[16]

While Townsend's inference that directors serve no useful purpose may be overstated, it is clear that the board cannot affirmatively manage the large corporation. It is generally unable to initiate action, serving instead as a sounding board or rubber stamp for management proposals. The potential for the board to fulfill the function of an affirmative check and balance upon management declines in proportion to the financial success and stability of the corporation. For the large corporation operating in noncompetitive markets with millions of shares outstanding, the realistic possibility of the board being converted from a House of Lords to one of Commons does not seem probable.

Where does all this lead us? I believe it is accurate to say that the American economy is dominated by a few hundred large economic entities, largely operating in noncompetitive markets, where management control is nearly absolute, and the legal and economic justifications for shareholders and a board of directors as we know them today no longer pertain. Further, the continuing myth of shareholder control is aggravating the maldistribution of wealth in our society, as it accumulates wealth in the hands of shareholders who do nothing to create or expand wealth. The political, social, and economic impact of this development is one of the most important issues challenging this nation. Whether we become a just, prosperous, peaceful, free, and democratic society turns on its resolution. If the problem is not recognized or if solutions are not premised on recognizable legal standards, it is not too much to say that we may well experience the rebirth of a feudal system as destructive of human values as any earlier feudalisms.[17] Of more immediate and practical concern is the absolute necessity to establish the basic economic, political, and legal premises legitimizing the modern corporation. Without this, it will be impossible to translate sound policy recommendations into a consistent and workable rule of law governing the modern corporation.

It is important to note what these conclusions do not say. They do not say, nor do I believe, that the officers and directors of large corporate enterprises are incompetent, evil, or unconcerned. Nor do they assert that private ownership of productive wealth is not the desirable or necessary way to order economic affairs and protect human freedom. What I am saying, however, is that any discussion of a federal corporation law must first consider whether the corporation is any longer the just or ideal device for organizing economic activity. Should these aggregations of a society's wealth, affecting the productive resources of many nations and the livelihood of millions of people, be clothed with a legal personality entitled to perpetual life with an infinite power to accumulate wealth, and be managed by a board of directors that does not direct, and owned by shareholders who do not own?

Just asking the question may suggest some of the dimensions of the problems a federal corporation act should consider. Should perpetual succession be permitted? Should the corporation be clothed with a legal personality? Should the concept of a board of directors be retained any longer? Who are the constituents of the corporation? How can management power be subjected to checks and controls while avoiding the dangers inherent in affirmative government control? To what extent should we rely upon the external check of the market versus reliance upon the internal check of corporate structure to harness management power?

It may be desirable, as well as politically necessary, to avoid facing the revolutionary and complex implications of rethinking these issues. It does not require humility, just honesty, to confess that one has no ready answers to these issues. Perhaps the key to unraveling the public purpose of the modern corporation requires a greater disclosure of the kinds of information necessary to make rational policy judgments. Disclosure is not only essential for a realistic deconcentration program, it is also imperative for making any practical proposals for re-ordering internal corporate relationships. For example, there is little public information about who ultimately owns the top five hundred corporations. Ownership interests are hidden behind a variety of fronts, which render impossible attempts to discover the ultimate control and concentration of wealth. Some trends revealing ownership interests, however, are apparent. The rapid growth of institutional investors, for example, has been widely noted but little understood. We know that institutional investors accounted for almost 50 percent of all public volume on the New York Stock Exchange in 1969 and that their structure and operation tend to further divorce ownership and control.[18] Some suspect institutional investors have the potential for increasingly concentrating economic power in the hands of a few, while also posing a potential threat to entrenched management. Perhaps the mere threat of a proxy battle, tender offer, or merger by an institutional investor may constitute a sufficient check upon arbitrary management power to warrant retention of the *status quo* of "shareholder democracy," no matter how mythical it may be.

If corporate democracy means a rule of law legitimizing management power and defining rights and liabilities within the modern corporation, we may be groping, however disorganized, in its direction. Shareholder interests (investment interests, not entreprenurial interests) are being given expanded legal protection through the development of private remedies under section 10(b) of the Securities Exchange Commission Act of 1934. Employee rights have been receiving expanded protection through labor legislation and civil rights legislation. Consumers have been granted powers to check abuses of management power through private antitrust litigation, consumer protection legislation, and expanded class action procedures. Environmental depredations by unchecked corporate power may be coming to an end by the passage of tough but practical anti-pollution legislation. It even seems possible that the disgrace of undue corporate political power may be curbed by legislation to control political campaign expenditures, unless the 1972 version is as loopholed and unenforced as its 1925 predecessor.

Yet these developments barely legitimize the existing structure and power of the large modern corporation. They do not tell us much about who owns them, how they operate, or what are their political, economic, social, and legal purposes. Nor do these developments offer adequate remedies for an increasing list of suspected adverse consequences of corporate power. There is reason to suspect that the maldistribution of wealth in our society may be caused in part by the existing internal structure and operation of large corporations.[19] There is increasing evidence that the abuse of political power by management needs to be subjected to meaningful internal checks and balances as well as external restraints like civil rights, labor, and antipollution legislation. The loss of control over one's economic, political, and social destiny in the corporate state[20] suggests a need to redefine internal corporate relationships. To do so in ignorance is risky; but not to begin a fundamental attack upon the problem will mean a continued failure to apply the rule of law to the corporation.

It is perhaps time to return to the process of studying problems through remedies rather than the common practice of exhaustive empirical and theoretical research of the problem first and remedies never. Testing specific remedies against existing reality and theory often does more to illuminate a problem than all the commissions, wringing of hands, and academic navel speculation put together. To do so requires that one have little pride of authorship in a suggested remedy and a willingness to re-examine all assumptions. Action in the face of ignorance can be a virtue, if it gets us off the dime.

My suggestions for action in the "corporate democracy" section of a federal corporation statute are predicated upon the following assumptions:

1. Before any rational action can be taken, reform of the political process, particularly its dependence upon large sums of cash, is essential.

2. Full corporate disclosure must be increased regarding the legal and beneficial ownership of the corporation, the process and content of significant economic, political, and social decisions made by the corporation, corporate resource allocation decisions, marketing policies, and profits.

3. Economic concentration—horizontal and vertical, industrial and financial, monopolistic and conglomerate—must be ended if we are to make the system manageable as well as competitive. Socialism of some or all of our large corporations should be avoided; the further extension of affirmative controls must be done with great caution lest we completely destroy the flexibility, freedom, and individuality of our economic system.

4. Shareholders in large corporations, where a separation of ownership and control exists, have no compelling right to share in the profits of our expanding economic base, vis-à-vis other interest groups affected by these corporations.

5. The recognition and protection of some exclusive domain of private individual property rights is indispensable to the protection of individual liberty, the development of individual social independence, and the efficient ordering of individual economic affairs.

6. Economic power, like political power, must be closely restrained if society is to maximize efficient utilization of its economic resources in a manner consistent with the preservation of a free democratic society.

7. The coalescence of political and economic power in our society is to be avoided because of its obvious danger for all concerned; not the least of which are the rights of individuals and the efficiency of economic activity.

8. There is a major maldistribution of wealth in our society. The existing system, including the Internal Revenue Code and all

the trappings of the welfare state, maintains and accelerates that maldistribution of wealth, as do the existing legal and economic structures of the corporation.

With these assumptions as a backdrop, a federal corporation act should contain the following provisions affecting corporate democracy:

PROXY SYSTEM

The present proxy system should remain intact and the evolution now occurring in the SEC and the courts should be encouraged—so long as we do not believe it effectively establishes shareholder democracy or controls the powers of management. As presently structured, the proxy system serves several purposes. It is an important source of disclosure of some information about the corporation; it is a vehicle for launching potentially beneficial attacks upon entrenched oligarchies, even though the attack may be on behalf of another oligarchy; it is a weapon for focusing public attention on the conduct of corporations in the social, political, and economic spheres; and it is a useful device for alerting corporate headquarters to issues managers might not otherwise know or be sensitive about. Campaign GM, a crushing defeat at the corporate ballot box, has been a resounding success in directing public attention to the political and social impact of the auto giant's action and nonaction. The efforts of the Medical Committee for Human Rights, to stop Dow Chemical from producing napalm, have established reviewability of administrative decisions which affect unchecked managerial power to allocate corporate resources; their efforts have opened a potential crack in the legalistic wall insulating corporate management and shareholders from legitimate demands of society.[21]

REDEFINING THE CORPORATE CONSTITUENCY

A federal corporation act must explore the possibility of redefining the corporate constituency and the weight given existing voting rights. Partisans of traditional corporate democracy have often suggested cumulative voting as a device for insuring minority representation on the board. Another suggestion is to change voting power from a basis of one share–one vote to one shareholder–one vote. Both suggestions may have merit in the small or medium-sized corporation but are impractical in the large public issue corporation with millions of shares and thousands of shareholders. Moreover, both proposals are premised upon a theory that shareholders have a legal, economic, or moral right to exercise control because they "own" the corporation. It is, at best, a shaky premise.

The present legal constituency—the shareholder—has not and cannot exercise the franchise in large corporations because of the wide dispersal of stock and the inherent power of management. Moreover, the shareholder's interest is not that of a proprietor but of a gambler in the stock market. Until the justifications for allowing one who toils not to enjoy the net profit of the productive wealth created by the economy are resolved, we should not become overly concerned about their corporate voting rights. Shareholder voting rights are premised upon assumptions that are no longer legitimate or justifiable. The voting record of shareholders indicate that they realize they do not really "own," do not contribute to, and do not control the corporation. Shareholders, however, do have an investment interest in the stock market crap game. As such, they are entitled to a societal guarantee that the rules of the game are equitable and adequately enforced so long as society continues to sanction the game. The protection of the shareholder's investment interest can perhaps develop adequately through Section 10 (b) of the Securities Act of 1934 and through an increased awareness by state courts of a need to insure honesty in stock transactions. The concept of shareholder ownership and control can also be used to fashion legal controls of management powers, by giving shareholders standing to bring direct or derivative suits for breach of fiduciary duties, self-dealing, sale of control, and a host of other potentially unfair management practices. Rather than redefining the constituency to represent more closely modern corporate reality, however, such a trend merely expands the questionable right of shareholders to control, based upon their unrealistic claim of ownership.

Other nominees for the constituency of the corporation have included the general public, the consumer of the particular corporation's product, the government, and employees of the corporation.[22]

To make the general public or the corporation's consumers the constituency is theoretically titillating but hardly workable. The common bond to give the constituency working cohesion is simply not there. Also, the practical expectation that individuals within these groups will rationally or consistently exercise the franchise seems far-fetched. Consumers should be given other methods for curbing the abuse of corporate power, like a truly independent consumer agency, class action rights, meaningful market information, and worthwhile warranty rights. The suggestion that the government have a seat on the board collides with my basic hostility to a coalition of economic and political power. Moreover, there is some evidence that government representation ón a corporate board has simply not made any difference as a practical matter.[23] While my concern on this point may be overcome, I can neither see nor envision a system for government representation that will avoid this dangerous combination of power.

The only cohesive, workable, and effective constituency within view is the corporation's work force. The time has come to recognize labor, white-collar and blue-collar, as a contribution to capital formation and an investment entitled to a voice in the management and a share of the profit. Halting steps in this direction have been made elsewhere. In Germany, the "co-determination" movement has secured equal representation with shareholders on the boards of supervision (the equivalent of our boards of directors) in the iron, steel, and coal industries. The Works Constitution Law of 1952 provides for a lesser degree of representation on boards of supervision in the rest of the economy, and extension of the "co-determination principle" is a major political issue with good prospects for further action in Germany.[24]

In Yugoslavia, an economy starting from a totally different theoretical base than ours, an interesting experiment has been developing. Workers Councils have been established throughout the economy with an objective of establishing self-management of economic enterprises. All employees are entitled to vote in the selection of the Council, which in turn selects an executive body and the managing board. The Council and the representatives of the municipality jointly select the director of the enterprise for a four-year term. Some have seen a great increase in productivity as a result, believing it to be caused by an increase in worker identity and interest in the enterprise.[25]

What claim does labor have to exercise a voice in management? An employee's investment of his entire productive career is a more compelling moral claim than that of the "shareholder," who has not contributed substantial "risk capital" or anything else to the venture. An employee's investment of a career has traditionally been rewarded by a salary and a gold watch at the end of fifty years, except for high-level managers entitled to participate as shareholders through stock option plans. If the legal and economic justification for stock options is to encourage and reward managerial efficiency, why should not that reward and incentive be extended to all employees responsible for increments of enterprise wealth? To permit the continuation of the current state of affairs in the large public issue corporation, where ownership and control are separated and capital formation is largely through internally generated funds, is to create a monolithic monster capable of endless wealth accumulation for the benefit of an undeserving few who contribute little or nothing to the enterprise.

Thus, a federal corporation law should seriously consider nominating the employees of the large corporation as the constituency with sufficient cohesion yet sufficient independence to serve as a meaningful check and balance upon corporate management. Such a proposal —to say the least—will be revolutionary. For example, the function of labor unions may be entirely changed or eliminated if the employee's interest changes from seller of his labor to owner of the enterprise. While a mutual association of employees may still be necessary for an effective use of the franchise, the objective of the association may be radically different from the current objectives of monopolistic large unions bargaining with a monopoly or oligopoly. Employee interests should coincide with company interests rather than industry-wide interests, assuming deconcentration of market control takes place in concentrated industries. Realization of the fruits of increased productivity may take the form of dividends or capital gains growth rather than inflationary wage demands. By the same token, inefficiency, poor workmanship, and unwise exercise of the franchise by employees would not be insulated from the economic retribution of the market place by union contracts or arbitrary union job security policies.

Admittedly, the implications and complications of employee ownership and control would be far-reaching and complex. But if part of the problem with shareholder democracy is the absence of a cohesive, interested constituency, I can see no other alternative but employee ownership and control.

IMPLEMENTING EMPLOYEE OWNERSHIP AS THE CORPORATE CONSTITUENCY

We may well be stumbling in the general direction of employee ownership and control. But if it is unknowingly accomplished, great damage can occur. Thus, the rise of pension trusts—to give employees the tax advantage of a deferred annuity and the security of a retirement income geared to stock values—has occurred in a vacuum of public regulation. The Senate Labor and Public Welfare Committee is beginning a two-year study which, I believe, will uncover widespread abuse of trust and a denial of beneficiary rights. A federal corporation act must confront the social, economic, and political implications of pension trusts as well as other institutional investors. For example, if trustee power to vote the stock of pension trusts is not carefully circumscribed, we will only further accelerate the separation of ownership and control and the concentration of economic power. If employee vesting rights are not clearly established and the portability of pension rights assured, we take a giant step toward feudalism by binding an employee forever to his employer or union, without an effective voice to control the destiny of his retirement investment and with a very strong club in the employer's or union's hand to control employee activity.

MALDISTRIBUTION OF WEALTH

Employee ownership as a device for redistributing wealth is an important facet of establishing the employee as the constituent of the corporation. In their book, *Two-Factor Theory: The Economics of Reality*, Louis Kelso and Patricia Hetter have put forward an intriguing plan for requiring the financing of corporate capital formation by issuing stock to an Employee Stock Ownership Trust to be paid for on credit by future dividends. The plan would require, *inter alia*, a prohibition upon retained earnings, the payment of net earnings in the form of dividends, and major revision of the corporate income tax. Kelso and Hetter's objective is to furnish over 90 percent of the population lacking capital with capital, with a second income, and with a means for minimizing the maldistribution of wealth. It can also create a viable corporate constituency by giving employees of an enterprise the status of shareholders in the enterprise. While I would not subscribe to all the claims and provisions of this suggestion, the plan deserves serious consideration in a federal corporation act dealing with corporate democracy.[26]

REVITALIZING THE BOARD OF DIRECTORS

The corporate laws of all fifty states bravely claim that the business of the corporation shall be managed by a board of directors. As indicated earlier, the board of most major corporations has withered on the vine in practice, if not in theory. The alternatives are abolishing the board and substituting direct election and control of management by the corporate constituency, however defined, or revitalizing the board of directors. In part, the securities laws have added some stimulus for a more active board by imposing some director liability for inequitable stock transactions and insider trading.[27] If political reality dictates working within existing institutions in drafting a federal corporation act, as it probably will, the federal corporation act must make the board of directors into a meaningful institution rather than abolishing it.

One alternative, consistent with my view of employees as the only viable, practical, and legitimate constituency of the corporation, would provide for employee election of all or part of the board. A second alternative is to impose high fiduciary standards of care and loyalty upon directors, regardless of who elects them. The states have not imposed a uniform, consistent, or high duty upon directors. Nor have the states established a uniform system for determining who may enforce the duty. A federal corporation act should consider imposing a uniform standard of trustee, liable for nonfeasance, misfeasance, and malfeasance, and subject to the highest fiduciary standards of loyalty. Such a standard should be coupled with a prohibition upon indemnification and liability insurance[28] in order to make the duty a substantial sanction forcing directors to carry out the theoretical duties imposed upon them by the new federal law. The duties thus imposed should be directly enforceable by shareholders, employees, and the government. Consumers damaged by some corporate action caused by director breach of duty might also be given a direct right of action. The action should be direct rather than derivative to avoid the procedural impediments and substantive complications of derivative suits. In order to avoid the evils of strike suits, secret settlements and contingent fees should be barred, and the courts should be required to set reasonable attorney fees and actual costs for the successful plaintiff.

The establishment of a coherent, equitable, and practical policy toward corporate democracy—whether included in a federal chartering statute or not—forces one to come to grips with the fundamental jurisprudential and economic implications of the modern corporation. The way we resolve the riddle of "shareholder democracy" will go far in determining the precise provisions of a federal corporation act. The way we resolve the issue of "corporate democracy" within or outside a federal corporation statute may well determine whether we will continue the drift toward a new feudalism or whether we organize our economic affairs in a manner consistent with the presumptions of a free democratic society.

VII

CORPORATE SECRECY VS. CORPORATE DISCLOSURE

WILLARD F. MUELLER*

It is fundamental that a market economy functions properly only in an atmosphere of extensive knowledge concerning financial and other aspects of corporate behavior.[1] Contrary to the assertions of many corporate spokesmen, corporate secrecy—not corporate disclosure— is the great enemy of a market economy in a free society. It was a point recognized as early as Theodore Roosevelt's first annual message to Congress in 1901, when he eloquently articulated the rationale for requiring extensive disclosure of the financial and other affairs of large corporations. "Great corporations exist only because they are created and safeguarded by our institutions; and it is our right and our duty to see that they work in harmony with these institutions."

A market-directed economy is premised on intelligent responses of businessmen and investors to profit opportunities. Investors direct the flow of capital funds into the most efficient enterprises. But as a firm becomes increasingly conglomerated, its public financial reports become less and less useful to investors. Additionally, a market economy places heavy reliance on the self-corrective mechanism of the market place to keep competition alive. When a firm holds a strong market position resulting in high profits, this dominance acts as a magnet inducing new entry. Or, conversely, when a firm has higher

---

* Professor of Economics, and a lecturer in law, at the University of Wisconsin; Director, Bureau of Economics, Federal Trade Commission, (1961–68); Executive Director, Cabinet Committee on Price Stability (1968); author of *A Primer on Monopoly and Competition* (1970).

than necessary costs, which result in unprofitable operations, this too
attracts entry and spurs on competitors to better the inefficient company. But again, the published financial statements of the large
conglomerate enterprise mask both the high profits and the losses of
its various operations.

Ironically, American businessmen today operate under two sets of
rules with respect to the disclosure of corporate financial information
—one set for large corporations and another for smaller ones. We
know a great deal about small and medium-sized corporations because, almost invariably, they are quite specialized. One need only
glance at the annual report of almost any industrial company with
annual sales under fifty million dollars to learn its strengths and
weaknesses in a line of business. But not so for large conglomerate
corporations, whose annual reports conceal more than they reveal.
Not surprisingly, therefore, it is the large corporation that invariably
resists steps to strengthen disclosure requirements—steps that in
practice would, at most, place it on a par with smaller corporations.
This is yet another example of allegedly equal treatment under the
law resulting in grossly unequal treatment among those covered by
the law. One is reminded of Anatole France's bitter characterization of the anomaly: "The law with majestic impartiality forbids the
rich and poor alike from stealing bread and sleeping under bridges."

Although proponents of greater disclosure generally have rested
their case on variations of the above arguments, I believe there are
even more compelling reasons for more public access to corporate
affairs. These arguments do not rest merely on the needs of the
investor or the proper functioning of a competitive market but on
the needs for knowledge in a democratic society by the public at
large: by consumers, by public regulatory agencies, by the press,
and by social scientists and others involved in the essential task of
probing and interpreting the changing nature of corporate organization and behavior. For only when important corporate affairs are
exposed to public inspection can the social legitimacy of the corporation be determined. Nor is mine a mere academic interest in urging
that more corporate affairs be open to analyses by social scientists
and others. I would hope most thoughtful Americans agree that it is
absurd to conceal corporate affairs so as to prevent serious and systematic study of an institution vitally affecting the lives of all Amer-

icans. Social scientists today have high-powered tools of analysis but little meaningful data to analyze. Too often our theories remain untested and our computers idle. The situation is akin to giving the scientist an electron microscope but refusing him specimens to examine.

The problems faced by President Nixon's recently created Price Commission provide a timely illustration of how our ignorance of corporate affairs may frustrate public policy. Although the President promised that corporate profits would not be controlled directly, he emphasized that the Price Commission would look to the profit records of certain strategic industries to determine whether particular price increases were justified—which is easier said than done. There are no reliable data readily available on the profits of particular industries. The only information currently available on profitability in manufacturing industries is gathered for the FTC *Quarterly Financial Report on Manufacturing*. In many cases, however, these "industry" data are worse than useless; not only are they extremely aggregated—*e.g.*, electrical machinery, equipment, and supplies—but also individual industries include the entire consolidated profits of large corporations operating across many industries. For example, the profits of International Telephone & Telegraph (ITT) are included in a single FTC "industry" despite the fact that nearly half its profits are earned from foreign operations, another substantial amount from nonmanufacturing industries, and the remainder from such diverse manufacturing industries as electronics, paper, baking, publishing, and chemicals. Yet powerful corporate interests have to date frustrated FTC efforts to require corporations to report their profits on an industry rather than a consolidated basis.

Nor can this problem be dismissed by arguing that the new Price Commission will be given subpoena powers to develop its own data. It is entirely unrealistic to expect that this can be done on an *ad hoc* basis in the crisis atmosphere within which the Price Commission inevitably makes its decisions. Despite all the loose talk about the vast powers of the federal government, the unfortunate truth is that it does not have sufficient economic facts to do this job. And, unhappily, this is only one of numerous examples where our federal government is so woefully uninformed of corporate affairs that even honest and well-intentioned men cannot effectively execute public policy.

This is an intolerable situation. In a free society, no institution vital to the public interest can maintain a claim to legitimacy if its affairs are shrouded in secrecy. Significant steps have been taken in recent years in opening to public view many more governmental affairs, though much more can still be done. The time is long overdue for similar steps to be taken to open the large private corporation, that institution which controls most of our nation's economic activity, to public view.

THE DECLINE IN PUBLIC KNOWLEDGE OF CORPORATE AFFAIRS

The need for more adequate disclosure of corporate financial affairs grows as American corporations grow in size and complexity. Our economic intelligence about much of business organization was better around 1900, when Roosevelt sought to expose the "mammoth" corporations to public view, than it is today. There were few big businesses in Roosevelt's time and these were quite specialized. The great trust movement of the period created only two industrial corporations with assets exceeding five hundred million dollars by 1909, and both of these, U.S. Steel and Standard Oil (N.J.), were specialized to a particular industry. In contrast, by the first quarter of 1971, there were 111 industrial corporations with assets of one billion dollars or more. Although there are about two hundred thousand corporations and nearly two hundred thousand partnerships and proprietorships engaged in manufacturing, by the beginning of 1971 the 111 largest of these held at least 51 percent of the assets and earned 56 percent of the profits of all corporations engaged primarily in manufacturing; the 333 industrial corporations with assets of five hundred million dollars or more accounted for fully 70 percent of all industrial assets, excluding their unconsolidated holdings. Indeed, by 1971 the two largest industrial corporations alone had combined sales of nearly forty-seven billion dollars, which is about as great (in constant dollars) as those of the over two hundred thousand manufacturing establishments operating in 1899.

But much more is involved than an increase in the absolute size of American corporations and the growing share of industrial activity controlled by a relatively few large businesses. Many large contemporary corporations operate across an increasing number of industries and across many national boundaries. Such multiproduct, multinational corporations enjoy far greater flexibility and discretion in deploying their resources than do their smaller, more specialized rivals.

The new dimensions of corporate control extend beyond the economic into the political. Corporate annual reports increasingly read like a state of the nation address, and in some cases like a state of the world address. Indeed, the tone and scope of a recent ITT annual report are not unlike what one might expect of a prime minister's characterization of the British Empire in its days of glory. ITT proudly proclaimed to its stockholders that its vast international organization "is constantly at work around the clock—in 67 nations on six continents, in activities extending from the Arctic to the Antarctic and quite literally from the bottom of the sea to the moon. . . ."[2] It might appropriately have added that its officers and directors have included such international men of affairs as former U. N. Secretary General Trygve Lie, director of ITT–Norway; former Belgium premier Paul-Henry Spaak, a director of ITT–Belgium; two members of the British House of Lords; a member of the French National Assembly; and, at home, John A. McCone, former director of the CIA, and Eugene R. Black, who has held such important posts as president of the International Bank for Reconstruction, special financial advisor to the Secretary General of the U.N., and financial advisor to the sheikh of Kuwait, as well as being a board member of dozens of large corporations.

As perhaps the outstanding example—and success story—of the modern multinational conglomerate corporation, ITT is a useful subject of an inquiry into the adequacy of existing corporate disclosure requirements.

ITT—A CASE STUDY IN INADEQUATE DISCLOSURE

Due to indiscretions concerning its 1971 antitrust settlement, ITT suddenly became a household word in early 1972. Yet its growth, and power, have been of longstanding duration. It grew nearly eight-

fold during the last decade to become one of the world's largest
international corporations; its assets grew from $1.1 billion in 1961
to $8.3 billion in 1970. The latter figure excludes properties valued
at $527 million that are owned by NASA and the Department of
Defense but operated by ITT.[3]

ITT was already a very large company before it became a highly
conglomerated organization. In the four decades following its found-
ing in 1920, it grew into a large international manufacturer of
telecommunications equipment and an operator of telecommunications systems. In the early 1960s, ITT embarked on a major diversifi-
cation-through-merger program in order to change its image from
what its chairman and president characterized as "primarily a
one-product company." During 1961–68 it acquired fifty-two
domestic and fifty-five foreign corporations, with the acquired domestic companies alone holding combined assets of about $1.5 billion.
During 1969 ITT's board of directors approved twenty-two domestic
and eleven foreign acquisitions. The three largest—Hartford Fire
Insurance Company, Grinnell Corporation, and Canteen Corporation—added over two billion dollars. Since 1969 it has acquired
another sixty companies, making it the most acquisitive corporation
of the current merger movement. (The 1971 settlement of three
Justice Department antitrust cases has only partially slowed down
this pace.) Before engaging in this massive merger program in 1960,
ITT ranked thirty-fourth among America's manufacturing companies and forty-third among the industrials of the world. In 1971 it
ranked eighth among America's industrial companies and, with
398,000 employees, it ranked as the fourth largest private industrial
employer of the world.

ITT has retained its telecommunications leadership, ranking as the
world's second largest manufacturer of such products and the largest
outside the United States. But as a result of this acquisition effort,
by 1970 its traditional line of telecommunications and electronics
manufacturing accounted for only 20 percent of its net income.
Much of the rest derived from the operations of leading firms acquired in such diverse businesses as industrial and consumer electrical, electronic, and other industrial products, life insurance, consumer finance, car rentals, hotels, baking, chemical cellulose and

lumber, residential construction, and silica for the glass, chemical, metallurgical, ceramic, and building industries.*

Significantly, most of ITT's acquired assets came not from small, ailing companies but from profitable corporations that were already leaders in their field: Rayonier Corporation had assets of 292 million dollars and was the world's leading producer of chemical cellulose; Continental Baking Company had assets of one hundred eighty-six million dollars and was the world's largest baking and cake company; Avis, Inc., had assets of forty-nine million dollars and was the world's second largest car rental system; Sheraton Corporation of America, with assets of 286 million dollars, was the world's largest hotel and motel system. Levitt & Sons, Inc., with assets of 91 million dollars, was the leading builder of single-family dwellings; Grinnell Corporation had assets of 184 million dollars and was the largest producer of automatic fire protection systems; Canteen Corporation had assets of 140 million dollars and operated one of the largest vending machine systems; Hartford Fire Insurance Corporation is one of the oldest and largest property and casualty insurance writers, with assets of 1.9 billion dollars.

Although ITT is primarily a manufacturing corporation, selling to and buying from thousands of other businesses, it also touches directly the lives of millions. As a consumer you can buy a home and live in one of ITT–Levitt's planned communities; buy furnishings for your home with personal loans from one of ITT's finance subsidiaries; fertilize your lawn with ITT's Scott fertilizer; insure your home at ITT–Hartford Fire Insurance; buy your life insurance from one of ITT's life insurance subsidiaries; invest your savings in ITT–Hamilton Management mutual funds; munch on ITT–Continental bakery products; savor an ITT–Smithfield ham; buy cigarettes and coffee from ITT–Canteen vending machines; stay at hotels or motels owned by ITT–Sheraton; rent a car from ITT–Avis; and buy books from ITT's Bobbs-Merrill publishing division or attend one of ITT's

---

* If another merger of major dimensions with American Broadcasting Company had not been abandoned in January 1968, after a challenge by the Department of Justice, ITT would have been established as a leader in U.S. radio and television broadcasting. It also would have been engaged in the operation of motion picture theaters and amusement centers, and the manufacture and sale of phonograph records.

technical and business schools. Moreover, part of each of your tax dollars spent on defense and space programs goes to ITT, which is one of the nation's leading prime defense contractors. ITT maintains Washington's "hot line" to Moscow, mans the Air Force Distant Early Warning (DEW) system and the giant Ballistic Missile Early Warning System (BMEWS) sites in Greenland and Alaska, the large NASA facility at Cocoa Beach, Florida, and DOD's Western Test Range in California.*

With its numerous foreign operations, ITT is an important force in international economic affairs. Since 1960 ITT has acquired over fifty foreign companies and now has about one-third of Europe's telecommunications business. So the story for Europeans is much the same as for Americans. And, as mentioned earlier, some ITT employees are better known in circles of international diplomacy than in business.** It is not unfair to ask whether such men are on ITT's board because of their business acumen or their prestige in international diplomacy.[4]

The growing multinational character of huge ITT-type conglomerates raises important issues concerning their national sovereignties and allegiances. Their composition creates dual loyalties that make it difficult to perceive the American national interest in their dealings at home and abroad. Perhaps Thomas Jefferson's observation is as apt today as when he made it in a much simpler world. "Merchants have no country," said Jefferson. "The mere spot they stand on does not constitute so strong an attachment as that from which they draw their gain." Perhaps more importantly, massive multinational corporations like ITT have dimensions of economic and political power extending beyond that held by the traditional large corporations which, while large in absolute terms, are more narrowly specialized

---

* The recent antitrust consent agreement required that ITT divest Canteen Corporation, Avis, Levitt, the fire protection division of Grinnell, and Hamilton Life and ITT Life Insurance divisions, a package involving assets of $792 million. According to trade reports, even financial analysts were baffled as to the probable impact of the divestiture on ITT's financial picture, as ITT's common stock fell from $62 before the settlement was announced to as low as $52.12½ a share immediately following the announcement.[7]

** As this book goes to press, Senator William Fulbright's Senate Foreign Relations Committee is beginning a detailed look at ITT's meddling role in the past Chilean election, as alleged by ITT memoranda released by columnist Jack Anderson.

in relatively few lines of industry. Such corporations truly fit into President Woodrow Wilson's characterization in 1919 of the great corporations of his period. In his view, "These great corporations are economic states. They are no longer private corporations." The large international corporations of today obviously are much larger "economic states" than those troubling Wilson five decades ago.

Despite the enormous growth of ITT over the last decade, we really know less about its constituent parts than we did in 1960, when it was still quite specialized. Each time ITT acquires a public corporation, it further diminishes our economic intelligence of American industrial organization, as the operating statements and balance sheets of the acquired companies are subsumed in ITT's consolidated statements. In 1970 ITT provided the public precious little financial information on its operations. Although it manufactured numerous products, it broke down its net assets into only four broad categories: "manufacturing," "consumer and business services," "telecommunications utilities," and "consolidated," with the largest share (49 percent) in the "consolidated" category.[5] It did little better with respect to sales and income information, which are detailed below:

PRINCIPAL ITT PRODUCT GROUPS, 1970[6]

| | Sales and Revenues | | Net Income | |
	millions	percent	millions	percent
Manufacturing				
Telecommunications Equipment	$1,244	19	$ 52	15
Industrial & Consumer Products	1,849	29	71	20
Natural Resources	287	5	30	8
Defense & Space Programs	316	5	8	2
Subtotal	3,696	58	161	45
Consumer & Business Services				
Food Processing & Services	1,241	19	30	8
Consumer Services	808	13	19	6
Business & Financial Services	386	6	21	6
Hartford Fire	—	—	88	25
Subtotal	2,435	38	158	45
Utility Operations	233	4	34	10
Total	$6,364	100%	$353	100%

Except for Hartford Fire Insurance Company, it is impossible to determine the financial contribution of the over one hundred operations acquired by ITT since 1960. With annual sales of near $350 million when acquired in 1969, Grinnell in 1970 was submerged in ITT's Industrial and Consumer Product group, which had reported sales of $1,849 million. Similarly, such important and diverse acquisitions as Avis-Rent-A-Car, Canteen, Levitt & Sons, Sheraton Hotels, and Bobbs-Merrill Publishing were included in ITT's Consumer and Business Services group along with divisions manufacturing frozen foods, providing technical education, running parking lots, and owning other industry or service categories.

ITT's reporting procedures recently were severely criticized by a leading financial analyst. Mr. David Norr, partner of the First Manhattan Company and recently appointed to the Accounting Principles Board, criticized ITT's annual report for not reflecting retroactively the results of the many companies it had acquired. Norr reportedly indicated that this was sufficient grounds for the New York Stock Exchange to halt trading in ITT securities.[8] Also, because ITT used the pooling-of-interest method of accounting, it reportedly overstated greatly the earnings generated by the companies it acquired during 1964–68. It paid $1,278 million for companies with net worth of $534 million. According to an analysis of these acquisitions by the staff of the House Antitrust Subcommittee, if this excess payment for "goodwill" had been amortized over a ten-year period, "ITT's reported net income for 1968 would be overstated by 70.4 percent."[9] Lest you assume ITT's financial reporting practices are below par for large corporations, let me remind you that for four consecutive years ITT received the top award of the Financial Analysts Federation for "excellence in corporate reporting." Obviously, ITT has much company when it comes to inadequate reporting.

THE SEC'S FAILURE
TO REQUIRE ADEQUATE DISCLOSURE

For many years the SEC had a rule that corporations subject to its jurisdiction had to disclose the relative importance of each product, service, or class of similar products that contributed 15 percent or more to gross sales.[10] This rule had long been criticized as being excessively broad, but the SEC remained unmoved. Then Senator Philip Hart's Senate Subcommittee on Antitrust and Monopoly held hearings in 1965 on the subject, and threatened to introduce legislation directing the SEC to require divisional or some other more definitive form of segmented sales and profit reporting. SEC Chairman, Manuel F. Cohen, subsequently informed Senator Hart that the SEC already had the authority to require adequate disclosure and that it was considering doing so.[11]

During the next few years, there was considerable discussion and controversy in the business community, particularly among public accountants, a number of whom had long been critical of this and other SEC reporting requirements.[12] But most of the accounting fraternity opposed stricter rules. Finally, on September 4, 1968, the SEC issued a proposed rule that would have required, among other things, corporations to report the sales and net income of each class of related or similar products which contribute 10 percent or more to sales or net income. These rules, however, are totally inadequate for large corporations, as was pointed out to former SEC Chairman Manuel Cohen prior to their adoption.[13] They require much more detailed disclosure from small corporations than from large ones, and, as noted above, international conglomerates the likes of ITT need disclose few details of the sources of their profits.

Not only did the SEC permit large corporations to report financial details of merely their largest product lines but it also failed to adopt rules guaranteeing comparability in reporting. Rather than establish criteria of its own, the SEC gave management discretion in deciding what constituted meaningful product categories. It did so on the premise that "management, because of its familiarity with company structure, is in the most informed position to separate the company into components on a reasonable basis for reporting purposes. Accordingly, discretion is left to the management to devise a reporting pattern appropriate to the particular company's operations and responsive to its organizational concepts."[14]

This episode argues forcefully for adopting a more direct approach to the question of corporate secrecy. Because the SEC has repeatedly demonstrated an inability or unwillingness to perform responsibly in this area, I think a new legislative mandate is required. Even were the agency to perform more responsibly in the future than in the past, new legislation is required because the SEC's authority is restricted almost entirely to financial disclosure relevant to protecting the investor. The consumer and general public are equally entitled to know about a corporation's activities and performance.

THE NEED FOR FEDERAL CHARTERING

But how best to go about requiring adequate public disclosure of corporate affairs? One essential first step in my judgment is legislation requiring federal chartering of all large corporations. This is not a new idea, as already noted in Ralph Nader's chapter. While some politicians have favored the idea, so have some academicians from time to time urged federal chartering of corporations; perhaps the strongest case was made by Henry C. Simons in his historic proposal for "A Positive Program for Laissez Faire": "As a main feature of the program, *there must be a complete 'new deal' with respect to the private corporation* . . . the corporation is simply running away with our economic (and political) system by virtue merely of an absurd carelessness and extravagance on the part of the states in granting powers to these legal creatures."[15] Simons, therefore, recommended "transfer to the federal government of the exclusive power to charter ordinary, private corporations, and subsequent annulment of all charters granted by the states."[16]

Because of this changed character of the American business scene, it is appropriate that large corporations be recognized and treated as quasipublic institutions. Federal chartering can be an appropriate first step in the transformation of the large corporation from a purely private enterprise to a quasipublic enterprise. Obviously, this effort is only one part of a more comprehensive program to assure this end. One of the virtues of adopting federal chartering, as opposed to a series of individual reforms aimed at the same goals, is that such action will require an explicit public decision recognizing the role that large corporations play in contemporary society. This decision will necessarily involve a great public policy debate on the future role and responsibility of the large corporation. In my view, such a debate is imperative to the continued social legitimacy of big business, for out of the discussion will come a new consensus of what it is reasonable and appropriate to expect from the large corporation.

One is tempted to settle for piecemeal reform, as witness the SEC compromise in setting disclosure standards. The politician's slogan, "half a loaf is better than none," has great popular appeal. But this siren call of pragmatism often serves only to frustrate adequate reform. For half a loaf is not better than none of it only dulls the appetite and the legitimate demand for a full meal. There are times when the wisest and most pragmatic course, then, is to take an uncompromising stand. I therefore propose a direct assault on the corporate secrecy issue across a broad front, an assault premised on what Justice Louis Brandeis emphasized as "the essential difference between corporations and natural persons." If a public consensus can be mustered to confront head-on the corporate secrecy issue, a federal chartering statute requiring extensive public disclosure would be preferable to a piecemeal attack on the numerous individual statutes and administrative rulings that presently protect the corporation from public view.

DISCLOSURE REQUIREMENTS
OF FEDERALLY CHARTERED CORPORATIONS

Perhaps such a charter need apply only to corporations with assets exceeding one billion dollars, which would embrace just over one hundred industrial corporations and perhaps another one hundred and fifty in all other fields. Not only do these corporations account for most economic activity in many strategic industries, but we know least about these corporations because of their multiproduct and multinational character. A federal charter should include the following provisions setting forth the public disclosure requirements of large corporations.

Segmented Reporting of Investment, Revenue, and Profit

Corporations should disclose their financial characteristics in much greater detail than now required by the SEC. Criteria for determining adequate disclosure should not be restricted to those necessary for investment purposes, as required by the Securities Exchange Act of 1934, but also for the broader public policy purposes discussed above. In addition, investment, revenue, and profit information should be disclosed in as narrow product lines as possible and should be sufficiently uniform to permit intercorporate comparisons. By establishing appropriate product lines or reporting segments, the chartering agency should have access to a corporation's records and files. When deemed necessary, the chartering agency should require a corporation to use accounting procedures and to maintain financial records that insure uniform reporting procedures.

Public Disclosure of Product Information

Corporations should make public the volume of the various products that they manufacture and distribute. The degree of detail contemplated by this provision goes well beyond that of the preceding provision, which recognizes that it often may be impossible to develop meaningful financial information on individual products. No such problems exist, of course, with respect to sales or shipments data for individual products. To reduce the reporting burden and to insure uniform reporting, the first step in implementing this provision should be to make public the data large corporations now report to the Bureau of the Census.[17] The chartering agency should then establish appropriate requirements where the criteria currently employed by the Bureau of the Census are deemed inadequate.

In this area, as in many others, corporations have succeeded in enacting legislation that cloaks in secrecy information that at one time was available to the public. Prior to the enactment of the Sherman Act in 1890, the Bureau of the Census reported information in considerable detail, publishing capital investment and sales data for individual manufacturing establishments on a county basis (and for 1839 on a city basis). As a result, disclosure of individual company operations was commonplace for the big businesses of that period. But commencing in 1890, corporations succeeded in shielding from public view details of individual companies reporting to the Census Bureau. Today governmental regulatory agencies are prevented access to this information, even where they do not disclose it. Indeed, in 1962 large corporations were successful in enacting the Henderson-Johnston Act, which prohibits a regulatory agency from subpoenaing from a corporation's files any copies of reports made to the Census Bureau. As a result, corporations may now destroy many historical sales records required for normal business operations, relying instead on their copies of reports to the Census Bureau, thereby forestalling regulatory agencies from obtaining information for any but the most recent years.

Disclosure of Corporate Tax Returns

The public should have access to income and other federal tax returns of large corporations. Currently, the same degree of confidentiality is accorded corporate income tax returns as is accorded the returns of individual citizens. Indeed, the degree of confidentiality has been increased by administrative action in recent years; consequently, regulatory and other government agencies have little or no access to such records despite their great amount of information relevant for the effective functioning of these agencies. For example, in 1965 an appropriations subcommittee of the United States Senate intimidated the Federal Trade Commission into promising not to seek access to the tax returns of individual corporations, although it was legally entitled to do so. Shortly thereafter the Bureau of the Budget of the Executive Office of the President revised its procedures in order to greatly restrict access to corporate tax returns by all government agencies.

There was a time when the public had complete access to corporate tax returns in some states, but such access has been greatly eroded in recent decades. For example, until 1953 the State of Wisconsin's revenue statute gave the public free access to and almost unrestricted use of the State's corporate tax returns. The only restriction provided that, "No person shall divulge or circulate for revenue or offer to obtain, divulge or circulate for compensation any information derived from income tax returns." The statute emphasized, however, "that this [provision] shall not be construed to prohibit publication by any newspaper of information derived from income tax returns for purposes of argument nor to prohibit any public speaker from referring to such information in any address." This statute was amended in 1953 to permit the public access only to information of the net income tax paid (which, of course, was already reported in corporate annual reports), not to the tax return itself. However, complete access is still available to officers of the State or its political subdivisions or their authorized agents, members of legislative committees or their agents, the federal government, and persons examining such returns pursuant to a court order upon showing to the court that the information in such returns is relevant to a pending court action. The leading champions of the 1953 bill greatly restricting the degree of public access to tax returns were the Wisconsin Automotive Trade Association and the Wisconsin and Milwaukee Chambers of Commerce.

Disclosure of Intercorporate Holdings

Corporations should make public all their holdings in other domestic and foreign corporations, including wholly and jointly owned subsidiary corporations. In the case of jointly owned subsidiaries, corporations should also disclose the holdings in such subsidiaries of other major corporate stockholders, both domestic and foreign. Existing SEC rules require corporations to report information only for those corporations over which they "exercise control" and which constitute 15 percent or more of their aggregate assets. As a result, the larger a corporation, the less information it need disclose. For example, in 1968 Standard Oil (N.J.) had investments of about one billion dollars. It was not possible, however, to identify from public sources even the names of all the corporations in which it had investments, and it was not possible to identify the value of the assets of *any* of these corporations.

Disclosure of Publicly Owned Facilities Operated or Leased by Private Corporations

Large corporations should be required to disclose any facilities that they operate for or lease from the federal government. The information reported should include detailed statements of the nature of business or services involved and the contractual arrangements governing the use and operation of such facilities.[18] In 1967 corporations operated federally owned properties with a value of at least $14.7 billion. This represents an enormous volume of "hidden" assets controlled by large corporations. It is virtually impossible for the public, and even Congressional committees, to obtain even the barest details of the extent and nature of such operations.

Disclosure of Foreign Operations

Multinational American corporations should be required to disclose the extent and nature of their foreign operations, including the identity of board members of their foreign-based subsidiaries and the financial interest and other ties that such subsidiaries may have with other U.S. or foreign corporations.

Disclosure of Social Costs

It is becoming increasingly commonplace for corporations to include in their annual reports—and advertisements—statements of the costs they incur in cleaning up the environment and in undertaking other efforts to improve the quality of life. In certain circumstances it would seem sound public policy that corporations also disclose the social costs of their operations, that is, costs they impose on society (*e.g.*, pollution) that are not reflected in the corporation's balance sheet. It might also be desirable to require corporations to disclose their expenditures in improving product safety and other aspects of product quality. Another important category of practices requiring public disclosure relates to minority employment practices. Recent studies indicate that corporations with market power have poorer records in employing minority groups than businesses in more competitive industries. In view of the critical nature of this problem in contemporary society, the public is entitled to know what our largest corporations are contributing to its solution. These disclosure requirements help society better evaluate a corporation's total benefits and costs to society.

Public Representation on the Board of Directors

The chartering agency should have the right to appoint at least one member to the board of directors of corporations where this is necessary to obtain information on corporate affairs especially critical to the public interest.

Such a public board member would serve as a window through which the public could view the inner workings of the corporations. Robert Townsend has emphasized the desirability of such public board members. In his view such a public representative on the board could be of invaluable assistance to the government agencies—*e.g.*, the antitrust authorities, the Department of Transportation, and the Department of Environmental Protection—in asking the right questions to determine whether corporations were complying with the law.

Organization and Procedures of the Chartering Agency

The chartering agency should have sufficient staff and develop sufficient expertise and management capability so that it can perform its functions effectively without heavy reliance on private accountants and industry experts. It should be required to consult with and obtain the views of the antitrust agencies, other appropriate governmental agencies, and public advisory panels (not including representatives of federally chartered corporations). Safeguards should be taken to insure that the agency remains independent of the corporations which it charters. I believe a properly constituted collegial agency independent of the President is most likely to accomplish this end. All aspects of such an agency's operations should, to the fullest extent possible, be open to public view. Among other things, it should hold public hearings when formulating new rules and should make public reports explaining its reasons for adopting particular rules. Participants in such hearings should include the chartering agency's staff, corporations affected by the rules, and interested members of the public.

This skeletal program for providing greater public disclosure of corporate affairs is clearly not an attack on our market economy but an effort to improve it. In truth, it is a rather conservative program. Nor is this proposal a substitute for a vigorous program to make competition more effective wherever possible. On the contrary, it complements efforts to improve competition by opening new opportunities for the operation of "natural" market forces. But though the program recognizes that competition is not dead (*pace* Galbraith in his *New Industrial State*)[19] as an important disciplining influence in most American industries, it also recognizes that giant corporations enjoy great discretion in making numerous decisions that affect our social, cultural, political as well as economic welfare. More complete disclosure by large corporations therefore serves the dual objectives of aiding natural market forces in doing their job and of providing the other broader benefits to society flowing from more complete information of corporate affairs.

What are the prospects for the adoption of this approach? Perhaps none in the short run. But breezes of change are blowing from many directions: public accountants, financial analysts, investors, and even corporate officials. A broader constituency than this, however, is required for those parts of the program unrelated to the investor. Smaller businessmen and labor are natural parts of this constituency since both are disadvantaged by the present aura of secrecy surrounding the operations of large corporations. The constituency also should logically include the consumer movement, environmentalists, and other broader public interest groups that increasingly question the legitimacy of the large modern corporation. For the public can only answer questions of legitimacy if it has access to what Theodore Roosevelt demanded seven decades ago, "knowledge, full and complete; knowledge which may be made public to the world."

VIII

THE ANTITRUST ALTERNATIVE

WALTER ADAMS*

In 1960 Paul Samuelson and Robert A. Solow published their land-mark article on the Phillips curve.[1] They showed that a post-industrial society like the United States could achieve price stability, but only at the cost of some unemployment, or could achieve the objective of full employment, but at the cost of some inflation. Price stability during the 1960s, they wrote, would involve unemployment of roughly 5½ percent; alternatively, unemployment could be reduced to the 3-percent level if we were prepared to accept a 4½-percent annual inflation rate. The implications were clear: the American economy was vulnerable not only to traditional demand-pull inflation but also, because of structural imperfections in the institutional fabric, to cost-push inflation.

The Samuelson-Solow analysis, however, was largely ignored. Economists indulged their penchant for irrelevance, heatedly debating the comparative virtues of monetary versus fiscal policy as anti-inflationary weapons. Only recently has there been some recognition that *neither* policy has successfully coped with inflation of the last decade. Professor Milton Friedman, for example, leader of the "conservative" monetarists, now concedes that if his predictions for 1969–70 had been accurate, the maximum rate of price increases would have been 4 to 4.5 percent instead of the actual 6.5 to 7 per-

* Professor of Economics at Michigan State University; acting president and president of Michigan State University (1969–70); co-author of *Monopoly in America* (1956); editor of *The Structure of American Industry* (1971), and others.

cent. Similarly, Arthur Okun, "liberal" fiscalist and member of President Johnson's Council of Economic Advisers, now admits to being deeply distressed by the failure of the 10-percent income tax surcharge of mid-1968 to dampen the inflationary boom. "When we were able to call the policy tune," he recalls ruefully, "the economy did not dance to it." And while neither monetary nor fiscal policy stemmed inflation, unemployment, of course, continued on its merry rise—with an average rate of 3.5 percent in 1969, 4.9 percent in 1970, and 5.9 percent in 1971.

Given this confusion among professional economists, it is understandable perhaps that politicians persisted in clinging to certain comfortable illusions. Thus, for two and one half years, President Nixon tried to deal with inflation as if economic power were not concentrated, as if a benevolently competitive market performed its traditional regulatory control over the economy, and as if orthodox monetary and fiscal policies could cope with structural problems like inflation in the midst of recession.

By mid-1971, finally, Mr. Nixon began to acknowledge what should have been obvious facts of life, *viz.* that the American economy was honeycombed with pervasive concentrations of economic power; that powerful unions could raise wages and giant corporations could raise prices; that government monetary and fiscal policy can be subverted by power groups immune from the discipline of the competitive market mechanism; in short, that cost-push inflation requires a candid confrontation with the existence of concentrated power and its consequences. Consequently, on August 15, 1971, the President peremptorily imposed a wage-price freeze to be followed, ninety days later, by Phase II of his New Economic Policy. Under Phase II—for a period yet unspecified—wages and prices in major industries are to be regulated by a troika of government agencies. These agencies, not the impotent "competitive" market in which he had formerly placed his trust, are to protect the public from the rapacious exploiters inhabiting the New Industrial State.

THE ILLUSION OF DIRECT CONTROLS

This game plan, I submit, is musty wine in old bottles. It is a public policy, dating back to the age of the robber barons, when wily tycoons first learned that government regulation of prices posed no threat to their vested power.

In 1892, Richard S. Olney, a railroad executive slated to become Attorney General in the Cleveland Administration, explained to another railroad mogul why it would be counterproductive to abolish the Interstate Commerce Commission:

> My impression would be that looking at the matter from a railroad point of view exclusively it would not be a wise thing to undertake. . . . The Commission, as its functions have now been limited by the courts, is, or can be made, of great use to the railroads. It satisfies the popular clamor for a government supervision of the railroads, at the same time that that supervision is almost entirely nominal. Further, the older such a commission gets to be, the more inclined it will be found to take the business and railroad view of things. It thus becomes a sort of barrier between the railroad corporations and the people and a sort of protection against hasty and crude legislation hostile to railroad interests. . . . The part of wisdom is not to destroy the Commission, but to utilize it.

Testifying before the Stanley Committee in 1911, Judge Elbert H. Gary, president of the U.S. Steel Corporation, also endorsed regulation as a public control mechanism. He made it very clear that he preferred a regime of regulation to the discipline of competition:

> . . . [I]t is very important to consider how the people shall be protected against imposition or oppression as the possible result of great aggregations of capital, whether in the possession of corporations or individuals. . . . I believe that the Sherman Act does not meet and will never fully prevent that. I believe we must come to enforced publicity and governmental control, even as to prices, and . . . I would be very glad if we had some place where we could go, to a responsible governmental authority, and say to them, "Here are our facts and figures, here is our property, here our cost of production; now you tell us what we have the right to do and what prices we have the right to charge." I know this is a very extreme view, and I know that the railroads objected to it for a long time; but whether the standpoint of making the most money is concerned or not, whether it is the wise thing, I believe it is the necessary thing, and it seems to me corporations have no right to disregard these public questions and these public interests.

And today, big business seems graciously acquiescent in the proposed wage-price controls, while erstwhile Nixon critics—notably Professor Galbraith—give the President an A-minus for embarking on the arcane mysteries of regulatory economics. If the new game plan is intended to replace competition as a protective mechanism for the public interest, I wish to register my dissent and predict its failure. I do so largely on the basis of our experience with the independent regulatory commissions which have proved to be near-disaster:[2]

1. Regulation is based on the dubious assumption that government commissions are a monolithic force, separate and apart from the economy, untainted and untouchable by the interests they are supposed to regulate. But experience indicates that what starts as regulation usually ends up as protection, that commissions like the ICC protect their industry from competition rather than the public from exploitation. The commissions, originally designed as instruments of countervailing power, degenerate into handmaidens of coalescing power, never successfully dealing with the question, "*quis ipsos custodes custodiet?*"

2. Regulation is, at best, a negative force for right conduct. A government commission can refuse to recommend a price increase, but it cannot compel an industry to lower production costs. It has no power to force regulated firms to spend money on new plants or scrap old plants. It cannot tell firms to increase expenditures on research and development, or to be more progressive in invention and innovation. Even if the commission had a perfectly clear view of what potentially attainable cost reductions and correct conduct are, how could it gently admonish powerful firms to comply with its prescriptions? Regulated firms may be prevented from doing the wrong things, but they cannot be forced to do the right things to serve the public interest.

3. Regulation, even if desirable in the short run, is not a substitute but a complement to competition; that is, it cannot function effectively wtihout some exogenous force to discipline the conservative bias of both regulatees and regulators. I note in passing that it is not the "public interest" regulation by the Civil Aeronautics Board but the peripheral competition of charters, excursions, and group plans which threatens the high-fare stranglehold of the

cartel run by the International Air Transport Association. The history of the regulated industries is replete with examples to document the proposition that competition, not regulation, forces innovations on bureaucratic managers and their permissive guardians.

4. It has been argued that regulation is justified because competition is a twentieth-century anachronism, the implementation of which would require the restructuring of practically the entire manufacturing economy. Regulation, it is said, is nothing but a rational response to the economic inevitabilities and technological imperatives of modern industrialism. In this view, a relic from our age of innocence, firms are big because they are efficient; firms are big because they are progressive; firms are big because they are good; firms are big because consumers have made them big. But, as we should already know and as I will show presently, industrial concentration in some sectors of the economy is not the result of natural law, or the outgrowth of inexorable technological imperatives.

THE VIABILITY OF COMPETITION

John Kenneth Galbraith is probably the most articulate and influential economist to propagate the view that a trade-off is necessary between competition, on the one hand, and efficiency, progressiveness, and planning, on the other. He urges that we accept the inevitable and foresake the "charade of antitrust" in favor of a more realistic regimen of direct controls. Unfortunately, he offers little empirical evidence to support the claim that competition is an anachronism and that its euthanasia is justified in the public interest.

Efficiency

In the mass-production industries, firms must undoubtedly be large, but do they need to assume the dinosaur proportions of some present-day giants? The unit of technological efficiency is the plant, not the firm. Thus, while there are undisputed advantages to large-scale integrated operations at a single steel plant, for example, there is little technological justification for combining these functionally separate plants into a single administrative unit. United States Steel is nothing more than several Inland Steels strewn about the country, and no one has yet suggested that Inland is not big enough to be efficient. A firm producing such divergent lines as rubber boots, chain saws, motorboats, and chicken feed may be seeking conglomerate size and power; it is certainly not responding to technological necessity. In short, one can favor technological bigness and oppose administrative bigness without inconsistency.

Two major empirical studies document this generalization. The first, by Dr. John M. Blair, indicates a significant divergence between plant and company concentration in major industries dominated by oligopoly. It indicates that between 1947 and 1958 there was a general tendency for plant concentration to decline, which means that in many industries technology may actually militate toward optimal efficiency in plants of "smaller" size.[3] The second study, by Professor Joe Bain, presents engineering estimates of scale economies and capital requirements in twenty industries of above-average concentration. Bain finds that "Concentration by firms is in every case but one greater than required by single-plant economies, and in more than half of the cases very substantially greater." In less precise language, many multiplant industrial giants have gone beyond the optimal size required for efficiency. Galbraith acknowledges the validity of Bain's findings, but dismisses them by saying, "The size of General Motors is in the service not of monopoly or the economies of scale, but of planning. And for this planning . . . there is no clear upper limit to the desirable size. It could be that the bigger the better."[4] If size is to be justified, then, this must be done on grounds other than efficiency. I shall return to this point in a moment.

Technological progress

As in the case of efficiency, there is no strict correlation between giantism and progressiveness. In a study of the sixty most important inventions of recent years, it was found that more than half came from independent inventors, less than half from corporate research, and even less from the research done by large concerns.[5] Moreover, while some highly concentrated industries spend a large share of their income on research, others do not; within the same industry, some smaller firms spend as high a *percentage* as their larger rivals. As Clair Wilcox points out, "The big concern has the ability to finance innovation; it does not necessarily do so. There is no clear relationship between size and investment in research."[6]

Finally, roughly two-thirds of the research done in the United States is financed by the federal government, and in many cases the research contractor gets the patent rights on inventions paid for with public funds. The inventive genius which ostensibly goes with size would seem to involve socialization of risk and privatization of profit.

The U.S. steel industry, which ranks among the largest, most basic, and most concentrated of American industries—certainly part of Professor Galbraith's industrial state—affords a dramatic case in point. It spends only 0.7 percent of its revenues on research and, in technological progressiveness, the giants which dominate this industry lag behind their smaller domestic rivals as well as their smaller foreign competitors. Thus, the basic oxygen furnace—considered the "only major breakthrough at the ingot level since before the turn of the century"—was invented in 1950 by a miniscule Austrian *firm* which was less than one-third the size of a single *plant* of the United States Steel Corp. The innovation was introduced in the United States in 1954 by McLouth Steel, which at the time had about 1 percent of domestic steel capacity—to be followed some ten years later by the steel giants: United States Steel in December 1963, Bethlehem in 1964, and Republic in 1965. Despite the fact that this revolutionary invention involved an average operating cost saving of five dollars per ton and an investment cost saving of twenty dollars per ton of installed capacity, the steel giants during the 1950s, according to *Business Week*, "bought forty million tons of the wrong capacity—the open-hearth furnace" which was obsolete almost the moment it was put in place.[7] Only after they were subjected to actual and threatened competition from domestic and foreign steelmakers in the 1960s did the steel giants decide to accommodate themselves to the oxygen revolution. Thus, it was the cold wind of competition, and not the catatonia induced by industrial concentration, which proved conducive to innovation and technological progress.[8]

Planning in the public interest

Modern technology, says Galbraith, makes planning essential, and the giant corporation is its chosen instrument. This planning, in turn, requires the corporation to eliminate risk and uncertainty, to create for itself an environment of stability and security, to free itself from all outside interference with its planning function. Consequently, it must have enough size and power not only to produce a "mauve and cerise, air-conditioned, power-steered, and power-braked automobile"[9]—unsafe at any speed—but also enough power to brainwash customers to buy it. In the interest of planning, producers must be able to sell what they make—be it automobiles or missiles—and at prices which the technostructure deems remunerative.

Aside from the unproved premise of technological necessity on which this argument rests, it raises crucial questions of responsibility and accountability. By what standards do the industrial giants plan, and is there an automatic convergence between private and public advantage? Must we, as a matter of inexorable inevitability, accept the proposition that what is good for General Motors is good for the country? What are the safeguards—other than the intellectual in politics—against arbitrary abuse of power, capricious or faulty decision-making? Must society legitimatize a self-sustaining, self-serving, self-justifying, and self-perpetuating industrial oligarchy as the price for industrial efficiency and progress?

This high price need not and should not be paid. The competitive market is a far more efficacious instrument for serving society, and far more viable, than its critics would have us believe. Let me illustrate:

    1. In the electric power industry, a network of local monopolies, under government regulation and protection, was long addicted to the belief that the demand for electric power was inelastic, that rates had little to do with the quantity of electricity used. It was not industrial planning, carried on by private monopolists under public supervision, but the yardstick competition of TVA which demonstrated the financial feasibility of aggressive rate reductions. It was this competitive experiment which proved that lower electric rates were not only possible but also profitable, both to the private monopolists and to the customers they served.

    2. In the airline oligopoly, also operating under the umbrella of government protectionism, the dominant firms long suffered from the same addiction. They refused to institute coach service on the

grounds that it would eliminate first-class service and, through a reduction in the rate structure, bring financial ruin to the industry. Again, a bureaucracy-ridden, conservative, overcautious, over-protected industry was shown to have engaged in defective planning—to its own detriment as well as the public's. And again it was the force and discipline of competition—from the small, nonscheduled carriers, operating at the margin of the industry—which showed the giants and their overprotective public regulators to be wrong. As a Senate committee observed, it was the pioneering and competition of the nonskeds which "shattered the concept of the fixed, limited market for civil aviation. As a result, the question is no longer what portion of a fixed pie any company will get, but rather how much the entire pie can grow."[10]

3. In the steel industry, after World War II, oligopoly planning resulted in truly shabby performance. There was an almost unbroken climb in steel prices, in good times and bad, in the face of rising or falling demand, increasing or declining unit costs. Prices rose even when only 50 percent of the industry's capacity was utilized. Technological change was resisted and obsolete capacity installed. Domestic markets were eroded by substitute materials and burgeoning imports. Steel's export-import balance deteriorated both in absolute and relative terms; whereas the industry once exported about five times as much as it imported, the ratio today is almost exactly reversed, and steel exports are confined almost exclusively to AID-financed sales guaranteed by "Buy American" provisos. If this deplorable performance is to be improved, it will come about through the disciplining force of domestic and foreign competition, and not through additional planning or an escalation of giant size. It will come about through an accommodation to the exigencies of the world market, and not by insensitive monopolistic pricing, practiced under the protectionist shelter of tariffs, quotas, and similar impediments to competition.

THE NONINEVITABILITY OF CONCENTRATION

As I read the industrial history of the United States, I find that the trend toward concentration of economic power is not a response to natural law or inexorable technological imperatives. Rather, it is the result of institutional forces which are subject to control, change, and reversal, such as the magnitude, velocity, and character of successive merger movements; the inadequacy of existing antitrust laws and/or the desultory performance of the enforcement agencies; and the unwise, man-made, discriminatory, privilege-creating actions of Big Government. These propositions can be illustrated by an admittedly cursory reference to two major industries, steel and oil.

The Case of Steel

The structure of the steel industry is a prime example of how massive mergers, antitrust forebearance, and governmental favoritism combine to produce an oligopoly with all the earmarks of non-competitive conduct and lackluster performance. Table 1 chronicles the number of steel mergers between 1899 and 1947. Though massive in scope, these mergers were allowed to stand after the Supreme Court proved reluctant to break asunder what promoters had illegally joined together.

TABLE 1

NUMBER OF COMPANIES ACQUIRED
BY 12 MAJOR STEEL PRODUCERS[11]

Period	Blast Furnaces	Steel Works & Rolling Mills	Fabricators
1899–1909	32	171	37
1909–1919	11	15	5
1919–1929	19	23	17
1929–1939	7	25	50
1939–1947	5	13	20

After World War II, a generous War Surplus Administration permitted U.S. Steel, Republic, and Armco to buy plants built at government expense, thus strengthening their oligopoly hold on the industry. U.S. Steel, for example, got the green light to purchase the Geneva Steel plant (built at a cost of 202 million dollars and sold to the Corporation for 47 million dollars) which increased its total capacity in the Pacific Coast and Mountain states from 17.3 to 39 percent, and brought its steel ingot capacity in the area up to 51 percent.

After the passage of the Celler-Kefauver Act of 1950, the government held the line on further mergers. In 1958, a U.S. District

Court blocked the proposed merger of Bethlehem and Youngstown which would have combined the second and sixth largest steel producers in the country. In 1969, Attorney General John Mitchell refused to approve the merger of Cyclops and Sharon which would have combined the seventeenth and eighteenth largest steel producers. At the time Mr. Mitchell warned that "superconcentration" posed a danger to our "economic, political and social structure." Two years later, however, in a startling *volte face*, he overruled his own Antitrust Division, and refused to challenge National's acquisition of Granite City, a consolidation of the fourth largest and eleventh largest producers, a combine with assets of 1.9 billion dollars and ranking third in a highly concentrated industry. If this is a precedent, mergers may again play their accustomed role of creating the oligopoly structures which facilitate conspiratorial conduct.

It is noteworthy, though hardly surprising, that conspiratorial conduct is the almost inevitable outgrowth of industrial concentration. Since 1960 alone, the Department of Justice has filed twenty cases against steel companies for price-fixing and collusive activity. Seven of these were civil cases, all settled by consent decrees, and thirteen were criminal cases, all settled by *nolo contendere*. The industry's conduct was not noticeably transformed by the settlement of these antitrust actions.

Indeed, the industry's policy of price escalation provided the prime stimulus to inflationary movements. Between 1947 and 1951, according to the Council of Economic Advisers

> The average increase in the price of basic steel products was 9 percent per year, twice the average increase of all wholesale prices. The unique behavior of steel prices was most pronounced in the mid-1950's. While the wholesale price index was falling an average of 0.9 percent annually from 1951 to 1955, the price index for steel was rising an average of 4.8 percent per year. From 1955 to 1958, steel prices were increasing 7.1 percent annually, or almost three times as fast as wholesale prices generally. No other major sector shows a similar record.

After a quiescent stage during the early 1960s, characterized by the "jawboning" and moral suasion of the Kennedy Administration, steel prices resumed their upward movement in 1964—on a gradual selective product-by-product basis at first, and on a general across-the-board basis in 1969. The imposition of "voluntary" import quotas in January 1969 and the Nixon Administration's refusal to engage in government-industry confrontations simply accelerated the trend.

The one factor which dampened the industry's enthusiasm for marching in lockstep toward constantly higher price levels was the burgeoning of import competition. Between January 1960 and December 1968, the composite steel price index increased 4 points, or 0.5 points per year. Starting in January 1969, however, after the U.S. State Department had successfully persuaded the Europeans and Japanese to accept voluntary quotas on their sales to the United States (*i.e.*, to enter into an informal international steel cartel), imports were cut back drastically and the domestic steel prices resumed their pre-1960 climb. The steel price index rose 7.8 points in 1969, 6.8 points in 1970, and a solid 9.1 points in the first eight months of 1971. Put differently, steel prices increased over five times as much in the two years and eight months since the import quotas went into effect than they had in the previous eight years. All this in the face of declining production and the idleness of roughly 25 percent of the nation's steel capacity.

As if the import quotas—supplemented by "Buy American" regulations and assorted trade barriers—were not enough to insulate the steel industry from competiton, President Nixon approved a temporary 10 percent surcharge on imports, including steel. In doing so, he perverted the "infant industry" argument for the benefit of lusty steel giants whose rambunctious excesses had undermined past attempts at inflation control. With this arsenal of import restraints, Mr. Nixon neutralized the perhaps most effective lid on steel pricing, while building up additional steam in an already overheated pressure cooker.

The case study of steel yields some incontrovertible conclusions: giantism in this industry is the result of massive mergers; the dominant firms are neither big because they are efficient, nor efficient because they are big; their technological lethargy, especially during the 1950s, put them at a comparative disadvantage in world competition; their insensitive, extortionate, oligopolistic price policy displaced American steel from world markets and opened the U.S. market to erosion by imports and substitutes; and, finally, the mercantilist protectionism of the federal government compounded the problems of the industry and the nation's economy. It gave legitimacy and endurance to a cartel which could not survive without government succor.

The policy conclusion, it seems to me, is not to create a regulatory bureaucracy which will interlock steel labor and steel management into a vertical power combine for escalating wages and prices under the umbrella of government benevolence and protection. If the objective is to control inflationary steel pricing, a much simpler policy is at hand: prohibit further steel mergers (*i.e.*, let companies grow by building, not buying; by competing for customers, not by purchasing competitors) and remove the obstacles to free international trade in steel; foreign competition will keep our steel barons "honest" as no government regulatory commission is inclined to do.

This policy can be implemented immediately, and even Professor Galbraith cannot dismiss it as impractical, long-range, or Utopian. It does not involve awaiting the results of seemingly endless trust-busting litigation. At the same time, it underscores the importance of a dissolution, divorcement, and divestiture program—at least with respect to the top three firms in the industry. Such deconcentration would yield not only more competition but also, I predict, greater efficiency.

The Case of Oil

Reflecting the tax advantages enjoyed by the oil industry, particularly the foreign tax credit and the depletion allowance, the giant oil companies have an annual cash flow approaching ten billion dollars. These internally generated funds make an admirable war chest for financing mergers and acquisitions. Their use for that purpose should not come as a surprise.

During the twelve-year period between 1956 and 1968, the twenty major oil companies absorbed twenty formerly independent firms engaged in petroleum refining.[12] Roughly one-third of these mergers brought together fully integrated enterprises operating in different regions of the country:

Standard Oil of California acquired Standard Oil of Kentucky (with assets of 142 million dollars);

Union Oil acquired Pure Oil (with assets of 766 million dollars);

Sun Oil acquired Sunray DX (with assets of 749 million dollars);

Atlantic Refining acquired Richfield (with assets of 500 million dollars);

Atlantic-Richfield acquired Sinclair (with assets of 1,810 million dollars, of which it had to divest itself partially to comply with an antitrust settlement. It sold 400 million dollars in assets to British Petroleum, but kept 1,410 million dollars).

In addition to these "market-extension" mergers, the major oil companies made fifty-two acquisitions in the field of crude oil and natural gas production. These mergers represented backward vertical integration.

But the oil giants did not confine their merger activity to the petroleum industry. They were also busy buying out producers of substitute fuels:

Continental Oil acquired Consolidated Coal (the nation's largest coal company, with assets of 249 million dollars);

Occidental Oil acquired Island Creek Coal (the nation's third largest coal company, with assets of 113 million dollars);

Standard Oil of Ohio acquired Old Ben Coal (with assets of 54 million dollars).

Smaller, but potentially more significant, were a series of acquisitions in the nuclear power field. Here Kerr-McGee bought five companies; Gulf, one; and Atlantic-Richfield, one.

As part of their forward vertical integration, the twenty major oil companies acquired eleven manufacturers of fertilizers, twenty-five manufacturers of plastics and products, and sixteen manufacturers of other chemicals. As a result, no less than eleven of the thirty top sellers of chemicals in 1968 were petroleum companies. Standard of New Jersey ranked sixth in chemical sales; Occidental eleventh; Shell thirteenth; Phillips seventeenth, and Mobil twentieth. In addition, the twenty majors contributed their share to purely conglomerate acquisitions by buying producers of crushed stone, sand and gravel, foods, paper, refrigeration machinery, brooms and brushes, and automatic vending machines. Their most comprehensive conquest was the fertilizer materials industry where the invasion of the oil giants left only one major independent (International Minerals & Chemical) in its wake.

All in all, the major oil companies completed a total of 226 mergers between 1956 and 1968. Their growth during the period was not "thrust upon them" by excellent performance in their chosen field; it was a tribute to their manipulative skill in a relentless strategy of industrial imperialism.

The government has been singularly ineffective in stemming this merger tide. The antitrust authorities, constrained by the limitations of existing law and the political curbs on their enforcement zeal, have fought little more than a modest rear-guard action. Indeed, in the name of conservation and national defense, the government has played a positive role in promoting an *imperium in imperio*, and provided the indispensable legal underpinnings for an industrywide cartel.[13] It has done for the oil companies what they could not legally do for themselves without violating the per se prohibitions of the antitrust laws against price-fixing and market allocations. The process is familiar. The Bureau of Mines in the Department of Interior publishes monthly estimates of the market demand for petroleum (at current prices, of course). Under the Interstate Oil Compact, approved by Congress, these estimates are broken down into quotas for each of the oil-producing states which, in turn, through various prorationing devices, allocate "allowable production" to individual wells. Oil produced in violation of these prorationing regulations is branded as "hot oil," and the federal government prohibits its shipment in interstate commerce. Also, to buttress this government-sanctioned cartel against potential competition, there is a tariff of 10.5 cents per barrel on crude oil (in effect since 1943) and an import quota of 12.2 percent of domestic production of crude oil and natural gas liquids (in effect since 1963). Finally, to top off these indirect subsidies with more visible favors, and to provide the proper incentives for an industry crucial to the national defense, the government authorizes oil companies to charge off a 22 percent depletion allowance against their gross income and to apply a foreign tax credit to their overseas operations. In all, the industry has been estimated to receive annually special favors of 3.5 billion dollars (according to Milton Friedman) or 4.0 billion dollars (according to Morris Adelman) in addition to having a government-sanctioned cartel provide the underpinning for its control of markets and prices.

In this industry, as in steel and elsewhere, competition would seem to be a far simpler and more effective anti-inflation policy than a system of wage-price controls. And effective competition can be achieved by stopping the growth by merger of industrial giants who already are too big; and ending the mercantilist restrictions of government which serve to create and entrench the concentration of private economic power. Again, this is not to deny the desirability of dissolution, divorcement, and divestiture.

PUBLIC POLICY PROPOSALS

In designing a mechanism for protecting the public, we must first recognize that economic power is not a decorative thing. It is more than a mere corporate status symbol to be passively enjoyed. It is more than an object of boastful pride in the counting houses and country clubs. Economic power may be used with statesmanlike forbearance and diplomatic skill. It may be used only where circumstances absolutely demand it, or when the political climate is particularly propitious. It may be accompanied by sophisticated public relations campaigns to purify its venality or sanitize the corporate image. But the fact remains that, in the long run, the possession of power and its exercise tend to coalesce. Where great power exists, it will be used whenever a need and opportunity for it may arise—and evidence is plentiful to support this generalization.

Economic power comes in all shapes and sizes. First, there is *horizontal* power, which is market control in its pristine, classical form. It consists of dominance over an industry (in relative, percentage terms), and is manifested in entry controls, price leadership and followership, and other forms of oligopolistic cooperation. Second, there is *vertical* power, which derives from control over successive stages of production and distribution, and gives firms the power to squeeze their suppliers by denial of access, or their distributors by denial of supplies, or both by manipulation of price. Third, there is *conglomerate* power, created when a firm's operations are so widely diversified that its survival no longer depends on success in any given product market or any given geographical area. The firm's absolute size, its sheer bigness, is so impressive that it can discipline or destroy its more specialized competitors. A conglomerate giant is powerful, therefore, not because it has monopoly or oligopoly control over a particular market, but because (as Corwin Edwards says) it can outbid, outspend, and outlose its smaller rivals. It occupies a position much like the millionaire poker player who can easily bankrupt his less opulent opponents, regardless of his innate ability, intuitive shrewdness, or mastery over the dizzy virtues of probability theory.

Whatever the success of antitrust in dealing with horizontal and vertical power may have been in recent years, it has clearly failed to stem the flood tide of conglomeration. Not only "pure" conglomerates but "market extension" and "product extension" mergers have shown a remarkable imperviousness to antitrust attack. And, with the demise of the Warren court, it is doubtful whether the enforcement agencies can hope for sympathetic receptivity as their borderline prosecutions reach the Supreme Court.

If this voracious appetite for mergers and acquisitions is to be curbed, and the consequent erosion of the competitive market place arrested, new legislation is clearly in order. As a maximum, such legislation would require the substantial restructuring of an oligopoly-dominated economy. As a minimum, it would call for, as Nader suggests, the federal incorporation of giant corporations on the simple ground that their operations are so extensive and their impact on the nation's economic life so pervasive, that they are "affected with the public interest."

Under my proposal, a modest proposal, any corporation with assets in excess of 250 million dollars, or any corporation which ranks among the top eight producers in an industry where the eight-firm concentration ratio is 70 percent or higher, shall be required to obtain a federal charter. Such firms, under the charter, shall be prohibited from:

1. acquiring the stock, assets, or property of another company;
2. granting or receiving any discrimination in price, service, or allowances, except where such discrimination can be demonstrated to be justified by savings in cost;

3. engaging in any tie-in arrangements or exclusive dealerships; and

4. participating in any scheme of interlocking control over any other corporation.

In addition, such firms shall be obligated to:

5. perform the duties of a common carrier by serving all customers on reasonable and nondiscriminatory terms;

6. license patents and know-how to other firms on a reasonable royalty basis; and

7. pursue pricing and product policies, calculated to achieve capacity production and full employment.

Note that the foregoing provisos do not limit the growth of giant firms on the basis of superior efficiency, technological innovation, or market success. They are designed only to limit growth artificially induced via merger, and to prevent the extension of existing market power by means of selected restrictive practices. As such, these provisos are a forthright recognition of the fact that industrial giantism has social and economic consequences of pervasive impact. As in the case of public utilities, these decisions should not be entrusted to a private industrial oligarchy. Absent the unsatisfactory alternative of direct government regulation, "power that controls the economy," as Justice Douglas once said, "should be decentralized. It should be scattered into many hands so that the fortunes of the people will not be dependent on the whim or caprice, the political prejudices, the emotional stability of a few self-appointed men. The fact that they are not vicious men but respectable and social minded is irrelevant."[14] That is the philosophy on which an industrial democracy must be based. It is founded on a theory of hostility to the concentration of power in private hands so great that not even a government of the people can be safely entrusted with its exercise.

PART THREE

OTHER RESTRAINTS
ON CORPORATE POWER

IX

CORPORATE SOCIAL RESPONSIBILITY: SHELL GAME FOR THE SEVENTIES?

JOEL F. HENNING*

A frenzy of activity from proxy contests to bombs has recently agitated the big-business world. The cry uttered by all, corporate insiders and outsiders, is "corporate social responsibility." The cry is the same whatever the issue: war, environmental destruction, urban decay, racial and sexual discrimination, consumer protection, better education, mass transit, and humanized technology. The reason for lavishing attention on the supercorporation is clear. The resources for solving our urgent problems are largely controlled by them. The two hundred biggest companies control about two-thirds of the nation's manufacturing assets. Eighteen had sales of more than four billion dollars. Four corporations earned more than one billion dollars in *profit*.[1]

Corporate social responsibility sounds like a good idea. Politicians and protesters who agree on virtually nothing else demand almost unanimously that "social responsibility" temper corporate policies. But whose responsibility is corporate social responsibility? Is it that of corporate managers, or of shareholders, workers, other corporate constituencies, or some combination thereof? Or is affirmative government action required to determine the social obligations of private business? This essay focuses on these questions.

* Fellow of the Adlai Stevenson Institute of International Affairs, consultant to the Corporate Accountability Research Group, and a former corporate lawyer in Chicago, Illinois; he has published articles on corporate law in various law journals, magazines, and newspapers.

I. CORPORATE RESPONSIBILITY AND OTHER MYTHS

The Responsibility Hype

The fundamental issue is *power*. If corporations have no discretionary power to act, however big and wealthy, they cannot be held responsibile for anything but their survival. In the classic model of a competitive market, no company can survive if it attempts to do anything but produce and sell at optimum economic efficiency. But if corporations can act more or less free from market restraints, the discretionary decisions of their managers must find justification elsewhere.

Milton Friedman is, of course, the most loquacious contemporary advocate of the theory that "there is one and only one social responsibility of business—to use its resources and engage in activities designed to increase its profits."[2] Most big businessmen ignore the Friedman analysis because they do not operate in competitive markets nor have they any desire to do so.[3] Also, Friedman's competitive market theory assumes that the sum of all individual market decisions equals the public interest. This argument is difficult to support in light of such pervasive disasters as that which our millions of automobiles, all purchased by free choice, have perpetrated on us.

Management is not bound inexorably to market imperatives. To whom or what, then, is management accountable? The management myth is that corporations are bound by the same moral constraints and social obligations as people. Accordingly business leaders will naturally look after the interests of workers, consumers, and the public in general, as well as their own interests and those of their shareholders. President Theodore Roosevelt endorsed this view when he told Congress that "Business success, . . . is a good thing only so far as it is accompanied by and develops a high standard of conduct —honor, integrity, civic courage."[4] In 1911 J. P. Morgan's partner, George W. Perkins, rejoiced in the "great awakening of the business conscience."[5]

The myth successfully shielded some enterprises from the Sherman antitrust act. In 1921 a book appeared called *U.S. Steel: A Corporate with a Soul*. The notion that U.S. Steel was a good soul, and Standard Oil a bad one, helped preserve U.S. Steel intact whereas Standard Oil had been broken up in an earlier monopolization case.

Reliance on corporate civic virtue as a substitute for public policy was challenged in 1912 by Presidential candidate Woodrow Wilson. Corporate leaders, he said, were being portrayed as "pitiful and kind," "patriotic," and "benevolent." This, he complained, was merely an "enterprise . . . of making the monopolies philanthropic."[6] In 1932, the myth was assaulted once again by A. A. Berle, Jr. "One recognizes," he wrote, "the occasional benevolences of the many corporate managers whose sympathies are warm and whose aspirations are magnificent. The gross result, however, appraised from the angle either of government or economics, has not been either benevolent or idealistic."[7]

Berle's seminal work should have laid to rest the myth of corporate morality. It is therefore with some astonishment that one finds that it still prevails, sustained by distinguished scholars. The economist Carl Kaysen, for example, has written, "No longer the agent of proprietorship seeking to maximize return on investment, management sees itself as responsible to stockholders, employees, customers, the general public, and, perhaps most important, the firm itself as an institution. . . . The modern corporation is a soulful corporation."[8] Most curious of all, Berle departed from his previous view and, shortly before his death in 1971, came to believe that corporations are managed in the interests of a "public consensus." He attributed his conversion to "more responsible, more perceptive and (in plain English) more honest" principles and practices of big business.[9]

Today the myth flourishes in the care of business leaders who use it to legitimate their autonomy. David Rockefeller points with pride to the "positive participation by the private sector in meeting the challenges that face our nation."[10] Westinghouse shareholders were told by its chairman of the board at a recent annual meeting that "the future growth and success of Westinghouse rests on how well we meet the urgent needs of people." The president of Gulf Oil told the Columbia Graduate School of Business that "the first responsibility of business is to operate for the well-being of society."[11] One brokerage house, Paine, Weber, Jackson & Curtis, even advertised for peace in Vietnam.

Alas, what they say is more inspiring than what they do. Chase Manhattan has perhaps done more in this area than any other financial institution but still less than it might. As of June 1971, it had placed nine million dollars in loans through its urban redevelopment portfolio, out of total resources of more than twenty-two billion dollars. The relatively tiny Hyde Park Bank in Chicago, 1/315 the size of the Chase, had extended more than four million dollars in comparable urban redevelopment loans. Westinghouse is meeting the needs of the Pentagon more than those of the people. The net value of its military prime contracts in fiscal 1969 was about one-half billion dollars, representing more than 30 percent of its total sales.[12] Gulf Oil's massive investment in the Portuguese colony of Angola is an important source of support for Portugal's anachronistic colonial relationship with African Angola. The dovish Paine, Weber did not follow up its peace ad with an adjustment in its portfolio to support peace-related companies.

The principal beneficiary of the current flood of corporate social concern has been the media. The so-called "public" utilities spend well over three hundred million dollars per year for advertising, much of it expressing their concern for the environment. One might think they were in the business of wilderness preservation rather than energy production, until one examines their dismal record of environmental protection.[13] Their ads do not reveal that the utilities rank at rock bottom when it comes to hiring and promoting blacks.[14] The four biggest can makers, calling themselves "The Can People," have been heavily advertising their "recycling centers," but privately the industry admits that the campaign involved no investment in new facilities and will have no real effect on the problem of solid waste disposal. "Since people want to feel that they're doing something, we want to go along with them," said one of the Can People.[15] The classic abuse of social responsibility advertising was recently perpetrated by Potlatch Forests. Its ad depicted an idyllic river scene with the caption, "It cost us a bundle, but the Clearwater River still runs clear." Indeed it does, where the photo was taken, *upstream* of Potlatch's pulp plant.

The Present Reality

In other words, business as usual, as the late Whitney Young, executive director of the Urban League, discovered. "Many companies" he said, "limit their concern to press releases, empty speeches, or less." He recalled "listening to the head of a major corporation brag about all his firm was doing. After some close questioning, I found the sum total of these grand efforts added up to less than two dozen summer jobs for Black youths in only three of the 60 cities in which that company operates."[16] When Gordon Sherman, president of Midas-International, demonstrated a solid commitment to corporate responsibility with financial contributions to Saul Alinsky's activities and others like them, he was forced out of the company in a bitter proxy battle against the company's chairman, Nate H. Sherman, Gordon's father.

Minority enterprise and capital investment, the natural means by which business was determined to support urban redevelopment, have hardly justified the fanfare with which they were initiated only a few years ago. A study published in 1971 by the Conference Board, a business research organization, reported that most minority enterprises "have encountered greater difficulties, incurred higher costs, employed fewer people, and met with less success than had been anticipated at the outset."[17] The insurance industry's much publicized two-billion-dollar pledge for low-income urban housing and related projects began with a bang in 1967 but is fizzling out. As the program ends, the balance of the funds is going increasingly into commercial loans to business, not into housing. In 1969 Westinghouse, General Electric, Alcoa, International Telephone and Telegraph, Boise-Cascade, Martin-Marietta, and U.S. Steel all submitted winning prototypes to the federal government's Operation Breakthrough, designed to facilitate low-cost housing construction. Since that heralded beginning, few projects have been completed, and they are all in suburban areas.

Some business efforts may be socially unproductive because they raise expectations which cannot be fulfilled. When employment was high, manufacturers would hire the hard-core unemployed because they needed them, not in fulfillment of their social responsibility.

When the economy turned down, the hard-core were, of course, among the first to go. As the recent recession deepened, Chrysler cancelled a $13.8 million federal contract to train 4,450 hard-core unemployed workers. Zenith almost simultaneously laid off around 3,000 workers, more than one-third of whom were black. Ling-Temco-Vought Aircraft Company of Dallas recruited more than 1,500 Mexican-Americans during 1968 and 1969. But these workers lost their jobs during cutbacks in 1970. In 1971 the program was completely phased out. Leaders of the JOBS program find it increasingly difficult to place the hard-core. "I just wonder," said Douglas Frazer of the United Auto Workers, "whether we haven't done more harm than good with this program. We build up hopes and then we pull the rug out from under them."[18]

New York's Consolidated Edison and Chicago's Commonwealth Edison initiated serious efforts to limit the pollutants they were putting into the air only after confrontations with outraged, intense, broad-based citizens' groups who threatened lawsuits and the withholding of electric bill payments. These companies are resisting with equal vigor the modification of their nuclear installations to reduce the risks of thermal pollution. The automobile industry rejected safety programs in automobile design and advertising in favor of style changes and subsexual promotions—until GM's indiscretions toward Ralph Nader backfired, compelling a reluctant Congress to pass the National Highway Safety Act of 1966. The same industry is running behind schedule in meeting federal exhaust emission standards. Under GM's new chairman, Richard C. Gerstenberg, the pace of social action is not apt to accelerate. "I don't think we've taken more [socially responsible steps] than we have had to take," he says.[19]

Even in the conventional and benign area of charitable contributions, corporate performance is unimpressive. One study indicates that corporate charitable gifts go overwhelmingly to conservative and inoffensive organizations, engaged in marginally productive welfare programs.[20] And overall corporate beneficence is dwindling. In 1969 corporate charitable giving dropped below 1 percent of pretax profits, compared with 1.11 percent as recently as 1967.[21] The bigger the corporation, the smaller the percentage of net income it gives away.[22]

Although education has received a substantial share of corporate philanthropy, that share is shrinking. A front-page editorial in *Barron's*, the national financial weekly, may explain the decline:

> The cadres marching on American business have trained at Berkeley, Wisconsin, Cornell and hundreds of other schools. . . . Isn't it incredible that American businessmen and financiers are still so naive as to think they are being charitable when they support institutions and individuals who, measure by measure, move us all closer to the end of the capitalist system.[23]

The Business of Business

The conclusion seems irresistible that the reputation of big business as social benefactor is self-made and unfulfilled. But even if the conclusion were otherwise, there is ample reason to resist the concept of corporate social responsibility.

First, if business has any expertise, it is management and technology. Our current social crises have moral, legal, and political dimensions which only incidentally (if at all) require business skills. For example, our current crisis in education is, in part, technological and managerial; we must have improved physical plants, advanced mechanical teaching aids, improved data retrieval, and more efficient bureaucracies. But the crisis is substantially deeper, involving basic social questions such as who should be taught, what, when, by whom, at what cost, and where should control of such decisions reside. None of these questions is within the special competence of business, nor is there persuasive argument that corporate managers should make such decisions for the rest of us. Obviously the appropriate answers to these questions are not necessarily consistent with corporate profitability. To the extent that competitive markets still exist, even the most enlightened and publicly responsive corporate management would have to make such decisions in relation to its competitive situation.

Business has not even been able to compose a meaningful articulation of its social responsibility. After five years of gestation, the Committee for Economic Development issued a policy statement in 1971 called *Social Responsibilities of Business Corporations*. All that came forth was an acknowledgement that business has "served society well" but now must expand its social activities in pursuit of

"enlightened self-interest." The document is intellectually and empir-
ically thin. It is unloved even by some of its creators. "Flawed by the
carelessness of the scholarship . . . this kind of unrestrained—indeed
unmerited—adulation is not going to do [business] any good, because its deficiences are still so numerous," said two dissenting members of CED's research and policy committee in the appendix.[24]

It is no wonder that business could not agree on its social responsibilities. Recent examples of businessmen's "moral" decisions suggest that their standards can deviate from the rhetoric of social
responsibility quoted above. The president of Dow Chemical Company told his shareholders at the 1967 annual meeting that the
company would renew its napalm contract even though it was not
financially rewarding and "we could be hurt in many ways." Why?
"We as a company have made a moral judgment."[25] Honeywell's
chairman responded almost identically when shareholders questioned
its war contracts. Corporate responsibility to Patrick Frawley, Jr.,
head of a substantial business empire that has included Schick and
Technicolor, means hiring a man "to make speeches on free enterprise and against Communism at local groups." One such employee,
John Fergus, was convicted of conspiracy to libel former U. S. Senator Thomas Kuchel, a liberal.[26] Scores of printers have demonstrated their social responsibility by refusing to print material "against
our good conscience," much of it involving opinions inconsistent
with the printers' own politics.[27]

Business leaders are inevitably isolated from reality. Chief executives of corporations that are as big as nations are, like government
leaders, subject to what George Reedy, Lyndon Johnson's Presidential press secretary, called "the most important and least examined
problem of the Presidency, . . . maintaining contact with reality."[28]
If the problem afflicts those who are dependent upon political support
of the people, how much more acute it is for relatively autonomous
corporate executives, who generally work too hard to keep up with
events beyond those of immediate and obvious concern to their companies.* As a result of this isolation, Jules Cohen of Harvard Business School found that

---

* GM's new chairman Gerstenberg is candid about his lack of time for non-
business reading. "Oh, I read a book about fishing once a while, or duck
hunting. I started to read *Wheels* [by Arthur Hailey] and I got through a

few companies have made efforts to identify and evaluate the many
new, community-based self-help groups. . . . Board chairmen who
could rely at one time on personal acquaintanceships with the leaders of charities soliciting their aid, or on lifelong familiarity with the
work of established groups, are not likely to have rubbed elbows with
Black militants or to have a sense of who's who in the ghetto
community.[29]

It remains to be seen whether the incipient movement to make corporate boards of directors more representative will diminish this
problem. There have not as yet been appointments from previously
unrepresented groups to justify optimism.

Even if businessmen in general shared an enlightened and com-
passionate *Weltanschauung*, the structure of the corporate system
does not provide practical standards upon which the social performance of corporate managers can be judged. Presently shareholders
and potential investors have relatively simple standards to apply in
evaluating management—profits and losses, return on investment,
capital growth—all of which can be reduced to numbers. Social issues
are not easily reduced to comparable terms for evaluation, although
"social accounting" is currently a topic of much conversation. Even
if sophisticated social accounting can be developed, social programs
will be evaluated against their costs and the commercial demands of
the business. The result will at best be a compromise, at worst a
fraud. "Sound business reasons for calling a halt to any lavish demonstration of corporate conscience" were found in "declining profits
caused by the economic recession of 1970–71."[30] Our social problems intensify in economic hard times, when the ability of business to
deal with them is reduced.

Finally, an anomalous situation confronts the corporate manager
even in old-fashioned cultural and philanthropic charity. In return
for the bestowal of corporate benevolence, the managers *personally*
receive significant social rewards: publicity, positions on socially elite
boards of trustees, civic honor, and power—all in a sense purchased
with other people's money, that of the shareholders. Thus autonomous corporate management has the power "to treat modern cor-

---

hundred pages of it and I haven't picked it up anymore." Russ DeYoung,
Goodyear's chief executive officer admits that his "social life and my family
life don't mean anything to me. They can't."

porations with their vast resources as personal satrapies implementing personal political or moral predilictions," as a federal court recently stated.[31]

II. THE ROMANCE OF CORPORATE DEMOCRACY

In all but a few of our largest industrial corporations, stock ownership is widely held by individuals, investment trusts, and institutional investors. In these publicly held companies, the conception that managers are responsible to shareholders or other so-called corporate constituencies is misleading as a description of reality and dysfunctional as a device for accomplishing social goals.

The Diminishing Rights of Shareholders

As Professors Dahl and Flynn elaborate elsewhere in this volume, shareholder democracy is largely a fiction, unsupported by corporate law. In modern corporate statutes, the classic duties that an agent in a position of trust (the corporate manager) owes to his principal (the shareholder) have been so vitiated as to be hardly recognizable to a student of common law. Common law liabilities for self-dealing by corporate officials have been limited by statute in several states including California, Delaware, and New York. These management-oriented legal "reforms" suggest that whether the classical corporate structure was democratic or not, the modern corporation is no more democratic than the current government of Greece.

The enactment of the two principal federal securities laws in 1933 and 1934, creating the Securities and Exchange Commission, has been the only significant legal development offering some protection to shareholders. These acts were designed primarily to provide a form of consumer protection for investors by requiring disclosures by management when stock is offered to the public and when it is traded by corporate insiders. One section of the securities laws provides some support for shareholders who wish to exercise their voting rights. It authorizes the SEC to promulgate such rules with respect to the solicitation of proxies as might be "necessary or appropriate in the public interest or for the protection of investors." Pursuant to this vague mandate, the SEC issued a rule which provides that any shareholder entitled to vote may submit to management a proposal for action at a shareholders' meeting, and if the proposal is timely delivered, "the management shall set forth the proposal in its proxy statement." Management is elsewhere required by the securities law to distribute its proxy to all shareholders and to provide a proxy ballot on which each shareholder can vote for any proposal on the proxy statement. On their face, these rules would seem to provide shareholders with an enormously effective device for manifesting their interests in the formulation of corporate policy. The SEC has, however, sharply limited the usefulness of its enabling rule. The two most devastating exceptions allow management to omit a shareholder proposal "if it clearly appears that the proposal is submitted . . . primarily for the purpose . . . of promoting general economic, political, racial, religious, social or similar causes," or if it "consists of a recommendation or request that the management take action with respect to a matter relating to the conduct of the ordinary business operations" of the company.[32]

Great artistry is required to frame a proposal that is neither so general as to be eliminated by the former exception nor too specific to fall victim to the latter. Proposals requiring that a specified quantity of a company's earnings be paid out as dividends, prohibiting certain advertising policies, directing the sale of a subsidiary, and urging an end to segregated seating on buses have all been denied a place on management's proxy by the SEC. During the great napalm controversy at Dow Chemical, the SEC refused to compel that company to carry shareholder resolutions restricting the marketing or the manufacture of napalm. Curiously, the company and the SEC appeared to rely on both the "social cause" and the "ordinary business operations" exceptions, ignoring the apparent conflict. The United States Circuit Court of Appeals remanded the case to the SEC, holding that proposed resolutions related to specific action by a corporation should qualify for inclusion.[33] Senator Muskie has introduced the Corporate Participation Act to limit the reach of the "social cause" exclusion so that resolutions proposing action within the control of the company (such as in the Dow case) will be acceptable even if in some way related to a social cause. Most recently, a Honeywell shareholder was denied access to its shareholder list and records dealing with its weapons contracts by the Minnesota Supreme Court. The court said that the stockholder's purpose, to solicit proxies opposing weapons production, was not "proper", since it did not deal with the return on his investment.[34]

A hardy band of "professional" minority shareholders—including Lewis and John Gilbert, Wilma Soss, and Evelyn Davis—have for decades occupied themselves with proposing resolutions at the annual meetings of our largest companies. Litigation initiated by them has marked the narrow trail of shareholder resolutions acceptable to the SEC. These include such issues as shareholder voting rights, staggering the terms of directors, location, conduct, and reporting of annual shareholder meetings, limitations on executive compensation, pensions, and stock options, and selection of certified public accountants. All of these issues concern either intracorporate due process or management perquisites. None challenges the conduct of the company in relation to the society in which it operates. Whatever the cost in dollars and the extra time wasted at annual meetings, the *quid pro quo* management receives from this dauntless and zany band of minority shareholders is substantially more valuable. Their questions, comments, and theatrical hokum regularly reach the nation via the accommodating financial press, thus sustaining the romantic notion that shareholder democracy lives. It does not.

The Renaissance of Shareholder Dissent

In spite of this abundant evidence that corporate democracy is phony, an expansion of minority shareholder activity into issues concerning the role of the corporation in society has recently occurred. In addition to the carefully organized and widely publicized Campaign GM, some form of attention has been called to social problems at the recent annual meetings of many companies including AT&T (military contracts), Atlantic-Richfield (pollution), Bank of America (Vietnam), Boeing (military contracts), Columbia Broadcasting System (women's liberation), Commonwealth Edison (pollution), Dow Chemical (military contracts), FMC (military contracts, pesticides, and phosphates), General Electric (military contracts, pollution, women's liberation, Gulf (colonial investments), Honeywell (military contracts), IBM (military contracts), Kennecott Copper (pollution), National Tea (consumer protection), Standard Oil of New Jersey (Vietnam), Union Carbide (pollution), and United Aircraft (military contracts). Only a few of these shareholder efforts have involved serious proxy solicitations.

Although modern shareholder insurgency was largely inspired by Saul Alinsky, his technique appears to have been misunderstood. Alinsky's original use of corporate proxies was tactical, not strategic. Proxy solicitation and shareholder protest were first used by him as incidental tactics in community action projects employing a range of other devices as well. In 1965 he organized a Rochester, New York, civil rights group called FIGHT (Freedom, Integration, God, Honor, Today). Rochester is in many ways Eastman Kodak's company town; Kodak employs more than forty thousand Rochester residents out of a population of four hundred and fifty thousand. FIGHT acquired a few shares in the company to confront it at the 1967 annual meeting on the issue of minority hiring. Local and national church groups supported FIGHT by withholding proxies from management. The shares withheld, however, amounted to less than 1 percent of the 161 million shares issued and outstanding, and the total vote for management was higher than that at the previous annual meeting, when no proxy battle was waged.

FIGHT reformed Kodak's hiring policies but the proxy battle was only one of many tactics used. Since Kodak dominates Rochester economically and politically, the issue of hiring, consequently, was local, concrete, and intimately connected to the welfare of the protesters and the company. Alinsky's troops were in the field not because they were stockholders of Kodak but because they were directly affected by the company's social policies. The proxy fight was simply a way of bringing the issue of minority hiring into the open.

Of all the recent corporate protests, the most successful was the one that approximated the conditions of the Kodak-FIGHT confrontation. A broadly based Chicago group called Campaign Against Pollution (CAP) organized chapters throughout the area served by Commonwealth Edison Company. Chapters encompassed groups as diverse as affluent suburbanites and blue-collar workers from Chicago's southwest side. When the campaign began in early 1970, Commonwealth Edison was producing over 65 percent of the sulphur dioxide in Chicago's air. The company had been instrumental in prevailing upon Mayor Daley to suspend enforcement of his air quality ordinance for an extra year. CAP collected proxies merely to gain admission to the utility's meeting and raise the issue of air pollution. It had no resolutions on the agenda. In Chicago, CAP's members were deeply concerned about the company's policies not as stock-holders but because of its direct impact on their lives—in this case, as involuntary consumers of air pollution. Shortly after the Common-wealth Edison annual meeting, which was held with a massive CAP presence outside, the company announced plans to reduce the sulphur content of its fuel to an acceptable level. CAP also effected changes in Commonwealth Edison's nuclear power station plans, and in the federal standards relating to thermal pollution. It was largely respon-sible for a new city air pollution ordinance and for the denial of a rate increase to the utility until it had implemented a comprehen-sive antipollution program.

Kodak was the major employer in Rochester, Commonwealth Edison the major polluter in Chicago. Both were issues of immediate and vital concern to the local people. CAP, like FIGHT, used other tactics as well. More important than their demonstration at the Edison meeting, CAP leaders testified and paraded their forces at several Chicago City Council hearings and meetings; members of CAP confronted their respective aldermen, who had previously run their wards on the mayor's orders with no dissension from constit-uents. Such restlessness in the ranks was reported up the political hierarchy with much effectiveness. For these reasons, Edison, like Kodak, was almost bound to respond constructively regardless of the success of the proxy effort itself.

Campaign GM was the most highly visible of recent shareholder efforts. It has submitted shareholder resolutions to General Motors an-nually since 1970 for inclusion in its proxy materials. Its first round of proposals included an enlargement of the GM board by three seats (from twenty-three to twenty-six) to be filled by "public repre-sentatives."* The Campaign also proposed formation of a special shareholders' Committee for Corporate Responsibility to be ap-pointed by GM management, Campaign GM, and the UAW. Other resolutions offered would have amended the corporate charter to for-

---

* Campaign GM suggested Betty Furness to represent consumers, René Dubos to champion the environment, and Channing Phillips to represent the black community.

bid GM to undertake any activity inconsistent with the public interest and would have imposed on the company specific policies relating to air pollution, minority employment, auto safety, product warranties, mass transit, and employee health and safety. Not unexpectedly, GM refused to include any of the proposals in its proxy statement. The SEC, however, ordered GM to include in its proxy the two proposals which the agency considered appropriate for shareholder concern: enlarging the board and establishing the shareholders' committee. The resolutions were concrete, procedural, and—whatever their social purpose—related specifically to shareholder-management relations.

Campaign GM therefore arrived in Detroit for its first annual meeting with a degree of legitimacy not even sought by other social dissidents, namely seeing their resolutions and supporting arguments in the proxy statement mailed to every one of the 1,350,000 GM shareholders. Yet the project failed to attract as many votes for either of its proposals as received by the Gilbert-style shareholder resolutions with which it shared the ballot, one involving limitations on executive compensation and the other proposing cumulative voting for directors. Other than the brief supporting comments in the proxy statement, these proposals, unlike the Campaign's, did not receive any significant publicity nor did their sponsors actively solicit the support of shareholders prior to the meeting.

In round two, Campaign GM submitted proposals in 1971 to compel additional corporate disclosures, expand shareholder rights, and widen the corporate constituency represented on the board of directors beyond shareholders to workers, dealers, and consumers. The Gilbert-style proposals in 1971 were once again intended to increase profits or facilitate the exercise of existing shareholder rights. The latter received approximately twice the votes of the former (more than 4 percent to less than 2 percent) Campaign GM's voting support declined in round two.[35] By round three in 1972 the campaign was barely able to attract media attention. At the GM meeting it proposed a study of whether stockholder interests would be served by breaking GM into several separate companies; it also submitted various other proposals in 1972 to Ford, Chrysler, AT&T, and six pharmaceutical companies.

Nevertheless, the Campaign has achieved three victories of sorts.

First, GM made some noteworthy gestures between rounds one and two. A public policy committee was appointed as a standing committee of the board of directors. A new vice president in charge of environmental activities was hired and a distinguished black activist, Leon Sullivan, was appointed to the board. To date no concrete results have been attributed to any of these reforms; budgets, staffing, and jurisdiction of the new offices remain undisclosed. Second, it raised public consciousness of GM's enormous influence over all of us, a valuable piece of learning. Third, it revealed a pervasive national establishment that has a dominant influence on corporate, philanthropic, and educational institutions.

The Campaign attempted to identify its theoretically natural constituency, those institutions which combine large endowments with an enlightened and concerned view of society. In particular, universities and foundations were solicited. The result was, as Betty Furness said, that these institutions were found to be "vacillating, hypocritical and overly cautious."[36] In 1970 Harvard, MIT, Syracuse, Rutgers, California, Princeton, and the Universities of Michigan, Pennsylvania, and Texas all voted with management. A very few colleges, including Antioch, Oregon, Tufts, and Amherst, voted at least in part with Campaign GM. In 1971 several universities, including Yale, Rockefeller, and Georgetown, avoided controversy by dumping their GM stock. One mutual fund polled its shareholders to determine how it should vote its General Motors shares on the social issues raised by the Campaign GM proxy proposals; they voted against the Campaign GM proposals.[37]

These incidents reflect the general nature of shareholder interest in corporate affairs. There are twenty-five million shareholders in publicly held American corporations. Yet in 1970 only twenty-five stockholders submitted 241 proposals for inclusion in all corporate proxy statements. More than half were submitted by the Gilbert brothers.[38] Shareholder interest could hardly be justified since no minority proposal has ever succeeded against management opposition.* Shareholders, after all, are not compelled to suffer the eco-

---

* Such shareholder interest as there is largely appears to be a reaction *against* the social protesters. In 1970 CAP dissenters were tripped in the aisle by other Commonwealth Edison shareholders. Campaign GM round two was neutralized by the appearance of former Postmaster General, Arthur E.

nomic losses or the social depredations of their companies. They can sell, like the colleges that dumped their GM stock to avoid dealing with the issue.

Even if dissenters somehow did achieve a significant impact at these meetings, management could respond by changing the rules. There is no legal requirement that a code of parliamentary procedure, such as Roberts Rules of Order, be observed. At its 1971 annual meeting, Gulf Oil's chairman, E. D. Brockett, was asked if he operated according to Roberts Rules of Order. "No sir," he answered, "*I'm* operating this meeting." The questioner, a black doctor from San Francisco, was thereupon thrown out.[39] When management tires of the annual meeting ritual, the meetings can be done away with entirely under the Delaware Corporation Law.[40] So long as shareholders vote on the basis of their holdings (one share, one vote —not one shareholder, one vote), the end of annual meetings cannot be mourned as a major blow to corporate democracy.

Some reformers would agree with the analysis presented so far: namely, that corporate managers and shareholders are either uninterested or unable to assert significant influence over corporate power on behalf of social concerns. But these reformers say that if corporations were *true* democracies, with power being shared by *all* groups who have a vital interest in their affairs—including employees, dealers, and consumers as well as shareholders and managers—big corporations would be operated in the public interest. But it is doubtful that appointing such representatives to corporate boards or otherwise involving them in corporate policy-making is an effective means of influencing corporate policy toward social responsibility. The most impressive social gesture made after round one of Campaign GM was the appointment of Reverend Leon Sullivan to GM's board. Sullivan is a tough, independent black leader, but his appointment is not evidence of impending change in company policy so much as proof of the marginal importance of "outside" directors.

"In the years that I spent on various boards," Robert Townsend says in *Up the Organization*, "I never heard a single suggestion from

Sumerfield, Jr., who led hundreds of GM boosters to the meeting, outnumbering the dissidents and delivering paeans of praise to the company and its beloved chairman. At the 1971 Bank of America meeting, the social protesters were greeted with disdain not from management, but from the shareholders.

a director made *as* a director *at* a board meeting that produced any result at all."[41] The General Motors board meets only twelve times a year. It is difficult to know how the most dedicated director, one of twenty-three, not intimate with the operations of a twenty-billion-dollar company and without independent staff, can have much impact on policy. Professor Myles Mace of Harvard Business School has recently written that the chief executive alone determines what the board does.[42]

If "constituency" board members (as in Campaign GM's proposal) had knowledge and power, other problems would arise. Adding workers' representatives to boards of directors would not necessarily accelerate conversion from military to peacetime production, at a loss in profits and jobs, or increase corporate attention to environmental issues, at a similar cost. Workers have in many cases strongly supported management in opposition to pressures for pollution abatement. The interest of consumer representatives on the board may be in direct conflict with those of minority representatives. Increased employment for the hard-core may diminish quality control. Minority representatives may not support conservationist board members who urge reduced consumption in order to preserve our energy resources and minimize pollution.

This is not to say that corporate democracy is not a good thing. The supercorporation is, indeed, as Professor Dahl discusses in his essay, a political system in which self-perpetuating rulers exercise arbitrary power over others.[43] Such oligarchies ought to be transformed into democracies. But internal corporate reform alone will not by itself correct the maldistribution of goods and services. It will not itself insure that corporations undertake serious programs for hiring and promoting minorities. While it can play a contributory role, corporate democracy does not guarantee corporate social responsibility.

III. PUBLIC SOCIAL RESPONSIBILITY

The purpose of this discouraging analysis of corporate social responsibility is not to imply that all hope is lost for a more humane and civilized America but rather that corporate social responsibility is not itself going to effect substantial improvements. The best results one can expect are isolated pragmatic responses by individual corporations. Sometimes these responses are praiseworthy, as, for example, Xerox's recently initiated social service leave program that allows employees up to a year's leave at full pay to offer volunteer social services. Almost all corporate decisions are in some respect "social." Every plant relocation, price increase, product, and work safety improvement deeply affects large numbers of people. Humane, enlightened decision-making of this sort is essential and ought to receive as much praise from social critics as acts of corporate venality receive condemnation.

But if we learned nothing else from the decade of the 1960s, we should now understand that pragmatic and occasional responses to important public issues are insufficient, whether from public or private institutions. Recognizing the discouraging record of governmental failure in the past, we must nevertheless attempt to develop just and efficacious public policies to compel corporate accountability. Although the record of government here has been far from ideal, the autonomous exercise of corporate power *must* be legitimized. Perhaps the wiser for his experience in the insurance industry's two-billion-dollar social investment program, one corporate executive, at least, now understands that "business needs government at all levels, to reorder its priorities and eliminate waste and inefficiency or the nation's social resource gap will never be filled—no matter what private enterprise does."[44]

Reference to government instantly gives rise to the specter of discredited, wasteful bureaucracies, and industry cooptation of sprawling agencies charged with fuzzy mandates to regulate in the public interest. But government policy need not mean more ICCs, FPCs, and the like. It can mean use of the market mechanism through deconcentration of industries and tax incentives and penalties. It can mean pervasive new disclosure laws that will generate information upon which citizens can act in their own interests as shareholders, employees, and consumers. Government can also provide citizens with self-enforcement tools such as class actions.

Radical critics will dismiss the political approach, insisting that power in America rests in its giant corporations and that therefore the government necessarily serves their ends. Corporations do in fact exert enormous influence over government. This influence must be effectively countered if comprehensive social change is to be effected. If the political process is inadequate for this purpose, the process itself must be changed. In any event, the conclusion remains that efforts to evoke a corporate social conscience boil down to pleas for charity. And corporate charity is too tenuous a solution for our nation's pressing problems. We must demand from government that public needs be identified and systematically satisfied.

X

CITIZEN COUNTERACTION?

ANDREW HACKER*

At the outset, proposals for corporate accountability should be understood for what they are: a new, even radical, departure from the conception of business behavior as conceived in this country. For the American presumption has always been that the freedom to conduct a business in ways of one's choosing is a self-evident liberty; that short of placing arsenic in apple juice, any citizen is entitled to pursue profits to the best of his ability. Not the least reason why we declared our independence of Great Britain was the mother country's tendency to restrain entrepreneurial exuberance. Indeed, the entire European system decreed that business could only be carried on with official permission; the burden lay on industrialists to show that their efforts ran parallel with public policy. Not so the United States. Untrammeled by mercantile economics and unencumbered by guild restrictions, for Americans the right to make money seemed so much a matter of course that it could go uncited in the Constitution. Short of incorporation, no forms need be filled in for a citizen to set up a sausage factory in his stable or an ironworks in his barn. "To cherish and stimulate the activity of the human mind, by multiplying the objects of enterprise, is not among the least considerable of the expedients by which the wealth of a nation may be promoted," said Alexander Hamilton in 1791.[1] And his words could easily have been

---

* Professor of Political Science at Queens College; Professor of Government at Cornell University (1955–71); editor of *The Corporation Takeover* (1964); author of *The End of the American Era* (1970) and many other books and articles.

engraved on the capitol rotunda, since the precept that official interference damages the gross national good has been accepted by law-
makers from his time until now.

Regulatory bureaus, inspection agencies, administrative tribunals,
in fact entire Cabinet-level departments, have seen themselves as
handmaidens of private industry, anxious to show sympathy and be
of assistance. And well they might. For business is the central institution of American society—its success rate far surpasses that of the
family—and hardly anyone questions the assumption that we will
only have certain amenities if someone can make a profit in the
process. I say all this with full realization that we have a Food and
Drug Administration, an Interstate Commerce Commission, a Federal Trade Commission, a Bureau of Mines, an Antitrust Division,
and even, at this writing, a Pay Board, a Price Commission, and a
Cost of Living Council. I am as aware as anyone of local zoning
rules, safety regulations, and the statutes concerning labeling, interest
rates, and sanitary slaughtering.

Yet the very recital of these laws and agencies can serve to make
my point. Government can only require certain behavior of businesses on an item-by-item basis. Any and all practices not specifically mentioned in duly processed statutes or adjudications are regarded as acts to be countenanced in and by a free society. Thus,
any new proposal for further intervention or regulation is regarded
not as a prima facie extension of government's inherent powers but
rather as a case which must bear the burden of proof. A paper mill
begins with the freedom to spew acids into the nearby waterways;
to limit that liberty, one must undertake the arduous effort of muster-
ing a legislative majority. Ours is still an economy operating on the
premise that citizens may use the productive process as a means of
self-enrichment. Few Americans are prepared to question such tenets
of a capitalist culture.* Not only is there a presumption against
significant new reforms, but it also takes no great imagination to
issue paper programs suggesting limits on corporate activity. Nevertheless, proposals for public directors, federal charters, criminal

---

* To lay my own ideological cards on the table, I confess not only to being
a registered Republican who has voted for Richard Milhous Nixon four times,
but also to having contributed to both the *Wall Street Journal* and the *National
Review*.

sanctions, and more extensive disclosure of information are ideas worth introducing into public discussion. On federal charters, one must note that some of our most swashbuckling railroads—for example, the Central Pacific and the Union Pacific—were incorporated by the federal government under the Pacific Railroad Act of 1862. The issue, I think, is not which level of government does the chartering but whether that government is inclined to exact accountability. But if one has to begin somewhere, it is best to put first things first. And the primary issue is *power*—the power enabling large corporations to preserve and expand their areas of enterprise in ways of their own choosing. Given this priority, some of the accompanying essays in this volume seem to read like reports to a graduate seminar. While coherent enough as analyses of institutional irrationalities, they end up like *Frankenstein* with the monster left out.

Despite the New Freedom and the New Deal, the New Frontier and the Great Society, American corporations remain as powerful as they were at the opening of this century. For every legislative limitation imposed upon business firms in the last seventy-five years, these institutions have discovered new fields of endeavor in which to extend their influence in and over society. While power cannot be measured by arithmetic indices, revenues offer some indication of ongoing activities. In 1954, for example, the five hundred largest industrial corporations rang up $1.57 in sales for every tax dollar received by all levels of government. A decade and a half later, in 1969, the five hundred biggest firms took in an even $2.00 for every tax dollar gathered by government.[2] That is, while corporate sales were doubling in this period, tax revenues expanded by less than 60 percent. And sales surely constitute some sign of a company's finding new fields to conquer. Our political science textbooks have so fixated us on the growth of "big government" that we spend little time looking into the even faster growing power of organizations our tradition tells us are private.

This is not the place to detail how the productive process shapes the contours of our countryside, or the manner in which a capitalist culture affects our mentalities.[3] I will simply indicate that business has sufficient control over our structure of government not to be unduly discommoded by regulatory forays which purport to be in the public interest—a point Senator Harris discusses. Inspection will serve as good an example as any to measure official intervention. And here the figures themselves are less important than asking why we have the numbers that we do. We might inquire, therefore, why is it that the Food and Drug Administration has, at current writing, only 212 inspectors to examine the nation's sixty thousand food plants? Or why is it that the Occupational Safety and Health Administration can afford only four hundred inspectors to make the rounds of the country's four million business establishments? Why, indeed, does the Federal Communications Commission's common carrier bureau maintain a staff of only 165 individuals to oversee our largest utility, the American Telephone and Telegraph Corporation, which itself has more than seven hundred and fifty thousand employees?[4] The short answer of course is that the Congress keeps the FDA, the OSHA, and the FCC on token budgets: just enough to insure that those agencies' names remain on the organization charts, but not nearly the amounts necessary to hire personnel who might challenge corporate conduct in any serious way.

The overriding fact, then, is that those who make our laws and appropriate public funds have tacitly accepted the assumption that business ought not to be interfered with. To be sure, there are occasional increments on the governmental side: after a series of disasters, for example, the Bureau of Mines was allowed to increase its staff of inspectors from 249 to 560.[5] But even if current forces are doubled, it will still mean that the nation's businesses remain substantially immune from thoroughgoing scrutiny. If the food industry were to be held accountable for obeying even the laws now on the books, what would be needed would be more like twenty thousand inspectors, each having the power to close down a plant on his own authority. What would have to happen, in a word, is that government agencies be permitted to become as powerful as the businesses they confront. But this is a parity which our state and national legislators cannot bring themselves to envisage. Moreover, a new breed of personnel would have to be found to staff these agencies; i.e., individuals having the determination to carry out their duties, even though their careers might be pleasanter and more placid were they to show themselves sympathetic to the enterprises they supposedly oversee. Even envisioning inspectors garbed as Castro's militiamen, striding into plants and offices with automatic rifles slung over their shoulders, the underlying question remains whether an adversary posture is not preferable to civil servants prone to identify with the institutions they should be bringing to account. And, it should be added, subsequent employment in the industries they once purported to regulate. Indeed, the very availability of executive positions—not to mention partnerships in law firms or brokerage houses—constitutes a permanent threat to the pursuit of public purposes.

Or more broadly, the issue is whether a power can be mustered to match the corporate presence. Simply because a statute contains words granting theoretical authority to a government agency does not mean that the instrument will be used. One doubts that the Department of Justice, under this or any foreseeable administration, will file suit to "break up" General Motors into a congeries of smaller companies. It is perhaps necessary to show that I am not unaware of the extent of antitrust activity. What I have said is with full consciousness of the facts that Procter & Gamble was made to divest itself of Clorox; that International Telephone and Telegraph was not permitted to acquire the American Broadcasting Company; and that the Federal Trade Commission has filed a monopolization suit against the four largest cereal companies. Actions of this sort have been going on since the days of Thurman Arnold, but they have not hampered the overall growth of corporate concentration and power. Moreover, the majority of antitrust suits call not for the breakup of big firms but rather for the cessation of certain practices.[6] In this instance, the problem lies not in the Antitrust Division's shortage of lawyers, although its being kept on a skeletal staff is symptomatic of Congress's unwillingness to invest that bureau with more than symbolic power. Rather, General Motors will not be decomposed because that company is accepted as an integral component of the country's structure, having parity with at least the Commonwealth of Pennsylvania.

Surely, then, such talk should be preceded by some inquiry into the parameters of the power necessary to mount such a challenge. My colleague, Robert Dahl, remarks that "if large numbers of Americans" became aware of their powerlessness, then the force of numbers might be massed in opposition to our corporate concentrations. But I wish he had told us the circumstances under which this eventuality might be anticipated. For my own observation has been that it takes more than words to inform individuals of their objective condition. Shaking a population loose from its false consciousness requires a rude awakening going well beyond the appeals of publicists.

As matters currently stand, government does not even deserve to be called the executive committee of the bourgeoisie. Rather, as indicated, it is a subsidiary branch of the corporate community. (DuPont's hegemony over Delaware, as revealed in the recent report sponsored by Ralph Nader, *The Company State*, has its counterparts across the country.) Any company worth its dividends can and does learn to live with the fleabites of such public oversight as an emaciated officialdom offers. At issue, therefore, is the *kind* of government this country would have to have were corporations to be faced with a power capable of bringing them to account. For example: a government having the power to command General Electric to stop this nonsense of manufacturing refrigerators in sixteen different colors (a scandalous waste of resources). To tell General Foods that it must cease putting crinkle cuts on its French-fried frozen potatoes (a dubious contribution to "economic growth"). To instruct Western Electric that it must find better uses for its productive capacities than turning out Princess telephones (they might be working on cheaper kidney machines). Indeed, to direct any given corporation that it does not have permission to desert the central city, to send dollars abroad, or to embark on new investment programs unless it can first be shown that the goods and services which will eventuate deserve such priority. Can we visualize a government prepared to inform companies that they cannot make or market snowmobiles or electric pencil sharpeners until more pressing productive needs have been attended to?

I have tried to imagine what manner of Congress we would require —and the kinds of Congressmen we would have to find—were such directives to be issued and enforced. Clearly they would have to be men and women impervious to the threats and blandishments of the business community. They would have to survive without campaign contributions, not only from corporation executives but also from local businessmen who finance candidates of all major parties. Moreover, they would have to pitch their appeals to voters who are employees of corporations, whose livelihoods depend on producing our cornucopia of superfluous products, ranging from oversized airplanes to undernourishing cereals; they will certainly be aware that official interference will jeopardize their jobs. To elect such a Congress would require the perceptions of politics quite different from those now held by the majority of American voters.

What would be called for, indeed, is some variant of the Marxian script—the creation of a new consciousness so that citizens cease identifying their own well-being with that of a capitalist culture. Instead of wanting more personal income for private comforts and pleasures, they would desire a just and rational economy where production's first obligation would be the satisfaction of social priorities. There must also be a willingness to accept administrative orders, to punish transgressors, and to turn a deaf ear to the siren songs of surplus consumption. For while most Americans are not exploited proletarians of the Marxian model, they have been corrupted by a culture which encourages them to prefer wall-to-wall carpeting to rebuilding slums, prisons, and public hospitals a few miles from their doors.

And I should emphasize here that this corporate accountability will prove costly. If large companies carry out the duties demanded of them, even their own inflated profits will prove insufficient to these tasks. Of course every corporation should stop polluting unwilling citizen victims; they should hire semiliterate workers and teach them to read once they are on the payroll; and there is no question that utility companies must build cooling towers alongside their nuclear reactors. But it must also be acknowledged that these measures will cost money. And the funds will come from one of two sources. Either companies will have to raise their prices, which means that consumers will have to satisfy themselves with a shorter ration of purchases each year. Or companies will be granted public funds for job training or other social purposes, and the consequent higher taxes will diminish our ambit of private spending. It should be obvious that we must pay a price for corporate accountability. But it is not self-evident that Americans are in a mood to make such sacrifices. As matters now stand, we keep more of our incomes for private consumption than do the citizens of any other industrialized nation. And we seem to prefer it that way.

I cannot detect serious signs that this country is ready to undergo a profound transformation in its social character. It will not do to say that if only "leadership" were to come forward, we would subsume our private pleasures to the public good. The effectiveness of leaders depends on the willingness of citizens to assume the role of followers. How many Americans have the temperament for swallowing their opinions and objections, for foregoing their tendency to cavil and criticize whenever a would-be leader's position is not wholly consonant with their own? The political battlefield is littered with the bodies of leaders who failed to measure up to the exacting standards of overopinionated and easily disaffected supporters. The average American digs in his heels, juts out his jaw, and in effect declares: "Just try to lead me! I dare you!" The irony is that so many of these citizens are the very ones who continue to call for "leadership."

If a constituency for political counteraction is to emerge, some evidence is needed of widespread opposition to corporate conduct. Can the American species of challenging citizens, just described, take up the cudgels? Obviously there is more such sentiment now than in the recent past. Enough Congressmen have got this message, for example, to vote against subsidizing a supersonic transport; to nearly defeat a loan for Lockheed; to blow the whistle on special favors for El Paso Natural Gas; and to pass bills requiring that the automobile industry make safer and less polluting cars. Yet these cases can be construed as several more instances of piecemeal reforms, of the sort to which industry has been subjected on and off for the last three-quarters of a century, and which have not overly curtailed corporate freedom. Moreover, survey results allow a variety of interpretations. "As far as the people running major companies are concerned," Louis Harris asked in 1966 and then again in late 1971, "would you say that you have a great deal of confidence, or only some confidence, or hardly any confidence at all in them?"[7] Of those who had views, the responses ran:

	1966	1971
"A great deal of confidence"	55%	27%
"Only some confidence"	35%	50%
"Hardly any confidence at all"	5%	15%

The percentage of people who once had a "great deal of confidence" has fallen by more than half, and this is clearly a substantial defection. The proportion having "hardly any confidence at all" has trebled in the last half decade, a significant sign of disillusion. Still, it should be noted that this 15 percent refers to "the people running major companies" and not to those institutions as such. And over three-quarters (27 percent and 50 percent) continue to maintain at least "some confidence," which is still an impressive majority. Finally, the Harris interviewers also asked these individuals how they felt about those presiding over science, education, and our legislative process. The descent in confidence expressed in those areas paralleled that applied to corporations, suggesting that there exists a generalized mistrust of those presiding over the country's dominant institutions and that business management's decline in popularity is part of a more pervasive malaise.

Even so, a time of malaise may be the best period in which to cash in whatever chips one has. Thus, Daniel Yankelovich found that between 1970 and 1971 the proportion of people professing to desire more government regulation of business rose from 50 percent to 69 percent; another Harris survey showed that among those having opinions, 95 percent felt that "it's good to have critics like Ralph Nader to keep industry on its toes."[8] And that the public is aroused over pollution—which is intimately interwoven with the corporate power issue—cannot be doubted. There would appear to be a body of opinion favorable to further moves toward greater measures of corporate accountability.

My own perplexity centers on the depth of the commitments inhering in these opinions. That there exists a liberal constituency in this country cannot be questioned. Almost a quarter of a million Americans have sent checks to Common Cause, presumably concerned over structural imbalances in our political system. At the same time it may be observed that a shortage of contributors forced the withdrawal of the one Presidential aspirant—Senator Fred Harris of Oklahoma—willing to campaign against corporate concentrations. Not the least problem is that citizens of liberal or left-leaning persuasions find that they must divide their energies and emotions across a wider range of issues than at any time in the past. Poverty and street crime must compete with traffic congestion and racial tensions; while the reform of state prisons, migrant labor camps, and inner-city hospitals take attention from the issues of overburdened courts, strip-mined landscapes, and the rise of venereal disease. On top of all this, individuals of goodwill are asked to support the liberation of women, homosexuals, and Soviet Jews; not to mention winding down our Asian involvements and worrying about conspiracy trials, official surveillance, and the fate of the Bill of Rights. People who take the predictable positions on these issues can probably be counted upon to favor making corporations more accountable. Even so, the question remains whether the fractions of themselves they can devote to this matter will add up to an impact of any magnitude.

The proletariat in the Marxian characterization—and, for that matter, the peasantry in the Maoist emendation—were much more single-minded: their overriding preoccupation was to end their exploitation by the propertied class. Their hopes and hatreds, therefore, could be channeled toward a straightforward goal: the abolition of production for private profit. In addition, the success of revolutionary movements has been in inverse proportion to a citizenry's sophistication. In China and Cuba, to take two recent examples, simple slogans and a forthright focus attracted a population having little to lose by a social upheaval. Any cause which wishes to call itself a "movement" must be able to involve its members so that they will take risks, make sacrifices, and eschew diversionary activities. Corporate power will not face a serious challenge in this country while those professing such an aim are simultaneously preoccupied with Lesbian liberation or opening delivery rooms to expectant fathers. But Americans are not peasants. We are too literate, too argumentative, indeed too individualistic, to be members of movements. If our opportunities for travel, education, and interesting occupations have made us wise to the ways of the world, these very experiences may have brought us to an eminence where we can no longer engage in populist politics.

Nevertheless, there is something to be gained by raising the whole subject of corporate accountability at this time, if only to start amassing a record of problems, proposals, and principles. After all, the *Fabian Essays* were published over a half century prior to the advent of Britain's first Labour government, and almost seventy-five years intervened between the *Communist Manifesto* and the emergence of the Soviet Union. While none of the essays in this volume call for so drastic a transformation as proposed by Marx and Engels, or even Shaw and Webb, the implications inhering in these essays should not be minimized.* Put very simply, they will be fought at every stage by organizations having skills, resources, and experiences for this kind of struggle.

My own inclination, therefore, is to continue the enterprise of gathering information, exposing operations, and sounding warnings. Corporate accountability is an idea whose time has not yet come; grievances against the business system have yet to assume paramountcy in the public mind. If this time is to come at all, it will be when the United States has its next serious depression. For as unemployment and economic insecurity begin to blanket people who have previously held steady jobs, they and many of their neighbors will be willing to elect officeholders prepared to impinge on corporate immunities. Issues such as fluoridation, sex education, and overcrowded airports will recede into the background, and attention can then focus on the assumptions underlying corporate capitalism. At such a time, too, popular mandates are so broad that a wide range of actions can be undertaken in the public's name. (When voters elected the 73rd Congress, for example, they were not sanctioning the Tennessee Valley Authority.) This is not an argument for mass unemployment—which, by the way, could also bring a regime of the right—but simply an indication that the American people will have to be made a lot angrier than they are now before they will commit themselves to transforming our economic system. Until that time occurs, those having the interest and the determination can do a lot worse than continuing to pick away at Prometheus's liver.

---

* At this point, a word on nationalization is appropriate. If only several industries are brought under public ownership—say, about 20 percent of productive capacity—then the odds are good that the companies remaining in private hands will influence government policy to insure that the nationalized firms serve as acquiescent adjuncts to the private sector. This has been the experience in Great Britain under both Conservative and Labour governments.[9] Hence the Marxian insistence on total nationalization, so as once and for all to abolish private centers of power having the capacity to undermine the goals of social ownership.

XI

DETERRING CORPORATE CRIME

GILBERT GEIS*

STREET VS. SUITE CRIME

An active debate is underway in the United States concerning the use of imprisonment to deal with crime.[1] Enlightened opinion holds that too many persons are already incarcerated, and that we should seek to reduce prison populations. It is an understandable view. Most prisoners today come from the dispossessed segments of our society; they are the blacks and the browns who commit "street crimes" for reasons said to be closely related to the injustices they suffer. But what of white-collar criminals, and the specific subset of corporate violators? If it is assumed that imprisonment is unnecessary for many lower-class offenders, it might be argued that it is also undesirable for corporation executives. In such terms, it may appear retributive and inconsistent to maintain that a law-violating corporation vice president spend time in jail, while advocating that those who work in his factory might well be treated more indulgently when they commit a criminal offense.

I do not, however, find it incompatible to favor both a reduction of the lower-class prison population and an increase in upper-class representation in prisons. Jail terms have a self-evident deterrent

---

* Professor, Program in Social Ecology, University of California; former chairman of the Section on Criminology of the American Sociological Association; editor of *White-Collar Criminal* (1968); co-author of *Man, Crime, and Society* (1970).

impact upon corporate officials, who belong to a social group that is exquisitely sensitive to status deprivation and censure. The white-collar offender and his business colleagues, more than the narcotic addict or the ghetto mugger, are apt to learn well the lesson intended by a prison term. In addition, there is something to be said for *noblesse oblige*, that those who have a larger share of what society offers carry a greater responsibility also.

It must be appreciated, too, that white-collar crimes constitute a more serious threat to the well-being and integrity of our society than more traditional kinds of crimes. As the President's Commission on Law Enforcement and Administration of Justice put the matter: "White-collar crime affects the whole moral climate of our society. Derelictions by corporations and their managers, who usually occupy leadership positions in their communities, establish an example which tends to erode the moral base of the law. . . ."[2]

Corporate crime kills and maims. It has been estimated, for example, that each year two hundred thousand to five hundred thousand workers are needlessly exposed to toxic agents such as radioactive materials and poisonous chemicals because of corporate failure to obey safety laws. And many of the 2.5 million temporary and 250,000 permanent worker disabilities from industrial accidents each year are the result of managerial acts that represent culpable failure to adhere to established standards.[3] Ralph Nader has accused the automobile industry of "criminal negligence" in building and selling potentially lethal cars. Nader's charges against the industry before a Congressional committee drew parallels between corporate crime and traditional crime, maintaining that acts which produce similar kinds of personal and social harm were handled in very different ways:

> If there are criminal penalties for the poor and deprived when they break the law, then there must be criminal penalties for the automobile industry when its executives knowingly violate standards designed to protect citizens from injuries and systematic fraud.[4]

Interrupted by a senator who insisted that the witness was not giving adequate credit to American industry for its many outstanding achievements, Nader merely drove his point deeper: "Do you give credit to a burglar," he asked, "because he doesn't burglarize 99 percent of the time?"[5]

Death was also the likely result of the following corporate dereliction recounted in the *Wall Street Journal* which, if the facts are as alleged, might well be regarded as negligent manslaughter:

> Beech Aircraft Corp., the nation's second-largest maker of private aircraft, has sold thousands of planes with allegedly defective fuel systems that might be responsible for numerous crash deaths —despite warnings years in advance of the crashes that the system wasn't working reliably under certain flight conditions.
>
> Though Beech strongly denies this, it is the inescapable conclusion drawn from inspection of court suits and exhibits in cases against Beech, from internal company memoranda, from information from the Federal Aviation Agency and the National Transportation Board, and from interviews with concerned parties.[6]

After 1970, the fuel systems in the suspect planes were corrected by Beech at the request of federal authorities. Before that, the company had been found liable in at least two air crashes and had settled two other cases before they went to the jury. In one case, tried in California and now under appeal, a $21.7 million judgment was entered against Beech. Of this, $17.5 million was for punitive damages, which generally are awarded in the state only when fraud or wanton and willful disregard for the safety of others is believed to exist. At the moment, suits are pending which involve the deaths of about twenty other persons in Beech planes.[7]

Those who cannot afford a private plane are protected against being killed in a crash of a Beech aircraft, but nothing will help the urban resident from being smogged. Again Nader has pointed out the parallel between corporate offenses and other kinds of crime and the disparate manner in which the two are viewed and treated:

> The efflux from motor vehicles, plants, and incinerators of sulfur oxides, hydrocarbons, carbon monoxide, oxides of nitrogen, particulates, and many more contaminants amounts to compulsory consumption of violence by most Americans. . . . This damage, perpetuated increasingly in direct violation of local, state, and federal law, shatters people's health and safety but still escapes inclusion in the crime statistics. "Smogging" a city or town has taken on the proportions of a massive crime wave, yet federal and state statistical compilations of crime pay attention to "muggers" and ignore "smoggers". . . .[8]

Corporate crime also imposes an enormous financial burden on society. The heavy electrical equipment price-fixing conspiracy alone involved theft from the American people of more money than was stolen in all of the country's robberies, burglaries, and larcenies during the years in which the price fixing occurred.[9] Yet, perhaps it can be alleged that corporate criminals deal death and deprivation not deliberately but, because their overriding interest is self-interest, through inadvertence, omission, and indifference. The social consciousness of the corporate offender often seems to resemble that of the small-town thief, portrayed by W. C. Fields, who was about to rob a sleeping cowboy. He changed his mind, however, when he discovered that the cowboy was wearing a revolver. "It would be dishonest," he remarked virtuously as he tiptoed away.[10] The moral is clear: since the public cannot be armed adequately to protect itself against corporate crime, those law enforcement agencies acting on its behalf should take measures sufficient to protect it. High on the list of such measures should be an insistence upon criminal definition and criminal prosecution for acts which seriously harm, deprive, or otherwise injure the public.

OBSTACLES TO PUBLIC OUTRAGE

The first prerequisite for imposing heavier sanctions on corporate criminals involves the development of a deepening sense of moral outrage on the part of the public. A number of factors have restricted public awareness of the depth and cost of white-collar crime. That the injuries caused by most corporate violations are highly diffused, falling almost imperceptively upon each of a great number of widely scattered victims is undoubtedly the greatest barrier to arousing public concern over white-collar crime. "It is better, so the image runs," C. Wright Mills once wrote, "to take one dime from each of ten million people at the point of a corporation than $100,000 from each of ten banks at the point of a gun." Then Mills added, with wisdom: "It is also safer."[11] Pollution cripples in a slow, incremental fashion; automobile deaths are difficult to trace to any single malfunctioning of inadequately designed machinery; antitrust offenses deprive many consumers of small amounts, rather than the larger sums apt to be stolen from fewer people by the burglar. It is somehow less infuriating and less fear-producing to be victimized a little every day over a long period of time than to have it happen all at once. That many very small losses can add up to a devastating sum constitutes impressive mathematical evidence, but the situation lacks real kick in an age benumbed by fiscal jumboism.

Take, as an example, the case of the Caltec Citrus Company. The Food and Drug Administration staked out the Company's warehouse, finding sugar, vitamin C, and other substances not permitted in pure orange juice being brought into the plant. Estimates were that the adulteration practices of the Company cost consumers one million dollars in lost value, thereby "earning" the Company an extra one million dollars in profits.[12] For the average customer, the idea of having possibly paid an extra nickel or dime for misrepresented orange juice is not the stuff from which deep outrage springs —at least not in this country at this time.

There are additional problems stemming from the class congruence between the white-collar offender and the persons who pass official judgment on him. The judge who tries and sentences the criminal corporate official was probably brought up in the same social class as the offender, and often shares the same economic views. Indeed, one Washington lawyer recently told a study group examining antitrust violations that "it is best to find the judge's friend or law partner to defend an antitrust client—which we have done."[13] Also, the prosecutor, yearning for the financial support and power base that will secure his political preferment, is not apt to risk antagonizing entrenched business interests in the community. In addition, the corporate offender usually relies upon high-priced, well-trained legal talent for his defense, men skilled in exploiting procedural advantages and in fashioning new loopholes. The fees for such endeavors are often paid by the corporation itself, under the guise that such subsidies are necessary to protect the corporate image, to sustain employee morale, and to provide an adequate defense. Finally, in the extremely unlikely event that he is sentenced to imprisonment, the corporate offender is much more apt to do time in one of the more comfortable penal institutions than in the maximum-security fortresses to which *déclassé* offenders are often sent.

White-collar criminals also benefit from two prevalent, although contradictory, community beliefs. On the one hand, neighbors of the corporate criminal often regard him as upright and steadfast; indeed, they will probably see him as solid and substantial a citizen as they themselves are. Witness, for example, the following item in the hometown newspaper of one of the convicted price fixers in the 1961 heavy electrical equipment antitrust case:

> A number of telegrams from Shenango Valley residents are being sent to a federal judge in Philadelphia, protesting his sentence of Westinghouse executive John H. Chiles, Jr. to a 30-day prison term. . . .
>
> The Vestry of St. John's Episcopal Church, Sharon, adopted a resolution voicing confidence in Chiles, who is a member of the church. . . .
>
> Residents who have sent telegrams point out Chiles was an outstanding citizen in church, civic and community affairs and believe the sentence is unfair.[14]

At the same time there is a cynicism among others about white-collar crime in general, a cynicism rooted in beliefs that the practices are so pervasive and endemic that reformative efforts are hopeless. "As news of higher immoralities breaks," Mills wrote, "people often say, 'Well, another one got caught today,' thereby implying that the cases disclosed are not odd events involving occasional characters, but symptoms of widespread conditions."[15] Wearied by expected exposé, citizens find that their well of moral indignation has long since run dry. This lack of indignation can clearly benefit the white-collar criminal. For example, the following courtroom speech, delivered by an attorney for Salvatore Bonanno—allegedly a leading figure in the network of organized crime—reflects public leniency toward such offenses: "It does not speak of the sort of activity where the public screams for protection, Your Honor," the lawyer said, his voice rising. "I think that in the vernacular the defendant stands before you convicted of having committed a white-collar crime and, having been convicted of a white-collar crime, Your Honor, I most respectfully . . . suggest to the court that he should be sentenced in conformity with people who have been convicted of white-collar crimes, and not being sentenced on the basis of his being Salvatore Bonanno."[16]

These are some of the barriers to generating public concern; what are the forces that need to be set in motion to surmount them?

Foremost, perhaps, is the firm assurance that justice can prevail, that apathy can be turned into enthusiasm, dishonesty into decency. History notes that corruption was rampant in English business and government circles until in the late 1800s, when an ethos of public honesty came to prevail, largely through the efforts of dedicated reformers.[17] Similarly, at their origin the British police were a rank and renegade force; today they are respected and respectable. In fact, at least one writer believes that the decency of the English police is largely responsible for the mannerly and orderly behavior shown by the general public.[18] Thus, change can be achieved, and such change can have eddylike effects on other elements of social existence.

Following this alteration in the psychology of the polity, the facts of corporate crime must then be widely exposed and explained. This process requires investigation, analysis, pamphleteering, and continual use of mass media outlets. It is a formidable task, but one made easier by the fact that the ingredients for success are already present: corporate offenses are notorious and their victims—especially the young—are increasingly concerned to cope with such depredations.[19] Also, when confronted with a problem, Americans respond by taking action to resolve the difficulty, an approach quite different from, say, that of the Chinese. As Barbara Tuchman has noted, the Chinese, at least in pre-Communist times, regarded passivity as their most effective tactic on the assumption that the wrong-doer ultimately will wear himself out.[20] The ideological basis of the American ethos was set out by Gunnar Myrdal in his now classic analysis of racial problems in the United States. We had to work our way out of the "dilemma" involved in the discrepancy between our articulated values and our actual behavior, Myrdal believed[21]; that resolution has proceeded, largely through the use of legal forces, though at a painfully slow and sometimes erratic pace.

So too, perhaps, with corporate crime. Part of the public may be unduly sympathetic, and part cynical, toward revelations of such crime, but a latent hostility is also evident. The Joint Commission on Correctional Manpower, for instance, found from a national survey a strong public disposition to sentence accountants who embezzle more harshly than either young burglars or persons caught looting during a riot.[22] Similarly, a 1969 Louis Harris Poll reported that a manufacturer of an unsafe automobile was regarded by respondents as worse than a mugger (68 percent to 22 percent), and a business-man who illegally fixed prices was considered worse than a burglar (54 percent to 28 percent).[23]

Corporate offenses, however, do not have biblical proscription—they lack, as an early writer noted, the "brimstone smell."[24] But the havoc such offenses produce, the malevolence with which they are undertaken, and the disdain with which they are continued, are all antithetical to principles we as citizens are expected to observe. It is a long step, assuredly, and sometimes an uncertain one, from lip service to cries of outrage; but at least principled antagonism is latent, needing only to be improved in decibels and fidelity. It should not prove impossible to convince citizens of the extreme danger entailed by such violations of our social compact. "Without trust, a civilized society cannot endure," Marya Mannes has said. "When the people who are too smart to be good fool the people who are too good to be smart, the society begins to crumble."[25]

It should be noted that Americans are perfectly willing to outlaw and to prosecute vigorously various kinds of behavior on social grounds, *i.e.*, in the belief that the behaviors constitute a threat to the social fabric rather than a threat to any prospective individual victims. Thus, possession of narcotics, abortion, homosexuality, and a host of other "victimless" crimes[26] are proscribed as threats to the moral integrity of our civilization. A reading of historical records indicates without question that class bias and religious intolerance were the predominant forces which gave rise to the laws against such "immoral" behavior.[27] It is now time that the rationale offered for prosecution of victimless crimes—that they threaten the integrity of the society—be applied to where it really belongs: to the realm of corporate offenses. This rationale did not work with victimless crimes because there was no reasonable way to convince non-perpetrators, often members of the perpetrators' general social groups, that what the offenders were doing was wrong. Therefore, eventually and inevitably, the logic of the perpetrators' position moved other groups either to take on their behavior (*e.g.,* the smoking of marijuana) or to take their side (*e.g.,* the performance of abortions). But the rationale *can* work vis-à-vis corporate crime, given its quantifiable harm actually imposed on nonparticipating victims. Also, there is the possibility of isolating the offender from reinforcement and rationalizations for his behavior, of making him appreciate that nobody morally sanctions corporate crime; of having him understand, as the English would put it, that "these kinds of things simply are not done by decent people." It is a standard defensive maneuver for criminals to redefine criminogetic behavior into benign terms. "Businessmen develop rationalizations which conceal the fact of crime," Edwin H. Sutherland wrote in 1949 in his classic study, *White Collar Crime*. "Even when they violate the law, they do not conceive of themselves as criminals," he noted, adding that "businessmen fight whenever words that tend to break down this rationalization are used."[28]

By far the best analysis of this process—and the way to combat it —is by Mary Cameron on middle-class shoplifters caught in Chicago's Marshall Field's. Store detectives advised that Field's would continue to be robbed unless some assault on the shoplifters' self-conceptions as honorable citizens was undertaken. The methods used toward this end are described by Cameron:

> Again and again store people explain to pilferers that they are under arrest as thieves, that they will, in the normal course of events, be taken in a police van to jail, held in jail until bond is raised, and tried in court before a judge and sentenced. Interrogation procedures at the store are directed specifically and consciously toward breaking down any illusion that the shoplifter may possess that his behavior is merely regarded as "naughty" or "bad". . . . It becomes increasingly clear to the pilferer that he is considered a thief and is in imminent danger of being hauled into court and publicly exhibited as such. This realization is often accompanied by dramatic changes in attitudes and by severe emotional disturbance.[29]

The most frequent question the middle-class female offenders ask is: "Will my husband have to know about this?" Men express great concern that their employers will discover what they have done. And both men and women shoplifters, following this process, cease the criminal acts that they have previously been routinely and complacently committing.[30]

The analogy to the corporate world is self-evident. As a law professor has observed, "Criminal prosecution of a corporation is rather ineffective unless one or more of the individual officers is also proceeded against."[31] A General Electric executive, for example, himself not involved in the price-fixing conspiracy, said that although he had remained silent about perceived antitrust violations, he would not have hesitated to report to his superiors any conspiracy involving thefts of company property.[32] Corporate crimes simply are not regarded in the same manner as traditional crimes, despite the harm they cause, and they will not be so regarded until the criminals who commit them are dealt with in the same manner as traditional offenders.

Harrison Salisbury tells of Leningrad women taking a captured German pilot to a devastated part of the besieged city during the Second World War, trying to force him to understand what he had been doing.[33] Persons convicted of drunken driving sometimes are made to visit the morgue so that they might appreciate the kind of death they threaten. Corporate criminals, though, remain insulated from their crimes. F. Scott Fitzgerald made the point well in *The Great Gatsby*: "They were careless people, Tom and Daisy—they smashed up things and creatures and retreated back into their money or their vast carelessness, or whatever it was that kept them together, and let other people clean up the mess they had made."[34]

How can this situation be changed? Taken together, a number of possible strategies involve widespread dissemination of the facts, incessant emphasis on the implications of such facts, and the methods by which the situation can be improved. Specific tactics might include regular publication of a statistical compilation of white-collar crime, similar to the FBI's *Uniform Crime Reports*, which now cover traditional offenses. It is well to recall that in its earliest days the FBI concentrated mostly on white-collar offenses, such as false purchases and sales of securities, bankruptcy fraud, and antitrust violations[35]; it was not until later that it assumed its "gangbuster" pose. Well publicized by the media, these FBI statistical reports form the basis for a periodic temperature-taking of the criminal fever said to grip us. Numerical and case history press releases on corporate crime would publicly highlight such incidents. It is perhaps too much to expect that there will some day be a "Ten Most Wanted" white-collar crime list, but public reporting must be stressed as a prerequisite to public understanding.

Another possibility is the infiltration of criminally suspect corporations by agents of the federal government trained for such delicate undercover work. It would be publicly beneficial to determine why and how such corporations disdain the criminal statutes they are supposed to obey. The cost would be minimal, since the infiltrators would likely be well paid by the corporation, and the financial yield from prosecutions and fines would undoubtedly more than offset any informer fees involved in the operation. To some this tactic may appear too obnoxious, productive of the very kind of social distrust that the corporate crimes themselves create. But so long as infiltration remains a viable FBI tactic to combat political and street crime, its use cannot be dismissed to combat white-collar crime. But perhaps, as an alternative, large companies should have placed in their offices a public servant who functions as an ombudsman, receiving public and employee complaints and investigating possible law violations.

There are, of course, other methods of uncovering and moving against corporate crimes, once the will to do so is effectively mobilized. Mandatory disclosure rules, rewards for information about criminal violations (in the manner that the income tax laws now operate), along with protections against retaliation for such disclosures, are among potential detection procedures. The goal remains the arousal of public interest to the point where the corporate offenses are clearly seen for what they are—frontal assaults on individuals and the society. Then, journals of news and opinion, such as *Time*, will no longer print stories dealing with the antitrust violations under the heading of "Business," but rather will place the stories where they belong, in the "Crime" section.[36] And judges and prosecutors, those weathervanes of public opinion, will find it to their own advantage and self-interest to respond to public concern by moving vigorously against the corporate criminal.

ALTERNATIVE KINDS OF SANCTIONS

Sanctions against corporate criminals, other than imprisonment, can be suggested; they are milder in nature and perhaps somewhat more in accord with the spirit of rehabilitation and deterrence than the spirit of retribution. While perhaps less effective instrumentalities for cauterizing offending sources, they at least possess the advantage of being more likely to be implemented at this time.

Corporate resources can be utilized to make corporate atonement for crimes committed. A procedure similar to that reported below for dealing in Germany with tax violators might be useful in inhibiting corporate offenses:

> In Germany, . . . they have a procedure whereby a taxpayer upon whom a fraud penalty has been imposed is required to make a public confession, apparently by newspaper advertisement, of the nature of his fraud, that a penalty has been imposed, that he admits the fact, and will not do it again. This procedure is known as "*tätige reue*" [positive repentance].[37]

A former FTC Chairman has said that "the Achilles heel of the advertising profession is that you worship at the altar of the positive image."[38] The same is true of corporations; thus the value of the public confession of guilt and the public promise of reform.

There is, of course, the sanction of the heavy fine. It has been argued that the disgorgement of illegal profits by the corporation— in the nature of treble damages or other multiplicated amounts —bears primarily upon the innocent shareholders rather than upon the guilty officials. This is not very persuasive. The purchase of corporate stock is always both an investment and a gamble; the gamble is that the corporation will prosper by whatever tactics of management its chosen officers pursue. Stockholders, usually consummately ignorant about the details of corporate policy and procedure, presume that their money will be used shrewdly and profitably. They probably are not too adverse to its illegal deployment, provided that such use is not discovered or, if discovered, is not penalized too heavily. It would seem that rousing fines against offending corporations will at least lead to stockholder retaliations against lax or offending managerial personnel, and will forewarn officials in other corporations that such derelictions are to be avoided if they expect to remain in their posts. The moral to widows dependent upon a steady income will be to avoid companies with criminal records, just as they are well advised to keep their money out of the grasp of other kinds of shady entrepreneurs and enterprises. Then, perhaps, sanctions against white-collar criminality can be built into the very structure of the market place itself.

What of corporate offenders themselves? The convicted violator might be barred from employment in the industry for a stipulated period of time, just as union leaders are barred from holding labor positions under similar circumstances.[39] In the heavy electrical equipment antitrust cases, for instance, one convicted offender was fired from his $125,000-a-year job with General Electric, but was employed immediately upon release from jail by another company at about a $70,000 annual salary. All ex-convicts ought to be helped to achieve gainful employment, but surely nonexecutive positions can be found which would still be gainful. "Business executives in general enjoy the greatest material rewards available in the world today," it has been noted. "The six-figure salaries at the top would be called piratical in any other sphere of activity."[40] A brief retirement by corporate officials from what in other forms of work is disparagingly called the "trough" does not seem to me to be an unreasonable imposition. Why put the fox immediately back in charge of the chicken coop? I recall some years ago the going joke at the Oklahoma State Penitentiary—that Nannie Doss, a woman who had a penchant for poisoning the food of her husbands, was going to be assigned duty as a mess-hall cook and then released to take a job in a short-order cafe. It was a macabre observation, except that similar things happen all the time with corporate criminals.

There have been suggestions that the penalties for corporate crime might be tailored to the nature of the offenses. Thus, the company president who insists that he had no knowledge of the crime could, if found culpable for negligent or criminal malfeasance, be sentenced to spend some time interning in the section of his organization from whence the violation arose. The difficulties inhere, of course, in the possibility of creating a heroic martyr rather than a rehabilitated official, and in problems relating to the logistics of the situation. Yet, veterans on major league baseball teams are dispatched to Class C clubs because of inadequate performance; they then attempt to work their way back to the top. The analogy is not precise, but the idea is worth further exploration.

THE ISSUE OF DETERRENCE

The evidence gleaned from the heavy electrical equipment case in 1961 represents our best information on the subject of deterrence of corporate crime; no antitrust prosecution of this magnitude has been attempted since, and very few had been undertaken earlier. Government attorneys were then convinced (I interviewed a number of them when I was gathering information on the subject for the President's Commission on Law Enforcement in 1966) that the 1961 antitrust prosecutions had been dramatically effective in breaking up price-fixing schemes by many other corporations. By 1966, however, they felt that the lesson had almost worn off. Senate hearings, conducted after the heavy electrical equipment conspirators had come out of jail, shed further light on the subject of deterrence. One witness before the Senate Antitrust and Monopoly Subcommittee— William Ginn, a former General Electric vice president—granted that the "taint of a jail sentence" had the effect of making people "start looking at moral values a little bit." Senator Philip Hart pushed the matter further, and drew the following remarks from the witness:

> *Hart*: This was what I was wondering about, whether, absent the introduction of this element of fear, there would have been any reexamination of the moral implications.
> *Ginn*: I wonder, Senator. That is a pretty tough one to answer.
> *Hart*: If I understand you correctly, you have already answered it. . . . After the fear, there came the moral reevaluation.[41]

Other witnesses who had done jail time stated with some certainty that they had learned their lesson well. "They would never get me to do it again. . . . I would starve before I would do it again," said another former General Electric executive.[42] Another man, from the same organization, was asked: "Suppose your superior tells you to resume the meetings; will they be resumed?" "No, sir," he answered with feeling. "I would leave the company rather than participate in the meetings again."[43]

These penitents were the same men who had earlier testified that price fixing was "a way of life" in their companies. They had not appreciated, they said, that what they were doing was criminal (though they never used *that* word; they always said "illegal"); and if *they* had not met with competitors, more willing and "flexible" replacements were available. They were men described by one of their attorneys in a bit of uncalculated irony as not deserving of jail sentences because they were not "cut-throat competitors," but rather persons who "devote much of their time and substance to the community."[44]* O. Henry's Gentle Grafter, speaking for himself, had put it more succinctly: "I feel as if I'd like to do something for as well as to humanity."[46]

The corporate executives were model prisoners in the Montgomery County jail. The warden praised them as the best workers he had ever had on a project devoted to reorganizing the jail's record-keeping system. Thus, to the extent that they conduct themselves more honestly within the walls than they have outside, corporate offenders might be able to introduce modern business skills into our old-fashioned penal facilities. Though they were allowed visitors two days a week, the imprisoned executives refused to have their families see them during the time, slightly less than a month, that they were jailed.[47] It was shame, of course, that made them so decide—shame, a sense of guilt, and injured pride. These are not the kinds of emotions a society ought cold-bloodedly and unthinkingly try to instill in people, criminals or not, *unless* it is found necessary to check socially destructive behavior.

What of the financial sanctions? The $437,500 fine against General Electric was equivalent to a parking fine for many citizens. That the corporations still felt the need to alibi and evade before the public, however, was noteworthy for its implication that loss of goodwill, more than loss of money or even an agent or two, might be the sanction feared most. Note, for instance, the following verbal sleight of hand by General Electric about a case that involved flagrant criminal behavior and represented, in the words of the sentencing judge, "a shocking indictment of a vast section of our economy."[48] At its first annual meeting following the sentencing of the price-

---

* The convicted felons saw themselves in similar roseate ways. The GE vice president, for instance, had written: "All of you know that next Monday, in Philadelphia, I will start serving a thirty-day jail term, along with six other *businessmen* for conduct which has been *interpreted* as being in conflict with the *complex* antitrust laws." (Emphasis added.)[45]

fixing conspirators, General Electric dismissed suggestions that further actions might be taken to cleanse itself. The idea, advanced by a stockholder, that the Company should retrieve sums paid to the conspirators as "incentive compensation" was said to "ignore the need for careful evaluation of a large number of factors." These factors—the expense of litigation and the morale of the organization—boiled down to a concern that "the best interests of the Company are served."[49] The president of Westinghouse demanded that employees adhere to the antitrust laws *not* because failure to do so was a crime or because it damaged the public. Rather, such behavior was discouraged because "any such action is—and will be considered to be—a deliberate act of disloyalty to Westinghouse."[50]

GE president Ralph Cordiner observed in 1961: "When all is said and done, it is impossible to legislate ethical conduct. A business enterprise must finally rely on individual character to meet the challenge of ethical responsibility." But by then the president had come to understand how the public might achieve what the Company could not: "Probably the strong example of the recent antitrust cases, and their consequences, will be the most effective deterrent against future violations," he decided.[51]

So the lesson had been learned—but only partly. It was much like the mother who scolds her children about stealing by saying that their behavior upsets her and might hurt the family's reputation in the neighborhood. After several such episodes, however, and a few prison terms or similarly strong sanctions against her offspring, she might suggest that a more compelling reason for not stealing is that it is a criminal offense, and that when you get caught you are going to suffer for it. When such an attitude comes to prevail in the corporate world, we will have taken a major step toward deterring corporate crime and protecting its innocent victims.

XII

COURTS AND CORPORATE
ACCOUNTABILITY

ARTHUR S. MILLER*

The notion of corporate accountability or responsibility—the terms
are only roughly synonymous—has suddenly become fashionable, not
only within a small group of academic commentators but also within
the business community itself. Witness, for example, a statement in
the summer of 1971 by the Committee for Economic Development.
Said the CED (in part):

> In relations with their constituencies and with the larger society,
> American corporations operate today in an intricate matrix of
> obligations and responsibilities that far exceed in scope and com-
> plexity those of most other institutions and are analogous in many
> respects to government itself. The great growth of corporations in
> size, market power, and impact on society has naturally brought
> with it a commensurate growth in responsibilities; in a democratic
> society, power sooner or later begets equivalent responsibility.[1]

At least three things can be said about the CED's position: (1)
that the business community is beginning to recognize—at least, to
articulate—responsibilities larger than merely making profits for the
stockholders of the corporations; (2) that the business community

---

* Professor of Law at the National Law Center, George Washington
University; author of *Racial Discrimination and Private Education*
(1957), *The Supreme Court and American Capitalism* (1968), and
numerous law review and magazine articles.

maintains that ours is a "democratic society"; and (3) that those who exercise power in that society at some time will be brought to book for its exercise. The first point is beyond argument. Not only the CED but many corporate executives willingly acknowledge that corporations have obligations beyond the simplistic model of making money for the "owners." It is as yet unclear whether these statements are other than the product of public relations counsellors. The second and third points, however, are even less evident. They suggest the two assumptions on which this chapter is based:

First, despite the myth to the contrary, the United States is not "democratic" in the sense of widespread participation in decision-making. No thoughtful observer of the American polity can fail to discern the presence of elite structures—of a "governing class"— within the nation, elites that not only determine policy but also have such control of the media of communication that a near monopoly of information is the norm. Voting is not enough.

Second, it is simply not true that "power sooner or later begets equivalent responsibility." Examples are legion and, as William of Occam might have said, need not be needlessly multiplied. Included here are some who have not been held accountable or responsible: those who took American into the morass of Vietnam; the top management of Lockheed, which managed it into near bankruptcy; the Mafia; Representative Natcher of Kentucky, who held up money for Washington's subway; David Rockefeller of the Chase Manhattan Bank; the boards of trustees of any university; the heads of major labor unions; those who control the supercorporations; the director of the Federal Bureau of Investigation; the Army Corps of Engineers; senior partners in major law firms; leaders in various ecclesiastical organizations; the Supreme Court of the United States, to say nothing of state and federal judges generally; the Central Intelligence Agency; tenured professors at universities; newspaper columnists and television commentators; chairmen of the standing committees of Congress. And so on, if not ad infinitum, perhaps ad nauseam. All exercise significant social power in situations where little or no accountability is present. The lesson is simple: ours is not a "democratic" society and power quite often is not accountable—if by accountable is meant that something called "the public interest" is the guiding criterion for decision-making by powerholders and that there are institutionalized means to insure that those powerholders adhere to that criterion.

It is only by taking the CED statement as a projection of an ideal, rather than of an actuality, that it can be accepted. Institutionally, the political organs of government simply do not, perhaps cannot, effect accountability on the giant corporations. The legislatures, whether state or national, are next to hopeless; they show little evidence of being willing to take the initiative in governing. One need only point to the total absence of constructive action by Congress on the new Nixonomics to show that. And the bureaucracy is at least not, effect accountability on the giant corporations. The legislatures, equally hopeless. We live in the "administrative state," one which, as Washington lawyer Charles A. Horsky once said, is "emphatically a government of men, not of laws."[2] Discretion is the norm. Law in the sense of interdiction is by and large absent, particularly in the higher reaches of the public administration.

What chance does the judicial branch have to impose accountability upon the corporations? It is to courts and those who man them—the judges and the lawyers—that this chapter is chiefly devoted.

DEFINING THE PROBLEM

What can courts do? That question can be broken down into at least four: what have courts done in the past? what are they doing now? what can they do in the future? and what *should* they do? Each merits some attention.

The Lessons of History

In inquiries such as this, a page of history is worth a volume of empirical data. One need not be called a Marxist or economic determinist to suggest that the courts during the formative years of the republic, and up through the 1920s, were employed *by* the business community to protect *its* interests. The term "employ" is not used in an invidious sense; venal and corrupt judges there have been and are, but the situation is far more subtle and far more entrenched than instances of out-and-out criminality. It may be seen in both private and public law.

As for private law, for example, tort law was largely judge-made. Rules of contributory negligence, assumption of risk, and the fellow-servant doctrine all permitted burgeoning corporations during the nineteenth century to escape much of the human costs of industrial development. In the area of contract law, which merges into public law as well, the historical notion of Sir Henry Maine that the movement of "progressive societies" was one from "status to contract" was written into legal doctrine. What this meant is that the economic power of the corporation was said to be equal to, but no more than, the economic power of the workingman—an obvious fiction, to be sure, but one followed by the courts. Furthermore, that most pervasive of all "contractual" instruments, the "contract of adhesion,"* was considered by the judges to be no different from a true arms-length transaction. The core idea was freedom of contract, which was the legal analogue of a laissez-faire economic system. The social basis for that notion, however, was never valid; certainly it has not been since the Civil War. But the law, in its magnificent majesty, tells us that the rich as well as the poor are free to contract. The law and the judges have never caught up with an idea espoused in the eighteenth century: "Necessitous men are not free men." One other example bears mention. Judges sitting in courts of equity were quick to issue injunctions to protect the property of the business class; but they never in American history held that there was a property right in a job. The result was that both in common law courts and equity courts the new corporations that came into existence beginning about 1850 flourished under a protective legal umbrella that, by and large, favored them at the expense of others (such as farmers and laborers).

As for public law, during the early nineteenth century corporations were both feared and relatively small in number. Not until the 1850s did major moves toward incorporation take place. During that decade more were formed than existed during the previous years of the Republic.[3] It is well to recall, also, that the Federal government was noteworthy for *not* regulating business, even though it had the power to do so under the interstate commerce clause of the Constitution.

---

* A contract of adhesion is a take-it-or-leave-it proposition—a "nonbargain" transaction. A moment's reflection discloses that most contracts are of this type.

What it often did do was to intervene in behalf of business. Subsidies to the railroads are one classic instance, but there are many others.

Prior to the Civil War, it was a controversial question whether the corporation was a person, thereby receiving the protections of the Constitution. The issue was initially resolved shortly after the Fourteenth Amendment was promulgated. Said the Supreme Court in the *Slaughterhouse Cases*:[4] It is inconceivable that the Fourteenth Amendment could be used for purposes other than to aid the newly freed slaves, a theme echoed in *Munn v. Illinois*[5] where the Court told an owner of a grain elevator regulated by the state of Illinois that his remedy was legislative rather than judicial. In other words, if you don't like what is being done to you, don't come to the Supreme Court; elect some new legislators. (That message was carefully noted and resurrected by business in the post-1937 period.)

For whatever reasons—and no doubt they are multiple—the Supreme Court in its infinite wisdom saw new light in 1886. In an otherwise obscure case about railroad regulation,[6] when the lawyers were again trying to convince Their Serene Highnesses that corporations should be persons within the meaning of Section 1 of the Fourteenth Amendment, Chief Justice Waite stopped oral argument and announced to counsel that he need not discuss the point further. Waite said that all the justices were of the opinion that corporations were indeed legal persons. (A remarkable invention, it has been accepted since, save for an occasional aberration by Justices Hugo L. Black and William O. Douglas. Those profound students of the Constitution who in recent years have been complaining about "judicial legislation" conveniently neglect to remember that piece of judicial lawmaking, which neatly amended the Constitution without having to go through the cumbersome processes set out in Article V.)

But that was only the beginning. Owing to the power of the strong-minded Justice Stephen Field and influenced in large measure by the American bar, including the famous Roscoe Conkling, the Court soon found that it could not only invent a new category of person; in addition, it could amend the Constitution by reading the due process clauses in a new way. That familiar history need not be recounted here; it is the rise and fall of "substantive due process" in economic matters, a development that enabled the Court to operate, as John R.

Commons put it in 1924, as "the first authoritative faculty of political economy in the world's history."[7] Protection against deprivation without due process of law was the liberty of those artificial constructs, the corporations, and the liberty included freedom to contract. That freedom, said the Court in a series of decisions enacting Herbert Spencer's *Social Statics* into law, meant that the workingman was to be as free to sell his labor as were the corporations to buy it; legislatures could not intrude into that relationship by fixing minimum wages and maximum hours. The Supreme Court prevailed until the 1930s, when even the justices could see that hungry men are not free men. They understood that the intervention of government at times was necessary to rectify the power imbalances created by the growth of corporate power. The breakthrough came when New York's law permitting milk prices to be regulated was upheld in 1934. Another decision validated Minnesota's mortgage moratorium law, thereby permitting farmers to have more time to pay off their mortgages. On the other hand, the National Recovery Act and the first Agricultural Adjustment Act were both invalidated.

But then came 1936 and the landslide Roosevelt victory, followed by his proposal in early 1937 to add new justices to the Supreme Court. F.D.R. lost that battle but he won the campaign and the war. Since 1937 the Court is no longer an "authoritative faculty of political economy"; rather, it is an arbiter of social ethics and an interpreter of statutes. Control over economic policies has been ceded to the avowedly political branches of government, epitomized in the Employment Act of 1946 and culminating in the Economic Stabilization Act of 1970. In the latter, Congress also abdicated—now to the President—and it is that officer who now rides tall in the economic saddle. The nation has come a long way from 1886.

What must be emphasized is that public law—whether legislation or judge-made—tended to aid the burgeoning business enterprises. Only when the Granger and Populist movements captured the legislatures in the late nineteenth century, producing statutes that regulated business (as distinguished from aiding business), did the Supreme Court suddenly find that the Fundamental Law proscribed such laws. For a period of about fifty years, the High Bench acted as a buffer between the corporations and their would-be regulators. Businessmen looked to the nine justices as ultimate protectors of the business interests.

Not so, however, since 1937, neither for the Court nor for the businessman. No longer able to employ the Court to protect their interests, businessmen have followed the advice of *Munn v. Illinois*. They have elected and controlled legislators and administrators who favor policies that either protect business or that minimize harm to it. Examples are many. For instance, a few years ago the Federal Communications Commission, in a rare burst of energy and courage, took the National Association of Broadcasters at its word and said that it was going to enact the N.A.B.'s code concerning commercials into administrative rule. The networks then immediately ran, not to the courts where ostensibly their remedy was, but to Congress. There they found a complaisant committee, which quickly reported out a bill saying that the FCC did not have the power to do that. That bill passed the House with an overwhelming vote, whereupon the FCC saw new light, rescinded the proposed rules, and there the matter rests today. The point is that the corporations manipulated Congress. Much the same thing happened when the Federal Trade Commission proposed stringent rules on cigarette advertising in 1964. Congress, bowing to industry pressure, took the matter away from the FTC and enacted its own innocuous bill.

Several dozen times since 1940, businessmen have used Congress as a super court of appeals, either to overrule the Supreme Court (as in the bank merger act) or administrative agencies (usually to discourage proposed rulings, as when Congress in 1962 prohibited the FTC from intensively studying the top thousand firms). Normally, however, the bureaucracy imposes only minimal restraints on business or, at times, acts as a surrogate for the businessman. A ready example of the latter is the accelerated tax depreciation allowances ramrodded through the Treasury in 1971 by bureaucrats anxious to do the bidding of the White House.

With the legislatures and the agencies being "representatives" of the regulated, the courts now are asked to do something that historically they never did and that in all probability they cannot do: place substantial restraints upon the centers of social power, including corporations and the operations of public administration. Textbooks on administrative and constitutional law to the contrary notwithstanding, the courts are ill prepared and far from willing to do the necessary tasks. But here and there it is possible to perceive some change.

The Judiciary Today

Courts, as we have seen, historically simply did not control the corporations. They did not impose norms of accountability upon the corporate managers. Even the antitrust laws, which were the first real attempt by Congress to do something about giant business, were soon scuttled by the Supreme Court, which neatly amended them by reading a rule of reasonableness into the flat terms of prohibition of restraints of trade. The Congressional response then became one of creating "independent regulatory commissions" to take care of some of the more pressing problems in industries brought by new technologies. The first of these, the Interstate Commerce Commission in 1887, antedated the Sherman Act. Supposedly it was to regulate the railroads. Business, of course, at first did not like the ICC, and thus had to decide what to do about it. Should they get it declared unconstitutional by the Supreme Court? As Walter Adams pointed out, they were told to exploit it, and exploit it they did.[8]

It was a pattern successful not only for the ICC but also for the other regulatory commissions. They are spokesmen for the regulated, rather than protectors of "the public interest." (Not for nothing has Justice W. O. Douglas said that these commissions should have a ten-year life span, and that they should have to be re-enacted every decade.) The Washington office for the networks is the FCC. The CAB—whose organic statute was written by an airlines attorney— manages to raise air fares at the time that the companies are losing money; an "administered" price system results that is the counterpart of administered prices in such basic industries as steel and oil, neither of which need fear zealous enforcement of antitrust laws.

Courts should require the regulatory commissions to pay more attention to the "public interest" standards than to the interests of the regulated. One important reform should be the judicial acceptance of liberalized "standing" for plaintiffs—those people with sufficient interest to bring a lawsuit. Beginning a half dozen years ago, some federal Courts of Appeals began to allow conservationists and television consumers, to name but two outstanding cases,[9] standing to challenge administrative action favorable to business. The net result of this development is that the doctrine of standing has now become so splintered that many new classes of plaintiffs are recognized. When to this is added the class action movement, one can readily see that if the trickle becomes a stream, there is going to be a lot of judicial action in the near future. The Supreme Court did hold in *Sierra Club v. Morton* (1972) that the Sierra Club lacked standing to challenge the construction of certain resort facilities in California, but the Court added that individuals near the planned facilities might qualify. It appears that standing is becoming a less substantial barrier to judicial action. This does not mean that the new types of plaintiffs will always or even often win, but it does mean that federal judges will have to listen and decide cases on their merits rather than slamming the door in the faces of some plaintiffs.

In addition, some decisions impose "substantive" standards of conduct on the bureaucracy—and through them on the corporations. This tendency runs back at least as far as 1954, when the Supreme Court in the *Phillips Petroleum* case[10] decided that the Federal Power Commission could regulate natural gas at the wellhead, something the FPC did not want to do. Since then, there has been a steady, albeit uneven, tendency by some courts to impose higher standards of conduct upon the administrators. In the *Cascade Natural Gas* case[11] a few years ago, Justice Douglas castigated the Antitrust Division for knuckling under to El Paso Natural Gas Company, one of the litigants; the Court went to the extraordinary means of removing the case from the jurisdiction of District Judge Willis W. Ritter in Utah. (These decisions have prompted El Paso to get one of its senators, Warren Magnuson, to propose a bill exempting it from the antitrust laws.) The *Alaskan Pipeline* case and the DDT case won by the Environmental Defense Fund may also fit into this category, as does *CAB v. Moss*,[12] in which the Court of Appeals slapped down the Board on a rate increase.

But if one swallow does not a summer make, a few scattered judicial decisions do not a new doctrine make. We are still a long, long way from reasonable attainment of the goal of corporate accountability, or even of opening up the legal process, judicial and administrative, to greater numbers and varieties of plaintiffs.

WHAT COURTS CAN AND SHOULD DO

There are again two basic ways in which courts can and should act: either they can permit members of what might be called the internal corporate community greater access to judicial remedies against corporate managers, or they can permit people from outside that corporate community to call it to account for some of its actions.

More specifically, courts can and, I think, should do the following: (1) enforce the antitrust laws more stringently; (2) use mandatory orders to require the bureaucracy to pull up its sox and govern more adequately; (3) enlarge the class action category; (4) allow shareholders greater access to the corporate decisional process, perhaps by permitting shareholders to trigger the Securities and Exchange Commission into action; (5) permit *qui tam* actions to enforce anti-pollution laws; (6) further enlarge the category of those with standing to bring the administrative process or judiciary into operation; (7) apply constitutional norms to corporate activity; (8) allow more legal actions to be brought against the companies themselves, either by way of stockholders' derivative suits or by others who might want to sue for some reason. This will take the development of new law and new legal categories. As matters stand now, corporate managers have little to fear from direct legal action, in the sense that basic changes will be effected in the structure of corporate governance—as they will have to be if accountability is to come about. Each of these is a subject all its own; I merely mention them to indicate some, but not all, possible avenues of judicial activity. Two warrant greater attention here.

First, *qui tam*. In 1970 the Conservation and Natural Resources Subcommittee of the House Committee on Government Operations issued a report on the possible use of this type of action to help enforce the Refuse Act of 1899. Under that statute, violators are subject to criminal prosecution and fines up to twenty-five hundred dollars or imprisonment up to one year. A corporation or a person who discharges or deposits refuse matter onto the banks of or into navigable waters without a permit, or contrary to the terms of a permit from the Corps of Engineers, is thus punishable. (This statute is noteworthy for one outstanding fact: the Corps of Engineers has never enforced it.)

Under its terms, however, the statute says that "one-half of said fine is to be paid to the person or persons giving information which shall lead to conviction." It is this language that has suggested to some that a *qui tam* action can be brought (*qui tam* is a civil action by a citizen to collect a fine, penalty or forfeiture). In effect, if permitted, it provides for a set of private prosecutors of that segment of the criminal law. The action has a long history. Holdsworth's *History of English Law* describes its use in the fourteenth and fifteenth centuries, calling it "a common expedient to give the public at large an interest in seeing that a statute was enforced by giving any member of the public the right to sue for the penalty imposed for its breach, and allowing him to get some part of that penalty." In the United States, Justice Black, speaking for the Supreme Court in 1943, said that "*qui tam* suits have been frequently permitted by legislative action. . . . Statutes providing for a reward to informers which do not specifically either authorize or forbid the informer to institute the [*qui tam*] action are construed to authorize him to sue,"[13] citing an opinion by Chief Justice John Marshall in 1805.

One would think, with the emphasis given to law and order these days, that the Refuse Act of 1899 should be vigorously enforced by the Department of Justice. One would further think that federal judges, with the discretion permitted them in interpreting statutes, would allow *qui tam* actions brought by citizens interested in enforcing that long-neglected statute. That is distinctly not the situation. *Qui tam* has not been permitted in most cases thus far litigated. *Bass Anglers v. U.S. Plywood*,[14] decided February 10, 1971, by the U.S. District Court in Houston, Texas, is a good example. Judge Woodrow B. Seals, after noting that "the ecological scales are in danger of being uncontrollably tipped," refused to enjoin defendants from dumping refuse in Texas waterways without a permit and also refused to order the Army to enforce the Refuse Act. Said Judge Seals: "No room remains for implying that any others" than the Department of Justice can enforce the statute, rejecting Justice Black's 1943 statement quoted above. The judge said that the Supreme Court "appeared to state the law too broadly," an interesting example of what Professor Walter Murphy once called a "lower court check on Supreme Court power." Having refused to halt environmental degradation, Judge Seals finds he has no jurisdiction to permit the action. An odd decision, enough to make one wonder what a judge with more courage or an appreciation of the latitude given judges to interpret statutes would have done in the circumstances. But, as I have said, the *Bass Anglers* decision is only one of a stream of near unanimity pouring from the bench saying that *qui tam* is not to be allowed. Dean Swift or H. L. Mencken would no doubt have been amused by this display of judicial pusillanimity or perhaps judicial obeisance to corporate idols. Others merely shake their heads in despair. Congress passes a statute. The Executive does little to enforce it. A citizen seeks to get some sort of enforcement. And he usually fails. Why? Catch-22, perhaps; or as Kurt Vonnegut might say, "so it goes" on the *qui tam* front.

Second, there is the question of applying constitutional norms to corporate activity. Once the giant corporations are recognized for what they are in fact—private governments—then it is not too difficult to get over the conceptual hurdle of state action necessary to apply constitutional limitations to the supercorporations. The Constitution, it is often said, runs against governments only. It is only necessary to call the corporation a government and the task becomes easy. (Whether it *should* be done may present harder problems.)

The Supreme Court has in two cases taken that mental leap, and in a number of others has come close to doing so. In 1946 a member of a religious sect was permitted to invoke the First Amendment's freedom of religion provision as a bar to a trespass prosecution on the private property of the Gulf Shipbuilding Corporation in Chickasaw, Alabama.[15] Chickasaw was a company town; it looked much like any other small American town or suburb—drab and dreary, sprawling and ugly. The Court, speaking through Justice Black, had no difficulty in finding that it performed a governmental function and hence was subject to the First Amendment. Twenty-two years later that decision provided precedent for holding that members of a labor union had a constitutional right, under the First Amendment, to picket on the private property of a shopping center.[16] Other cases fit within the framework: the "white primary" decisions[17] holding that a corporate body, the Democratic Party, could not constitutionally exclude Negroes from voting in primary elections; the sit-in cases,[18] which come close to holding—Justice Douglas is on record as so believing—that a charter from the state is all that is necessary to connect the state and corporation to make the corporation fall within the rubric of state action; and the *Burton*[19] case, holding that a private company renting space for a restaurant in a publicly owned parking lot became sufficiently public in signing the lease. Additional decisions, both federal and state, fall within that incipient concept.*

In putting forth the notion of constitutionalizing the corporation, I am not suggesting what the limits of such action should be. Quite simply, I think it self-evident that were we to start anew and rewrite the Constitution of 1787, something would have to be said about the corporations. And the unions. And other important social groups.

I am not urging that we should be governed by the judiciary. Far from it. As that cult of libertarians who applauded the activism of the Warren Court is now finding, a change in personnel can bring different results. Courts are less well equipped than are other branches of government to make and enforce decisions that decide delicate balances of liberty and justice in our constitutional order. It is to that final point that I now turn.

IMPEDIMENTS TO COURT INITIATIVES

There are more than a few serious impediments to effective judicial action. First is the adversary system itself and the legal profession. The Anglo-American system of litigation is a product of feudal times, of a prescientific age; it is well suited to settling minor problems of corrective justice—what might be termed the penny-ante disputes that human beings get into. But today, all law is either public law or is greatly influenced by public law. The system, therefore, must work in a situation far different from that for which it was developed and for which it only by happenstance has real effectiveness. When national resources are allocated, for example, as in the granting of airline franchises—an instance of distributive justice—it is by a trial-type hearing, precisely what the adversary system should *not* be used for. With the impact of science and technology and the myriad

---

* The Supreme Court, however, failed to follow the logic of its previous decisions when it held in *Lloyd Corp. v. Tanner* in early 1972 that an anti-war group did not have a constitutional right to picket on the premises of a shopping center.

problems growing out of them, the system is being asked to carry a workload that both quantitatively and qualitatively it cannot support. Automobile accident litigation quantitatively bogs down the courts and puts them hopelessly in arrears. At most, that system is one that rewards the legal profession and that enables the insurance industry to delay paying valid claims. Those injured in auto accidents get financial returns in roughly the same amount as lawyers get fees in that litigation. This is being recognized, to be sure, by the advent of no-fault insurance; but here, as is so often true, it took a crisis to precipitate action.

Shortcomings in the system are apparent as well in the obvious lack of competence on the part of judges and lawyers to deal with many of the complicated problems brought before them. That has been recognized by the Supreme Court. In the *Rowan & Nichols* case thirty years ago, for example, Justice Frankfurter unabashedly conceded his comparative lack of expertise to those who manned the Texas Railroad Commission and gladly gave up any effective review of its activities. Chief Justice Taft is said to have dodged "radio questions" whenever he could, simply because he knew that he did not understand that newfangled method of communication. Do not think that the passage of time has increased the expertness of judges. In 1971, in *Ohio v. Wyandotte Chemicals Corporation*,[20] a case in which the state of Ohio tried to invoke the original jurisdiction of the Supreme Court to abate the dumping of mercury into Lake Erie, the Court, speaking through Justice Harlan, refused to take the case, although he admitted "that we have jurisdiction seems clear enough." Only Justice Douglas dissented from that neat repeal of part of Article III of the Constitution. The reason, among other things, was that "we have no claim to special competence in dealing with the numerous conflicts between States and nonresident individuals that raise no serious issues of federal law." Harlan added:

> This Court has found even the simplest sort of interstate pollution case an extremely awkward vehicle to manage. And this case is an extraordinarily complex one both because of the novel scientific issues of fact inherent in it and the multiplicity of governmental agencies already involved. Its successful resolution would require primarily skills of factfinding, conciliation, detailed coordination

with—and perhaps not infrequent deference to—other adjudica-
tory bodies, and close supervision of the technical performance of
local industries. We have no claim to such expertise. . . .

Accordingly, the Court decided it would be better to husband its
resources so as to further its "paramount role as the supreme federal
appellate court." To Justice Douglas this was perplexing, for the
Court had accepted jurisdiction in even more complicated cases, such
as the water dispute in *Arizona v. California*; there, through the
use of a Special Master, it had been able to find the facts and to
operate without harm to its "paramount role." I am inclined to agree
with Justice Douglas, and to call the *Wyandotte* decision a disaster,
but the case stands for an equally important proposition: judges do
not feel confident when dealing with complicated scientific questions.

So, too, with economic policy questions. Justice Frankfurter conceded in 1954 that he and his colleagues really did not know what
difference it made to the economy were they to decide an antitrust
case one way or another.[21] And as Mark Massel, noted Washington
economist and attorney, showed a decade ago, the quality of economic analysis that lawyers bring to courts in antitrust cases is woefully short of the need.[22]

Another difficulty with the judicial process is the fact that judges
tend, by and large, to be drawn from that stratum of society reflecting the values of the businessman. Many, consequently, find it difficult to perceive why greater burdens should be laid upon the business
class. A result is a corpus of law, built up over the decades, that in
the main protects business.

Still another impediment to corporate accountability via the courts
is that the lawyers tend to follow the money—and the corporations
have the money. The best legal talent, therefore, is at the service of
the richest corporations. Those lawyers are adept at getting favorable
laws enacted or at obtaining desirable interpretations from judges
and administrators. But when there is adverse judicial or administrative behavior, they either get the court or agency overruled by the
legislature or so delay the process that just as there is a doctrine that
one must exhaust his administrative remedies before going to court,
there seems to be a practice of corporation lawyers exhausting
opposing litigants. It takes money and it takes perseverance to prevail
against that line-up.

Finally, who listens to courts? This is terra incognita. No one knows in any systematic or comprehensive way just what the operative impact of a judicial decision is. The judges speak, but who listens? We do know a little, to be sure: sometimes a Supreme Court decision, as in legislative reapportionment, is widely followed, but sometimes, as in the school prayer case, it is not. We know also that judicial decisions affecting administrative agencies have an impact, if at all, only on the immediate agency before the bar of the court—and perhaps not then. When the Second Circuit knocked the FPC back in the *Scenic Hudson* case, that did not result in significantly different behavior by the Commission. So, too, with the FCC and the *United Church of Christ* case. It will take a lot more judicial supervision than is now apparent to get the agencies into line.

CONCLUSION

Accountability refers to the duties and obligations a corporation has to the constellation of interests that make up "the" enterprise plus the people at large. A suggestion that courts can impose norms of accountability upon corporations (and the people who control them) is based on the assumption that the judiciary in some way differs from the avowedly political branches of government. That assumption is probably invalid. Although the orthodoxy of the legal profession proclaims judges to be impartial decision-makers dispensing justice with an even hand, there are few thoughtful observers today who would maintain that human limitations of mind and spirit can be transcended by those who wear the black robes of judicial office.[23] Put another way, this means that, as with legislatures, courts cannot—and surely will not—escape the political *Zeitgeist* The implication is clear: law reflects the power interests of the community. It will be changed—accountability will be effected upon corporations—at such time as there are new configurations of power, in the political sense, operating throughout the nation. The name of this game is still "politics," not "law."

To expect more from the judiciary is to ask for the improbable, if not the impossible. Although Chief Justice Earl Warren's Supreme Court did attempt to act as the ethical conscience of the nation, particularly in the areas of civil rights and civil liberties, the Warren era has now ended; and by no means is it certain that lasting reforms were in fact imposed by the Court. Judge Learned Hand, speaking three decades ago, put the same thought in these words:

> . . . this much I think I do know—that a society so riven that the spirit of moderation is gone, no court *can* save; that a society where that spirit flourishes, no court *need* save; that in a society which evades its responsibility by thrusting upon the courts the nurture of that spirit, that spirit in the end will perish. What is the spirit of moderation? It is the temper which does not press a partisan advantage to its bitter end, which can understand and will respect the other side, which feels a unity between all citizens—real and not the factitious product of propaganda—which recognizes their common fate and their common aspirations—in a word, which has faith in the sacredness of the individual.[24]

We delude ourselves, then, if we expect too much from courts. In the past, even more than today, "judges [spoke] for the ruling classes."[25] Only if those classes, operating through the political processes, trigger the courts can it be expected that judges will respond.

Our further matter merits attention: power in the modern state has moved ever increasingly from the judiciary to the legislatures and from them to the public administration. This is indeed "the administrative state," with power shared between interlocking public and private bureaucracies. The consequence is that public policy tends to be the resultant of a parallelogram of conflicting political forces exerted by groups (of which government is merely one group).[26] For the judiciary to try to mediate the disputes that inevitably arise in this process, judges will have to become even more deeply immersed in politics than they have been. It is one thing for a judge to make decisions in public policy matters when most law was private law, but quite another when public law has become the center of the legal process, the fulcrum upon which the entire system rests. The fate of the judiciary in the modern state seems to be a diminution in importance.[27]

XIII

HALFWAY UP FROM LIBERALISM: REGULATION AND CORPORATE POWER

SIMON LAZARUS*

In a widely noted address early in his Presidential campaign, Senator Edmund Muskie castigated American liberals for achieving no new social change since the New Deal. Whatever the merit of his indictment (and, except for civil rights, I think it largely true), I was struck less by the charge itself than by the implied compliment Muskie paid to the reformers of the recent past. In making a throw-away reference to the New Deal, he evidently assumed it was the yardstick by which liberals should judge their works today. He pictured the thirties as the grand era of liberal triumph and progress.

To be sure, there is nothing unusual in Senator Muskie's reverence for the New Deal. Most Americans now share that view. At home, in school, from the press, they learned that Franklin Roosevelt's reforms were the levers which the American public grasped to control the nation's "economic royalists." In reflecting this view, Muskie was merely repeating dogma trumpeted by such eminent figures as Arthur Schlesinger, Jr., who told us as recently as 1962 that, thanks

* Washington attorney, formerly a Fellow at Harvard University's Institute of Politics (1970–71) and General Counsel to New York City's Department of Consumer Affairs; this chapter is based on *The Genteel Populists*, a book to be published by Holt, Rinehart and Winston in spring, 1973.

to F.D.R.'s reforms: "The capitalist state . . . far from being the helpless instrument of the possessing class, has become the means by which other groups in society have redressed the balance of social power against those whom Hamilton called the rich and well-born."[1]

Schlesinger's encomium catches the feature most ingrained in the contemporary image of what the New Deal was all about. As he sees it, the public was able to seize control of the state, and through affirmative state action—through regulation—to counter the power of the wealthy, of business, of the interests. In this view, the New Deal implemented the advice given by Teddy Roosevelt thirty years earlier; in order to "deal on terms of equality" with the big corporations, Roosevelt said, "It becomes necessary for ordinary individuals to combine in their turn . . . through that biggest of all combinations called the government. . . ."[2]

Liberals have not been alone in clinging to the grandiose image of the second Roosevelt's reign. Others have viewed this period as the womb of a new regime of pervasive business regulation. For two decades after the Second World War, conservatives believed this and denounced it. More recently, radicals have similarly accepted the notion that the New Deal created a vast new apparatus of state power and imagined that subsequent corruption of this governmental machinery has yielded a "corporate state."

IMAGES OF PAST REFORM

Yet this widely shared image of the thirties is largely inaccurate. The New Deal that contemporaries think they remember—whether with admiration or antipathy—never really happened. Except for the ill-fated National Recovery Administration—which, at least in design, really did resemble Charles Reich's corporate state—the New Deal neither conceived of nor implemented any comprehensive planning or regulatory schemes aimed at "redressing the balance of social power." The period did witness a proliferation of new regulatory laws and bureaucracies. But these hardly added up to a more prudent substitute for the defunct NRA—as current discourse seems to assume.

Eleven agencies born during the thirties had regulatory (as distinct from welfare) functions. Of these only two—the Securities and

Exchange Commission and the Federal Power Commission (the latter of which was actually created during the Hoover Administration)—can reasonably be said to have been imposed by the public on the industry in question.[3] The others were engineered by the industries or other affected interests themselves, often for the purpose of immunizing cartel practices from antitrust restraints. Included in this latter category are such well-known creations of the New Deal period as the Civil Aeronautics Board, the Motor Carriers Act of 1935 (extending ICC rate-fixing and entry-limiting jurisdiction to trucks and buses), and the Federal Maritime Commission. The unhappy consequences of these "reforms"—higher consumer prices, restricted output, arbitrary curtailment of service offerings, frozen technical development, resource misallocation—have been documented by a large and still increasing body of scholarly and muckraking literature.[4] Somewhat less well covered is the origin of these regulatory measures. But enough has been published to make it clear that the reforms were mainly the work of industry pressures, and that their "defects," as they have since come to be viewed by unhappy liberal observers, were designed-in. Their architects wanted to stabilize competitive and/or technologically volatile markets, and in this hope they have not been disappointed.[5]

Furthermore, those New Deal regulatory measures which did benefit disadvantaged groups—the Fair Labor Standards Act, the Wagner Act, and the Agricultural Adjustment Act seem the most important—were not produced by experts riding a tidal wave of public concern. They were tailored to the specifications of very well-organized interest groups. They too were designed to stabilize what would otherwise be competitive markets. In retrospect, they cannot be said to have unambiguously promoted the public interest, at least if that term is considered strictly coincident with the economic interest of consumers.[6] But the value to the public of these measures is not the point here; my main concern is with the process of their gestation and birth. The regulatory initiatives are best understood as parceling out government power to various organized economic interests to better enable them to control the public. This is a far more sensible view than the common assumption that the New Deal was a Grand Design executed by government reformers and backed by public opinion to enable the public to control private interests.

The regulatory reforms of the Progressive Era, enacted two decades before the New Deal, conformed more closely to the conventional image of the reform legislative process. The most significant Progressive agencies—the Federal Trade Commission and the Federal Reserve Board—were probably necessitated by an aroused public opinion, more disturbed about corporate power than Americans have ever been before or since. On the other hand, even in these cases, the specific provisions of these measures—as distinguished from the general objectives to which they were supposedly addressed —were hammered out in the main by the affected economic groups. The design of the FTC was much contested. Agents of big business wanted the Commission strong enough to give advance advice, and consent, to questionable mergers and other transactions. Small business representatives feared such collaborative possibilities. They fought to reduce the powers of an agency which they similarly assumed would fall under the influence of big business.[7] The final terms of the legislation satisfied neither set of interests, but the appointees whom President Woodrow Wilson picked to run the new Commission pleased them both, and appalled reformer Louis Brandeis, who dismissed the FTC's first commissioners as "a stupid administration."[8] The banking reform battle was similarly a struggle between the big New York banks, smaller metropolitan banks elsewhere, and the even smaller "country banks." Largely irrelevant to the actual terms of the struggle was the backdrop of public concern about the "money trust" whipped up by the famous Pujo Committee investigations of 1911.[9]

This is not to imply that the New Deal, or its predecessor, Progressivism, were coordinated conspiracies against the public, as has been suggested by some. Nor is it to forget that the Adamson Act, Social Security, progressive taxation, and other welfare measures were landmark advances on behalf of F.D.R.'s "forgotten man at the bottom of the economic pyramid." My point simply is that we tend today to hold a grossly overstated view of how successful these earlier reformers were, even at the outset, in making good on their rhetorical commitment to affirmatively supervise business. As Professor Galbraith observed, during a period when he was given to emphasizing the self-regulatory virtues of "countervailing power" in the economy, "The truth is that much of the American liberal's modern advocacy of state intervention and planning has been general and verbal." It has been, he said, "a massive deployment of words. . . ."[10] The words of the reformers were indeed stirring. They held aloft heady visions of a peaceful revolution, a veritable industrial coup on behalf of the people. "To the far-sighted," proclaimed Harold Ickes in 1934,

> it has long been obvious that the only way out is for the govern-ment to take control and develop a better system for the people . . . if it is our purpose to make industrialism serve humanity in-stead of laying ourselves as victims on the cruel altar of industrial-ism. . . .[11]

Such words had their effect. Indeed, they produced one of recent history's most impressive victories for public relations. The press believed the myth that the New Deal was creating a brave new regulatory state. They convinced the public. Historians believed the myth. They convinced later generations, even sophisticated politicians like Senator Muskie.

THE IDEAL OF AFFIRMATIVE DEMOCRACY

In truth, I think our well-burnished image of the New Deal tells us less about the past than it does about ourselves. Its primary function is not to explain the America of the thirties but to justify the America of today. The myth serves an ideological need which liberals in all eras seem to share: the need for faith that American democracy can work as high school civics lessons insist it should—that "the peo-ple" can maintain active and affirmative direction of the nation's affairs, including positive control over agglomerations of private power. This "affirmative" concept of democracy has consistently been posited by liberalism. But when industrialism spawned vast and powerful private organizations, the possibility loomed that the affirmative ideal had been destroyed. "Big business interests," worried Woodrow Wilson at the height of Progressive anxiety about corporate power in 1912,

> . . . are so great that there is an open question whether the gov-ernment of the United States with the people back of it is strong enough to overcome and rule them. . . . We have come to be one of the worst ruled, one of the most completely controlled and

dominated, governments in the civilized world—no longer a government by free opinion, no longer a government by conviction
and the vote of the majority, but a government by the opinion and
the duress of small groups of dominant men.[12]

Such thoughts greatly disturb most civic-minded Americans. Believing that past generations (including Wilson's) were able to strike
back at the special interests through regulation helps to keep the old
faith.

And of course, this image of the past is not entirely wrong. Some
of the agencies created by the Progressives and New Dealers, and the
laws which they administer, *were* the products of public concern
rather than special interest calculation. Some of them have managed
to function in rough consonance with their original aims.[13] But in
general the contemporary estimate of past reform achievements far
exceeds the facts. This rosy view, however, helps us maintain faith
in the same basic ideal that motivated the Progressives and New
Dealers themselves: that somehow, if the right legislative formula,
the right set of arrangements is found, the public can at last be put
in firm and positive command over the interests. We might question
the way in which old reforms have been implemented. We might
even question the form in which the reformers' objectives were cast.
But we shy away, as from the plague, from the possibility of challenging the ideal itself, this affirmative concept of democratic controls
over private power. This same hope has shaped most of the criticism
of the regulatory establishment, just as much as it underlay the
efforts to build it in the first place. It is a psychological and ideological goal from which the new wave of reformers seeking to tame
corporate power have only partially liberated themselves.

REFORM THROUGH PRESIDENTIAL CONTROL

So strong has faith in this ideal of affirmative government remained
that proposals to correct the alleged defects of the Progressive–New
Deal agencies have merely confirmed and even reinforced its dictates.
Before the New Deal had even ended, serious disquiet surfaced in
official circles about the regulatory agencies. President Roosevelt
appointed a commission under the direction of Cornell political
scientist Robert Cushman to investigate and recommend reforms.

The commission report and Cushman's subsequent book concluded that things were not all as they should be, but recommended that they would improve if the President assumed more direct control over the agencies.[14] Most of the agencies at that time (as is still the case) were considered "independent," in the sense that their commissioners served for fixed terms and could not be fired by the President. Cushman's cure soon took hold and became the dominant new liberal conception of how the regulatory establishment should be structured.

Only last year, President Nixon's Council on Executive Reorganization (popularly known as the "Ash Council" after its chairman, Litton Industries president Roy L. Ash) embraced this traditionally liberal concept of regulatory reform. Echoing the line of criticism originated by Cushman and thereafter repeated and refined by Marver Bernstein,[15] James Landis,[16] and most recently, by Philip Elman,[17] the Ash Council contended that the agencies would lose their parochialism and sympathy for the narrow objectives of client industries[18] if the President were empowered to assume full formal control over the now independent regulatory agencies. This faith in the magical healing powers of Presidential control derives from one of the touchstones of liberal thought in this century: the notion that the Presidency is the most beneficent locus of governmental power in the nation. This line of criticism does not look initially at the *objectives* of regulatory statutes and policies; nor does it question whether government is politically capable of maintaining control over powerful industries, or under what circumstances such control can be maintained. The only question asked is *where* the responsibility for control should be located as a matter of law. The answer to this question has until recently seemed quite clear, since mainstream liberalism has for decades assumed that the Presidency was the sector of government best equipped to bring the pressures of the public will into focus on a given problem.

Unhappily, however, giving the President more legal authority does not necessarily mean that actual control will follow. In particular, such a change does not necessarily mean that the agency will become less responsive to the industry it regulates and more responsive to public concerns expressed through the President. If the industry has substantial influence over relevant parts of Congress, especially the appropriations subcommittee for the agency, then the President may be equally helpless when facing the same pressures. Even if the option is available to him, moreover, he may well decide not to exercise it. It rarely makes political sense for a President to arouse the antagonism of a powerful industry. A President can expect political benefits only when the public is deeply disturbed by the industry's position; such benefits are likely to be somewhat speculative in any case. But the political damage which flows from opposition to an industry and its sympathetic regulators is, in contrast, predictable and measurable. In short, the risks of anti-industry action for the President will often seem greater than the gains. Hence, changing the legal relations between the White House and the agencies to increase Presidential control would not necessarily change the crucial political determinants of regulatory policy.

The recent historical record provides numerous examples of regulatory agencies subject to direct Presidential influence where subservience to industry wishes is as marked as in some of the independent agencies. The Department of Agriculture has housed a variety of regulatory functions involving important issues of protection for both consumer and environmental concerns. But the existence of formal Presidential control, through the power to hire and fire the Secretary of Agriculture, has not significantly interfered with the pronounced tendency of USDA's subagencies to favor agricultural interests in their discharge of these functions. Until recently, for instance, the Pesticides Regulation Division of Agriculture had primary responsibility for carrying out the provisions of the 1947 Federal Insecticide, Fungicide and Rodenticide Act. But the House Government Operations Committee concluded, after holding extensive hearings, "until mid-1967, the USDA Pesticides Regulation Division failed almost completely to carry out its responsibility to enforce provisions of the Federal Insecticide, Fungicide and Rodenticide Act intended to protect the public from hazardous and ineffective pesticide products."[19]

It can be argued that USDA regulation of pesticides is not strictly analogous to the structure which the Ash Council has in mind for the functions now performed by the independent agencies. Unlike USDA (or, say, the Food and Drug Administration, which is part of HEW), regulatory agencies revamped along the lines sketched by the Council would not disappear into large bureaucracies. They would remain individual entities and would report directly to the White House, rather than simply to a higher layer of bureaucracy within the same agency. Depending, however, on the White House's priorities, that fact could mean that the agencies would receive less supervision, rather than more.

More important, it is a misconception to think that the President is, in general, more likely to be responsive than a particular administrative entity to public interests. The White House has itself not infrequently been the vehicle for the triumph of industry pressures. Again, recent examples are not hard to locate. In 1969 opposition to oil import quota policies mounted, as inflation spurred popular anxiety about the five billion dollars to eight billion dollars annually which the import program costs consumers. A Cabinet-level task force, headed by George P. Shultz, then Secretary of Labor and now director of the Office of Management and Budget, recommended that quotas be replaced by a tariff system which would reduce prices (or at least assure that the public treasury would benefit from the exclusionary policies alleged to promote the national security). The task force report was ignored by the President, even though he had to cloak his support for oil interests in an elaborate and prolonged ceremony involving the appointment of a still another committee to review (and reject) the findings of the Shultz task force.

Another example was furnished in 1970 and 1971 by the Environmental Protection Agency and the Council on Environmental Quality, agencies which are under direct White House control. They did not oppose the aircraft industry's side of the SST battle, despite the contrary demands of their environmentalist constituency. Their position was dictated by White House policy. Similarly in 1970, the Office of Consumer Affairs in the White House found itself overwhelmed by industry pressures expressed through the White House. Although Mrs. Virginia Knauer, head of the office and the President's Special Assistant for Consumer Affairs, had publicly endorsed the concept of class action lawsuits in consumer cases, and had promised to introduce legislation establishing a right to bring consumer class actions in the federal courts, she soon changed her mind. The American Retail Federation and other industry groups opposed to class action legislation later gloated publicly how they had successfully turned the White House against Mrs. Knauer on the class action issue, with the result that her legislative proposal was substantially diluted. Ultimately, she appeared in congressional offices as a lobbyist against strong class action bills proposed by Democratic senators and congressmen.

All this is not said to picture the present Administration as uniquely hostile to consumer, environmental, and other public concerns. These examples merely indicate that Presidents—other Presidents as well as this one—are not unlikely to take the industry side of an argument about public policy. Presidential control of regulatory decisions, therefore, will not systematically counter industry pressure on regulatory agencies.

There is one point that can be made in favor of increased Presidential control of the independent agencies. In times when public enthusiasm for consumer, environmental, or similar regulatory objectives suddenly becomes very high, after a long period of public unconcern, it may be the case that agencies subject to direct Presidential control will respond more speedily than formal independent agencies. But even in such cases—and the present era is such a case—the results of formal control cannot confidently be predicted. In this period of increasing public consciousness of consumer and environmental needs, most federal regulatory agencies have shown at least some disposition to respond to the public mood. But whether the response has been more far-reaching and dramatic, for example, at the Food and Drug Administration of HEW, which is subject to direct White House control, than at the FTC, which is not, appears doubtful at best.

CURRENT REFORM APPROACHES: HALFWAY UP FROM LIBERALISM

The Ash Council report on regulatory agencies did not produce a chorus of acclaim from any quarter. Perhaps we may have lost some of our traditional faith that transfer of formal control to the White House would automatically improve agency performance. In general, there seems to be less confidence in the traditional ideal that democratic governments can, through broad grants of regulatory power, manage the course of one or more industries in the public interest.

On the other hand, outright rejection of this faith has nowhere been made explicit. Nor has it been replaced by any coherent new approach or approaches. What has happened in this time of great ferment about the federal regulatory establishment is that many approaches have been put forward, some already moving onto the agenda for serious public consideration and action.

I would divide the current approaches to regulatory reform into four categories; two represent efforts to revive the old New Deal–Progressive hope for an affirmative state role in managing special interests, and two reflect more fundamental critiques of and departures from the inherited creed.

Reviving the Affirmative Ideal: "Tinkering" Reforms

The first set of proposals constitutes an integral category mainly from the standpoint of convenience. It includes a host of relatively modest suggestions for improving the existing system, which I would call, not in any derisive sense, "tinkering" reforms. Most of the items on this laundry list are aimed at curing common symptoms of the political malaise which has enfeebled regulatory institutions. These include proposals to give greater emphasis to criminal sanctions, aimed both at the subjects of regulation and at errant regulators themselves; to expand legal rights of access to information presently controlled by public and private bureaucracies, and to create affirmative obligations on the part of such bureaucracies to make periodic disclosures; to require industry contacts by regulators to be made on the record; to make it more difficult for regulatory officials to obtain jobs with regulated interests, and vice versa.

None of these proposals harbors significant potential for harm. On the other hand, none of these proposals seems likely to trigger dramatic changes in the agencies' performance, at least not by themselves. Drastic personal sanctions for official misdeeds do not seem readily applicable to many instances where existing anticorruption statutes do not already govern. Industry-oriented judgments by regulatory officials may seem deplorable to many, but they cannot, except in rare instances, be made occasions for draconian reprisal. And simple corruption, to which such penalties could and should be applied, is not a significant part of the problem with the federal agencies at this time. Information access requirements would be

very useful, but only if their enactment coincided with the development of an active group of public interest lawyers and other profes-
sionals who would obtain and disseminate the data made available.
The same analysis applies to affirmative disclosure requirements. The
SEC and the Securities laws of 1933 and 1934 show that such disclosure can transform the climate in which an industry operates—if
there is an active constituency (in this case securities firms, lawyers,
and investors) ready to make use of the law.

Reviving the Affirmative Ideal: Creating New Agencies

A variety of new regulatory entities has been suggested and some
established in the current epoch. One of these, the National Highway
Traffic Safety Administration, has proven surprisingly successful in
making regulated interests responsive to the public interest in factors
relevant to highway safety. Another, a proposed consumer safety
agency, seems less promising but perhaps nevertheless necessary.[20]
Still another, President Nixon's Environmental Protection Agency,
has generally given effect to broad public concern about the
environment.

Two other proposals, recently billed as major innovations, seem to
me fated for the same dismal denouement which befell such older
Grand Designs as the Federal Trade Commission and the National
Industrial Recovery Act. The first, a new "Independent Consumer
Protection Agency," will likely be enacted in this or the next Congress. It will appear before other consumer regulatory agencies as a
legal representative of consumer interests. This proposal has generated considerable excitement among consumer advocates (and
antagonism from the Chamber of Commerce and the Nixon Administration). But both reformers and conservatives will, I suspect, be
surprised by the new agency, once it is actually established. Its performance will likely serve as a reminder that calling an institution
"independent" will not make it so. Indeed, this new consumer
agency is far less likely than its predecessors to discharge its public
obligations with zeal and integrity. For the President, who will
appoint the agency's director, will have an even stronger incentive
to clamp down on any adventuristic ambitions of the agency than he
presently does in the case of traditional agencies like the Antitrust
Division or the Federal Trade Commission.

Existing regulatory agencies threaten the interests of campaign contributors. That alone has proven sufficient to induce most Presidents to keep a rein on their operations. But the new CPA will directly threaten the President himself. The President is, after all, responsible for the performance of the federal bureaucracy and the integrity of its programs. It will hardly suit his political convenience if gadfly government lawyers are put in the business of revealing that one agency after another has turned out faithless to its statutory mandate. No President, Republican or Democrat, could ever afford to have one of his own appointees publicize such damning evidence of his own misfeasance. The basic concept of the consumer protection agency seems to impose such contradictory pressures on the agency and its director that his job will prove unworkable, or else an exercise in stagecraft and public deception. It will not be surprising if the director of the agency matches Mrs. Knauer's timidity in dealing with other Presidential appointees and the industries with which they are, presumably, excessively friendly.[21]

A second new regulatory scheme which has received considerable advance billing, as this volume of essays itself attests, is the Progressive concept of federal incorporation. Here again, a certain measure of skepticism is hard to avoid. If the legislative process follows the script prescribed by precedent, any statute establishing a chartering scheme for the nation's biggest companies will offer vague, not to say vacuous, standards for determining the requisites of getting and keeping a license. These standards will surely stop short of expressly requiring any major changes in existing corporate policies or structures. Instead, the law will pass the buck to a new enforcement agency. Is there much reason to believe that this new agency will apply stricter antitrust or antipollution standards than the Antitrust Division or the EPA, just because it will be authorized to invoke the new enforcement penalty of delicensing? In fact, I would imagine that such an agency would be far less eager to lift the license of GM for monopolizing auto sales than the FCC, for example, was eager to lift the license of WNBC–TV for flouting Commission standards for the broadcast of antismoking spot commercials. Federal chartering received its most sustained and serious political attention during the Republican Administrations of Theodore Roosevelt and William Howard Taft; it was then the pet project of

Wall Street forces who believed that it would cement a cooperative relationship between the federal government and big business. Though their hopes for a legalized corporate state now seem somewhat overblown in view of the feckless career of the NRA in the early thirties, their basic assumption—that a federal corporation agency would be more a captive of industry than its master—seems as valid now as it was then.[22]

Beyond the Affirmative Ideal: Deregulation

A third approach to improving the performance of some regulated industries is to "liberate" them from regulatory controls. The overwhelming weight of scholarly opinion, especially among economists, now favors the substantial deregulation of all "naturally competitive" industries which are presently subject to price, entry, and output controls.[23] These include motor and air carriers, and a substantial amount of rail and ocean freight. Moreover, much support exists for loosening regulatory controls over intercity communications and over agriculture.[24] The wealth of scholarship and polemic on this subject bars repeating the arguments here, save for the following brief comment.

It is often said that the CAB and the ICC, to take the worst examples, represent perversions of the regulatory ideal. This is not true in any literal sense. As noted earlier in this essay, both agencies were more or less consciously designed to do just what they have done: limit competition in the interest of the members of the industries in existence when the legislation was originally passed. On the other hand, the naive ideology held by reformers at the time blinded them to the real nature of these regulatory enterprises. Contemptuous of the market and cocksure of their own ability, politically and intellectually, to determine and enforce the public interest, New Deal bureaucratic leaders went along with industry-hatched plans for regulation which in fact had nothing to do with reform. Now we know better, but uprooting the regulatory regime appears destined to be a lengthy and perhaps a totally impossible task.

The precedents on this point are not encouraging. During the 1940s Thurman Arnold's aggressive Antitrust Division persuaded the Supreme Court to invalidate price-fixing systems in the insurance and railroad industries which had previously operated under the color of friendly regulation.[25] With astonishing alacrity, Congress was prevailed upon to overrule the Court and restore the *status quo ante*. In 1945 the McCarran-Ferguson Act effectively immunized state-regulated insurance companies from antitrust restraints. In 1948 the Reed-Bulwinkle Act conferred a similar favor on all carriers regulated by the ICC.

This outcome should serve as a caveat to present-day reformers considering ambitious schemes for government control of industry. Quite simply, special economic interests are usually far better equipped for battle in the low-visibility arenas which determine how a regulatory statute is to be applied than they are in the relatively well-publicized contests about whether a law is to be enacted and what its provisions will be. For this reason, it is no wonder that reform triumphs in Congress, once the scene shifts downtown, often turn out to be Pyrrhic victories. Indeed, often the public is better able to protect its interests in the market place, without any government intervention, than under a regulatory regime, simply because organized interests are relatively more dextrous at manipulating government procedures and statutory standards than they are at controlling the free market.

Beyond the Affirmative Ideal: Public Interest Advocacy

The most original contribution of the new consumer movement to the short list of ideas for reforming regulation is the concept of consumer, or public interest, advocacy. Though the point is not often noted by its proponents, this approach reflects an admission that the old ideal of affirmative government was too ambitious to be workable. A retreat was necessary to a more conservative theory of reform. The new approach tacitly concedes that hope for the integrity of regulation cannot be guaranteed from within government. This pessimistic premise seems entirely correct. Democratic governments will inevitably be dominated by those participants in the political process who are best equipped to succeed on its terms. In the politics of bureaucracy, that means the well-organized and wealthy interests, not the phantom entity known as "the people," "the public," or "the public interest." Hence, if the regulatory system is to be made more sensitive to unorganized, public interests, an elite of public interest lawyers must be created, outside of government. The functions of this group would be twofold: first, to represent the interests of unorganized publics to officials and judges; and second, to inform the public of their stake in matters under regulatory control, so that opinion can be mobilized sufficient to put some semblance of pressure on the government.

No one can expect these public interest advocates to accomplish the sort of dramatic "redress of the balance of social power" that earlier reformers expected from the regulatory state created by the New Deal and Progressivism. The underlying concept is defensive, even negative, rather than affirmative. The theory assumes that regulated interests will dominate any form of governmental overseer (since they command resources of wealth and organization in the political terrain of election, legislation, and administration). Therefore, the argument continues, let us at least try to see that all sides of an issue are articulated and that they are brought out into the open. Especially if the courts will stand behind the effort—as they have so far indicated they will—this approach can expose and minimize private manipulation and abuse of agency powers. Perhaps it may even be possible that sustained advocacy concerning a particular issue or agency can create a ground swell of public outrage potent enough to produce meaningful structural reform—such as the abolition of the anticompetitive regulatory arrangements now entrenched in the transportation industries.

Many will think it foolish to expect help from the federal judiciary. Such skepticism is understandable, in view of Presidential rhetoric about "strict constructionism" and Chief Justice Burger's recurrent sermons against using the judicial law for reform. But the omens are not all negative. The Nixon Court's retrenchment on individual liberties issues is largely a response to rising public anxiety about crime. In contrast, opinion seems to favor more active judicial protection for public rights against corporate and government bureaucracies. Indeed, many supposedly conservative leaders have shown concern about bureaucratic indifference to the public interest. Chief Justice Burger is himself an example. In his famous 1966 decision in *United Church of Christ v. the Federal Communications Commission*, he established for the first time the right of public representatives to intervene as parties in federal regulatory proceedings. In explaining this initiative, Burger provided the public interest law movement with a rationale as cogent as anyone else has managed to articulate:

> The theory that the Commission can always effectively represent the listener interests in a renewal proceeding without the aid and participation of legitimate listener representatives fulfilling the role of private attorneys general is one of those assumptions we collectively try to work with so long as they are reasonably adequate. When it becomes clear, as it does to us now, that it is no longer a valid assumption which stands up under the realities of actual experience, neither we nor the Commission can continue to rely on it.[26]

But the enthusiasm reflected by Burger's opinion cannot overcome the institutional limits of the courts as instruments of reform. Such straws in the wind, however, do suggest that the federal judiciary will not reclaim its pre-New Deal role as an ideological and political haven for corporate power.

CAN REGULATION EVER WORK?

Regulation of industry is one of the least successful enterprises ever undertaken by American democracy—a conclusion flatly contradicting the conventional liberal wisdom of only a decade ago. But need it always be so? Is there any sweeping change that might be proposed which could in the future make the New Dealers' dreams come true? Can specific types of circumstances be identified under which particular instances or approaches to regulation can succeed?

We can dismiss out of hand the possibility of an apocalyptic entrance upon a new era. As long as the Constitution guarantees that all can participate in the political process, then inevitably those who are best able to amass and deploy the ingredients of political influence—which I would categorize as persuasion, organization, and wealth—will participate most effectively. Formal institutional changes in government are, therefore, neither likely to effect radical changes in the underlying political process nor in the substantive impact of governmental policies. A change in the bias of governmental policy toward the public interest will almost always, unless provided sustained political support, prove to be temporary. In theory, it might be possible to wall off a regulatory agency from unwanted pressures by conferring on it the means of amassing truly autonomous influence. This seems largely a theoretical hope. Even if, for example, reformers wanted to empower a new consumer protection agency (few would, I suspect) to levy an excess profits tax from which to finance its own operations, it seems unlikely that many congressman would find the idea appealing.[27]

Putting aside the possibility of apocalypse, what conditions can bring about successful regulation? In general, the more modest the political demands made of an agency, the more likely it is to prove successful. To refine this general statement a bit more, I would add that there seem to be two kinds of regulatory institutions, at least at the federal level: those with "defensive" or policing tasks—such as the FTC or the FDA—and those with "offensive" or managerial responsibilities, like the CAB or the Federal Reserve Board. Agencies in the latter category represent far more ambitious undertakings. Their task is to structure all or part of an industry's operations and thereafter direct the industry's course in the public interest. In contrast, policing agencies are designed not to pre-empt the free market but to enable consumers to make better use of its processes by thwarting anticompetitive or deceptive or unsafe practices. In general, regulatory schemes in the second category are more dangerous than the first. Policing agencies, if they become neutralized by industry pressures—always a substantial risk—will usually not produce more social harm than would have obtained if the agency had never been created in the first place. But, through agencies with managerial responsibilities over price and entry, industries can accumulate far more power to serve their interests at the expense of the public than they possessed before the agency came into existence. Furthermore, the functions performed by many policing agencies—like the banning or labeling of unsafe products—are so important that their very presence may add some slight measure of concern by affected industries to these vital matters (even if the chances are slim that politics will ever permit the agency to become the vigorous regulator that it ought to be). In general, experience seems to teach that regulation of the "offensive" or managerial genre should never be instituted, at least on a permanent basis, unless public interest objectives are supported by the regulated interests affected by the scheme.

Other than these guidelines, it does not seem to me possible to draw up a blueprint for distinguishing worthy regulatory schemes from unworthy ones. In each case, one has to compare the objectives which the agency is supposed to serve—in the eyes of public and private interests—and then its prospective capacity to fulfill those aims in its political environment. If the public-oriented objectives are reasonably concrete (as in the case of the National Highway Traffic Safety Administration's mandate to force auto companies to protect the internal passenger compartment of automobiles); if private interests affected by the measure support its public interest objectives (as in the case of support by the banking community for the Federal Reserve Board's responsibility for maintaining a flexible currency); if public support for the objectives of the scheme is strong, informed, and deeply rooted—then one can be relatively confident that a particular regulatory scheme will "work." To the extent that these conditions are absent, one has to expect the impact of regulation to be minimal or pernicious.

CHECKING THE REGULATORS: A PROPOSAL

It is apparent that my estimate of the chances for improving regulation from within government is most pessimistic, and that my main hope for reform lies with the establishment of a counterweight of public interest lawyers. This hope itself is not obviously a practical one. The main limitation is the paucity of funds that might become available for such high-minded pursuits. In view of this scarcity, it is understandable that reformers would turn to the traditional idea of a government agency to house the functions of public interest advocacy. But I believe, as noted earlier, that this new consumer protection agency represents a perversion of the public interest law concept, since it will subordinate the advocates on its payroll to the political imperatives of the executive branch. To lessen the danger of a still-birth for this very promising new idea of public interest advocacy, revisions in the structure of the agency can be suggested to render its personnel more independent of political pressures than in its present form.

It appears that there are two ways to ameliorate the difficulty that an advocate agency would have in establishing genuine independence. The first approach would be to give the administrator a fixed term, perhaps coincident with the term of the President who appointed him; this approach will strengthen the hand of the administrator in some instances but cannot be considered a thoroughly reliable guarantee.[28] A second approach would be to place the agency under the control of institutions other than the Presidency. For example, the agency might be responsible to a board of directors, whose members are appointed partly by Congress and by the federal judiciary or the Supreme Court (or the Chief Justice), as well as by the President. Further restrictions on Presidential influence might include specification of the criteria for selecting certain members of the board—e.g., one slot could be reserved for an individual distinguished for contributions in the field of environmental protection, another for an individual distinguished for contributions to the study of administrative law, others for presidents of the American Bar Association, the National Bar Association, the American Association of Trial Lawyers, and so on. In another variation of the scheme, the chairman might be empowered to name some of the other board members himself. In effect, this conception is an effort to copy the Legal Services Corporation which poverty lawyers have proposed as a relatively safe home for their work. It appears to be a secure approach to the practice of law in the public interest, attuned to our loss of faith in the old ideal of government regulation in the public interest.

XIV

PUBLIC ENTERPRISE

WILLIAM G. SHEPHERD*

Public enterprise exerts a perverse sort of fascination, although in the United States it always seems to be put at the bottom of the agenda. The rest of this book has reflected the growing awareness that the other treatments for market power won't work very well. Real trustbusting, strict regulation, and especially the jailing of company presidents are not, let us face the facts, very likely to occur in this century. This leads us to consider (or fear, or hope) that the state may have to control big business directly: taking over, owning and managing possibly a large block of industry. But how far should it go, and in what forms? Can a democracy manage public enterprises efficiently and in the *public* interest? Hasn't it failed elsewhere, both in Soviet-bloc economies and in Western Europe? Isn't it alien?

On the contrary. Public enterprises are already extraordinarily pervasive in this country, as I will indicate, and some lessons from their experience are reasonably clear. Yet these facts and possibilities of public enterprise exist in a great void of public ignorance, mingled often with pathological fantasies.[1] My attempt here to abate the ignorance will turn on these simple truths:

1. public enterprise offers a wide variety of tactics, some good, some very bad, some mixed;

---

* Professor of Economics, University of Michigan; author of *Economic Performance Under Public Ownership: British Fuel and Power* (1965); and *Market Power and Economic Welfare* (1970); co-editor of *Utility Regulation* (1966).

2. the proper scope of public enterprise depends on very wide issues of social power and justice, and an obsession with big business alone is a sure way to go astray;

3. public enterprise tactics should be used *with* other remedies such as antitrust, not *instead* of them;

4. a large group of costly, defective public enterprises should be withdrawn or changed, while a number of new tactics should be tried.

To use public enterprise well, one must have clear objectives. I take them to be the achievement of economic efficiency, fairness in distribution, cultural diversity, and a dispersal of power and opportunity. The chances for reaching these goals are in turn deeply influenced by the existing patterns of family wealth, position, and opportunity. Can fiddling with public enterprises get at these deeper roots? Not *just* by nationalizing utilities nor, probably, industrial corporations. Yet as I will make clear, public enterprise is decidedly double-edged. While certain uses of public enterprise do appear to offer high benefits, much orthodox public ownership, on the contrary, is costly and harmful.

WHAT IS PUBLIC ENTERPRISE?

The topic is vast.[2] It includes nearly everything—apart from antitrust and commission regulation—which public policy does or might reasonably do to affect market structure and behavior. Public enterprises range from conventional "utility" cases, such as TVA, city transit, ports, and the postal service, to industrial and service areas, over into certain subsidies and welfare-state programs, and on into important "social" enterprises such as public schools and universities, mental hospitals, medical care, the courts, and prisons. Indeed, these enterprises define much of our cultural strengths and weaknesses. We are surrounded with public enterprises of many sorts, from factories to specific controls, as Table 1 indicates. They are the great phantom presence of America—used, abused, and rarely recognized for what they really are.

They all share two basic dimensions: public *control* and public *sponsorship*. At one extreme, there are cases where public control is tight and there is little or no subsidy from the public purse. At the other extreme are cases where the public pays much through subsidies or prices but has little effective control.[3] Table 1 arranges a variety of cases roughly on the basis of these two criteria. Many of these cases are commonly regarded as "programs" rather than "public enterprise." Yet they are part of the same family. I include the full range of them here purposefully, because they help to show how diverse the tactics of "public enterprise" are. They range far beyond the conventional cases of TVA, British Railways, and the local municipal waterworks.

TABLE 1.

SELECTED PUBLIC-ENTERPRISE ACTIVITIES IN THE UNITED STATES,
BY APPROXIMATE DEGREE OF CONTROL AND SUBSIDY

	Control	*Partial Control*	*Slight Control*
No Subsidy	Municipal utilities (water, sewage)	State liquor stores	Port of New York Authority
	U.S. Government Printing Office	National land management	FHA housing program
	Social Security	Amtrak	Sports stadiums
	Municipal parking facilities	SBA programs (including minority support)	Tennessee Valley Authority
	Municipal transit	FAA programs	Performing arts centers
	Federal courts	Airports	Public housing
	Public law programs	AEC enrichment plants	Medicare
	Child-care programs	Highway construction and maintenance	Medicaid
		State courts	Public universities
		Local courts	SST program
		Federal maritime program	Military R&D contracting
		Mental hospitals	Veterans Administration hospitals
		State and local law enforcement agencies	Weapons purchasing and management
Full subsidy	Primary education	Prisons	
		Corps of Engineers	
		Census Bureau	

Public *sponsorship* is doubly costly, since it draws on tax revenues whose incidence is often quite regressive, shifting from poor to rich, and which could be devoted to other public programs which have high yields and highly progressive impacts.[4] The point is often ignored by the young who, along with some of the very rich, do not pay taxes. Therefore, sponsorship should be minimized. For any given degree of sponsorship, control is to be maximized, except in certain unusual cases (broadcasting, education) where independence is itself a desirable feature.

One needs also to look at the degree to which the public enterprise is national or local in scope, since local units are usually more responsive to genuine social control. One should in addition know if the enterprise is a monopoly or faces tight competitive or countervailing constraints. Almost always, local controls are preferable to national ones and a competitive situation is superior to setting up a monopoly.

We can better comprehend these pivotal points by looking at public enterprise abroad and comparing it with our own varieties. Four comparative lessons emerge. The first lesson is an historical one: the pedigree of public enterprise is both ancient and ominous. One line is autocratic, from ancient statecraft through to the Organic State of Italy, Soviet-type economics, and other dubious political systems. Another is visionary, sentimental British and Continental socialism, which is embodied in national firms in certain utility and sick-industry cases. Still another line is the municipal utility common in this country, with a leaden drabness relieved only by occasional taints of corruption. All of these have, from time to time, been inefficient, unable to cover costs with revenues, slow to innovate, and wasteful of capital. Classic public ownership of these sorts appears to be more costly, alien, and dangerous than the market power it is meant to remedy. One should, therefore, be skeptical about public enterprise, but not paranoid.

The second lesson is that the popular stereotype of public firms as money-losing monopolies in sick industries fits some cases abroad, but not most of them. In Western European coal and railway sectors, for example, public firms have struggled amid red ink for twenty-five years to shrink and recast production. But for every such Charbonnage de France or British Railways, there are many other public firms growing, innovating, and making profits. Obvious examples are Renault, the British electricity authorities, and Entente Nacionale Idrocarbon in Italy.

Third, it is primarily in the industrial and financial sectors that the United States has sharply less public enterprise than is common in Western Europe. In other sectors, U.S. experience with public enterprises is rich and growing, and it is less confined to the "public corporation" format than is common in Europe. That format involves much public sponsorship, with capital coming from the treasury. And it explicitly limits public control by making the public firm "autonomous" in most respects. Little wonder that the "public corporation" now seems an expensive and ineffectual device.

Fourth, it is obvious but important that the U.S. economy is much larger than any other. There exists no public enterprise in any Western economy whose scope and size are comparable to "nationalization" in this country. Abroad, even the largest public enterprises are only on a regional or local scale by American standards. In short, "nationalization" and "public ownership" in the classic British and European style are special cases, not representative of all the possibilities.

Indeed, we need to refresh our whole vocabulary on the topic. Ownership of the production plant is only one among the many public enterprise tactics, and—to repeat—it should be kept as low as possible. In that sense, "public ownership" is the wrong phrase and image with which to approach the task of designing efficient public enterprises. "Socialism" is another sensitive term in this context. Public enterprises can be formed and operated in reactionary and anti-"socialist" ways, as I will shortly show. Also, the emotional overtones of the socialist label run counter to the clinical, objective frame of mind necessary to evaluate public enterprise as a tool. Indeed, socialists above all need to scrutinize public enterprise with the most skeptical eye, since it can be so easily converted into anti-socialist purposes.

Another semantic trap is to think that private is "versus" public. In fact, public enterprise often sustains and subsidizes private firms and persons, some of them quite powerful and rich. And private resistance to public enterprise is often just a bargaining tactic to raise the price which the public must pay. Almost every private entity has a high price at which it will eagerly seek conversion into a "public" enterprise. Peaceful extensions of public ownership in the past have almost always been peaceful *because* they were very liberal in paying the former owners for dubious assets. The British Railways and coal nationalizations are only two such examples, where the great ideological debate was partly a statagem to raise the price paid to the former owners.

Since public enterprise raises so many complications, how should we go about deciding how far to extend it, and in what forms? The basic method is simple: measure their costs and benefits and then choose a total combination of public enterprise tactics which maximizes the benefits and avoids waste.[5] The public's resources for these tactics are of several sorts: tax revenues, the absorption of risks, public managers' talents, and the country's natural resources. They are scarce, and they can be—and often are—wasted on inferior uses. In allocating public resources in this direction, we need to proceed with care, since the social objectives involved are controversial and the data will permit only rough estimates. Still the costs of a public enterprise are often perfectly clear, in millions of dollars of investment, hundreds of skilled managers, and so forth.

The possible benefits will be of three main sorts:

1. efficiency: the output wrung from inputs, both now (including corrections for external costs such as pollution) and in progress over time;
2. equity: fairness in the distribution of opportunities, wealth, and income;
3. furtherance of basic social, cultural, and political values.

To make policy choices, one then estimates these benefits and costs, so that those offering the best payoffs can be identified and applied. For example, turning the U.S. Post Office into a public corporation presumably offered higher benefits compared with costs—in efficiency, fairness toward mail customers and employees, etc.—than the old *status quo* or any other plan did. But the new Amtrak experiment with rail passenger service is now widely regarded as creating more costs than benefits. In any event, some benefit-cost test is the only way to judge the best form public enterprise should take, and it should be done thoroughly and carefully rather than be left to assertions and hunches.

The intelligent chooser must also explore packages of several tools, rather than just pit one against another (*e.g.*, antitrust "versus" public enterprise). The best solutions often combine some features of public enterprise with some antitrust and some regulatory controls. The postal service is an obvious example of such a policy mix; it is a public corporation, under regulation by the U.S. Postal Rate Commission, with important areas of competition (packages, couriers, etc.). In short, the policy tools are often complements to each other.

In the final stage of choosing policies, the net benefits of each choice are taken as percentage rates of return on the "investment" of public resources, and the best ones are chosen, down to the range where the marginal returns of a policy just barely equal its marginal costs. The exercise bristles with complexities in defining objectives, measuring and weighting. Yet, implicitly, similar calculations are already being made throughout the government in all the cases in Table 1. If these sums were done openly and more fully, they might be done far more correctly.[6]

A number of policy conclusions emerge from this analysis. Public enterprises with low or negative net benefits should be dropped or revised. (I will discuss such cases shortly.) Equally, all policies offering more than marginal returns should be undertaken. This goes beyond the old nineteenth-century Manchester liberal bias toward the least possible action. In the public enterprise area, Manchester attitudes have allotted to "the State" only the sick industrial cases, the uninsurables and unemployables, and whatever special items—such as grand opera—which those with wealth and influence cannot acquire in the market place. But this view of the State as a last resort leads to a public sector so lopsided with inferior, regressive programs that it is kept from using a wide range of higher yielding tools.

Also, each task taken up for public enterprise treatment—such as managing the coal industry or child-care centers—diminishes the degree of accountability and balance that can be achieved in other "public" tasks. Worse, wealth and privilege often bias the political process and warp the public enterprise in antisocial directions. The lessons are that public accountability—or publicity—alone may not be enough to get responsive control; and that "public" enterprise is only too likely to operate for the benefit of those who already have the wealth or other strategic advantages.

PROFILES OF WORST AND BEST FORMS

Among the worst cases of public enterprises, there are at least five distinct types. The first is high sponsorship with low control. This shades into straight subsidies, often from poor to rich, often via state guarantees against private risks. Obvious examples are free capital for military suppliers, the recent loan guarantee for Lockheed Aircraft Corporation, and large portions of the U.S. maritime subsidy program.[7]

Second is sponsorship of activities used mainly by the wealthy. Obvious examples include many subsidized programs for performing arts, much suburban commuter service (including large parts of the new Amtrak experiment), tax support of university education for children from upper economic levels, and public parks in most towns.[8] The system of justice, in the context of unequal access to legal counsel, can be regarded as a public enterprise with largely a regressive incidence, and not just in its treatment of more purely commercial matters.[9] Many such matters would not withstand an objective evaluation of their efficiency and regressive incidence.

Third is the syndrome of the sick industry, often using enormous amounts of capital and often selling to (and buying from) large private firms. Since the "sickness" is often industry-wide (with severe dislocations which invite a "unified" treatment), the common result is a centralized monopoly financed directly and extensively by the treasury. The classic form is the British public corporation, in coal, steel, and railroads; railroads are, in fact, in this status almost everywhere in the world.[10]

Many of the "social" impacts which the shrinkage of these industries causes—on local unemployment and stagnation—are external to the public corporations. They should be treated by state programs for retraining and investment; instead, governments have routinely failed to do their share, leaving these impacts as a burden on the public firms, which reluctantly meet them by slowing down closures and by cross-subsidizing the losing parts.[11] The public firm is routinely prevented from raising its prices—to help "stop inflation"—but at the same time it is also expected to raise wages rapidly. The main beneficiaries are industrial users and equipment suppliers, a most unneedy lot.[12] The resulting financial losses, redundancy, and demoralization in the public firm are then interpreted to discredit all forms of public enterprise. The unnecessary drain on public funds, on public administration talent, and on "socialist" political impetus which results has been enormous.[13] But the disillusion with public enterprise should lie only on this specific, benighted form of it.

A fourth, and less pernicious, type is the nationwide public firm in a "healthy" utility sector, such as electric power and telephones. "Healthy" means that revenues cover costs (often because of excess demand) and that there are few big external effects or social impacts. Yet these enterprises still absorb vast amounts of capital and administrative talent. The gains are often minor and, as with British telephones, mainly taken by private firms and upper economic groups.[14] TVA's biggest customers include aluminum firms, a far cry from the rural poor; moreover, the lack of competitive constraints can breed internal inefficiency which is just as great as private utilities in the United States, under regulation, are widely believed to suffer.[15] A switch to private bond financing can abate much of the direct drain on public funds, but the other costs (of inefficiency, demands on managerial talent) persist; consequently, economic and social yields often remain nugatory.

A fifth group, directly affecting culture, personal liberties, and amenities, is also important. It is more ominous than the others but less easy to appraise scientifically. It includes the proposed federal master data bank of personal information and much of the gathering and use of "information" by that counterpart of private investigation firms, the Federal Bureau of Investigation. The American Army newspaper is another example; in fact, the whole Department of Defense can be regarded as a public enterprise with large social effects. The interstate highway program has a variety of effects on urban stability and amenity, some of them clearly negative and regressive. The Atomic Energy Commission's stewardship of atomic power has generated a range of environmental costs. There are other cases of this sort, all of them controversial and many of them perhaps costly in the extreme. I do not claim to know their true costs; I do insist that they should be evaluated as public enterprises in a cost-benefit framework.

These are categories of public enterprises which probably should— on sound economic criteria—be cut back, revised in format, constrained, and put on different pricing and investment policies. Their objectives are often unclear and their use of tools inefficient. Their vices are primarily monopoly, drainage of public funds, regressive pricing, neglect of externalities, and rigidity of form. Their benefits go mainly to powerful, unneedy groups.

By contrast, "optimal" public enterprises have tight constraints (by competition or budgetary control), minimum use of public funds and talent, a progressive incidence, clear allowances for external effects on ecology and society, and flexibility in arrangements. They are experiments with short lives, not permanent fixtures.

One is the *public-firm competitor*, with a quarter or less of the market and, in most cases, some mixture of private-public ownership and motivation. It could force improved pricing and efficiency in tight oligopoly markets. Its continuing threat of taking over other firms in other tight oligopoly markets could indirectly induce better performance in them too, a point discussed in more detail shortly.

A second group is the public entity as countervailer against any private market power which escapes other constraints. An obvious instance is the British national health service as a buyer of drugs from private companies. It is paralleled, but only piecemeal, in this country by the Veterans Administration and certain hospital groups.[16] Weapons purchases occasionally, but not consistently, are done on this aggressive basis. The aim is to place a steady degree of constraint on the suppliers.

Third are activities with high, progressive benefits spread widely throughout society. A downtown public library is the obvious example, as is the provision of good quality legal services to poor people. Programs stopping contagious disease are another; so is universal primary schooling, if properly structured, and possibly nursery care. The social-critic and innovator aspects of public universities—as distinct from the teaching functions pure and simple—are also activities of this sort.

Fourth are units whose outputs go mainly to upper-wealth groups and which maximize profits. Prime examples are state universities, performing arts programs, and high quality medical care, if they are properly priced. This can be done by using price discrimination—charging what the traffic will bear—on a means test or some other basis. This group is the mirror image of the second "worst" type above; the objective here is a frankly progressive incidence consistent with the usual efficiency criteria.

Between these best and worst extremes lie many mixed cases. For example, the Social Security insurance enterprise yields certain high benefits. But its financing is strongly and unnecessarily regressive, a clear defect. Hospital and health insurance enterprises (Medicare, Medicaid, and others) are notoriously lax toward inefficiency. Public housing projects have had obvious bad effects, via isolation and poor design, which could probably be avoided. The three vast AEC uranium-enrichment plants absorb large amounts of public capital and subsidize a very narrow group of large firms and utilities which use their services. In these and other cases, it is the policies which are wrong, not the fact of public enterprise.

The Census Bureau, a public interprise fact-collector, deserves a special condemnation for its business reporting. A census, by collecting objective data and then publishing them, can and should be the main vehicle for corporate accountability. In this way, the census should be a powerful means of corporate restraint. Instead, by present law, the census now ignores much of the relevant facts on market power and performance, and it hides most of the details which it does collect. Profitability, market shares, entry, technological changes, minority employment, who owns what—all on an individual firm and plant basis—are the heart of industrial organization and corporate power. The available data are mostly peripheral and inferior to the facts gotten by private market-research firms and sold at high prices. Only the public is excluded from the facts about U.S. industrial organization, and these are the facts needed in order to know which public policies work best. Worse, this rot of secrecy is spreading. Minority employment data have needlessly been put under census rules, for example, as are pollution data. Worst of all, the secrecy is quite permanent, though no company could fear serious harm from ten- or even five-year-old facts.

On this matter we can go beyond Willard Mueller's proposals. A change in these rules to full disclosure is of first legislative priority, to make the census a responsive public enterprise. Presumably, release of data after two or three years cannot harm any legitimate private interests. Indeed, only powerful and affluent corporations have a real stake in secrecy. Why should the census serve their interests?

The resources, structure, and expertise in this public enterprise are presently adequate, but they are being misdirected.

In short, large cutbacks and changes are needed in nearly the whole range of existing public enterprises, to prune out wasteful cases and to free resources for good ones.[17] Few of the bigger public enterprises are giving good results, even by low *Realpolitik* standards. At the same time, there is probably a sound basis for extending and experimenting with new public enterprise tactics in new ways and sectors. The net changes would probably reduce, perhaps sharply, the total commitment of public funds and public managers' talent.

DIRECTIONS FOR EXPERIMENTATION

The basic lessons about public enterprise can be reduced to hornbook form: define the problem and the social objectives. Use clear words, not political ones. Evaluate policies together. Minimize sponsorship. Maximize supervisable control. Always have competition, if at all possible. Smaller is better. Remove regressive subsidies. Allow for externalities. No permanent experiments.

While these truths are being absorbed and Professor Dahl's vast hearings are occurring, we need to think in practical terms about possible experiments in this area, learning about the finer and newer points as we proceed. Industry and finance are obviously the main prospective areas in this country for new public enterprise experiments. I will explore these, and several related ones, to see what a balanced use of public enterprise tools might look like. The coverage is selective, both to illustrate variety and single out important cases.

Industrial and Financial Pacesetters

The technique would be for the government to acquire "sufficient" control of a lesser firm in a tight oligopoly or near monopoly and operate it "competitively." The resulting take-over discipline would also influence sluggish leading firms in other markets. Their behavior would become more competitive and efficient, one can presume, in order to forestall an actual take-over of them.

The proposal differs from the pre-1950 "yardstick competition" concept in two ways.[18] First, it would minimize public capital, operating through just enough portfolio holdings to gain the needed control, perhaps 5 percent to 25 percent in most cases. This degree of control would depend on the objectives sought, which could vary over a wide range. In all cases, public directors would be put on the board, representing the public shareholdings. Second, it would be funded and operate like an investment banker, with power, with a variety of industrial choice, and with first-class expertise. Related versions have been tried in Britain, Italy, and other countries.[19] Their success has varied, generally being higher where the initial capital has been large, the management is expert, the focus is on lesser firms, and the experiment has lasted ten to twenty years, not much more or less. Judging by past experience, it may be optimistic to expect an objective environment here for such experiments. Yet this program and its possibilities, when compared to real (not merely ideal) alternatives, are reasonably promising. In particular, it would probably be less drastic and more lucrative (and acceptable) to private shareholders than divestiture or complete public ownership. It would base accountability on the economic power of shareholdings, and it would itself be accountable to the public agency holding the shares.

Its main focus would be those major near monopolies and tight oligopolies (industrial and financial) whose structure seems stable and conducive to high excess profits and/or inefficiency. The choice of companies with market power can be made on reasonably objective criteria, one being a model of market structure and profitability which I have been developing and which pinpoints the main company candidates—not just "oligopolies"—as a broad group.[20] Abstract criteria are fairly obvious; a firm not too small to survive and have an effect, but still small enough to leave room for aggressive growth, and not subject to crippling cost disadvantages.[21]

The practical scope and cost of such a program can be estimated very easily. The main candidates, fairly well agreed on among specialists,[22] presently are in seven to twelve problem industries—including automobiles, computers, steel, photocopy equipment, oil, soaps, photographic supplies, electrical equipment, and drugs. Assume that share ownership of 20 percent will suffice, on the average, and that firms ranking second to fourth are usually selected, one to an industry. On this basis and for these industries, only three billion dollars of share purchases would presently be needed, at the most, and about thirty "public directors" would go onto boards of directors to represent these holdings. These are distinctly moderate amounts compared to the problems and to alternative remedies. Had the purchases been made in 1960 (at about only $1.2 billion), the subsequent capital gains for the public would have been substantial. And in two of the producer goods firms, improved management might have avoided no less than one billion dollars in private portfolio losses during 1960–70. Such cases should attract powerful private support for public shareholdings. The holdings would of course yield dividends for the public purse as well as deliver competitive improvements for the benefit of the consumers.

This is an estimate of a *maximum* program, assuming that there is little restructuring, regulating, or any other policy actions toward these industries. Its funding and staffing are entirely feasible. Any large new changes in market structure or patents—or via other public enterprise moves—would reduce the need for this tactic. This program's mixture of private and public constraints poses risks, as Italian and other experience with public industrial holding companies suggests. In this country, the Reconstruction Finance Corporation provides mixed, but of course quite incomplete, lessons about the possible hazards and benefits. Public directors may be coopted, as regulators often are.[23] Yet the gains, even after such discounting, are likely to outweigh the risks and costs, and the public shareholdings will both give the public directors power and provide a basis for scrutiny and possible recall. These are matters for further careful research.

More direct controls are probably needed in financial markets, especially banking and insurance, where the accountability has so far been negligible. Leading financial firms have powerful influences over industrial market structures. The objective would be to enter and constrain the relatively few financial groups holding critical sway over a number of the major problem industries. The public shareholdings in individual firms, to be gathered under one roof into a public holding company, would be the natural basis for this attempt. But more would probably be needed, both in funds for lending to new entrants and in insider expertise and advice, to achieve success. The core to be changed is the close, mutually sustaining relationships between firms and their bankers, investment bankers and underwriters. Unless these networks can be altered, freed up, and paralleled by equally good procompetitive sources of funds and counsel, most other policy treatments will remain superficial, verging again on a charade. Accordingly, public investment banks and public commercial banks with highest quality expertise would be appropriate in several of the largest cities, probably as branches of a large public parent holding firm.

Countervailing Entities

The use of vertical constraints on powerful buyers and sellers can be extended and strengthened from the shaky base which already exists. Important gains can be gotten from better, much better, use of the powers presently available to such federal purchasers and suppliers as the Defense Department, NASA, the Atomic Energy Commission, the Post Office, large hospital systems, and Amtrak. Other extensions are likely to develop as a matter of course, such as unified, aggressive drug purchasing under expanding federal health programs during the next decade.

Risk Absorption

Risks are already absorbed for many private groups such as house buyers, certain weapons companies, bank depositors, and, recently, a number of small black-owned businesses. The list of such groups is astonishingly long. Whenever such a program draws on public funds or guarantees, the drain on public credit is as genuinely costly as a direct subsidy, even though direct revenues received from the privileged borrowing group may cover direct costs. The benefits of absorbing private risks may be great, but they are all too often focused regressively on wealthy recipients, often contrary to the programs' stated purposes. The net effects can easily be negative, especially where it is dominant firms which get the protection. The weapons, aerospace, computer, and electrical equipment sectors have many examples of this effect.

By contrast, high yields are likely where aid goes to new entry by firms or by new managerial and financial groups. Since any real new entry will reduce the value of the established positions, it will be resisted. The use of public credit should lean against such resistance by actively favoring new entrants. Or, at the very least, the negative kinds of public risk absorption—tax-absorbing, entry-reducing, and regressive—should be eliminated. There are many cases of such cynical venting of the public purse, and they should be remedied unsparingly. Well-arranged support for outsiders, including blacks—providing sophisticated financial and legal counsel, as well as credit —probably offers high yields up to a large scale of public funding.

To take a specific case: promotion of business opportunity for blacks, women, and other minority groups illustrates how wide and novel some of the choices can be. The training of new managers might be done much more effectively by a specific public training and placement enterprise than by handing out small-business loans. An effective training program would enroll top-quality company and academic experts to train members with direct experience in financial and commercial affairs. An excellent source of finance would be a direct tax on large firms and banks in proportion to the gaps in their minority hiring in managerial jobs. For example, the initial target for each large firm would reasonably be 4 percent participation rates for black males and for women in upper white-collar jobs. The tax on hiring rates below 4 percent could be five hundred dollars a year per minority persons not hired up to that target rate. The tax could be aligned with scientific estimates of the discrimination coefficient, and the target might be raised gradually over time, and also refined to allow for the special characteristics of some factory locales.[24] Any such basis would penalize discrimination, apply strong incentives for improvement, and finance the learning process to solve the problem. It would be self-financing, precise, and eventually self-liquidating. This is the direction which effective "public" policies should take, using well-designed public enterprise tactics. The present programs are expensive paternalism on a small scale, at the periphery of the problem.

Weapons Producers

Large weapons companies are obviously candidates for more control and less subsidy. Galbraith's suggestion of "nationalizing" them covers a spectrum of possible actions: partial control, public directors, risk guarantees, etc. My own preference is not to legitimize the subsidies by assuming control but to try hardest to cut the subsidies. Weapons supply has been a serious problem in virtually every society in every period. The arms race now is a strong factor in evaluating how to organize weapons production in the U.S.; whatever system minimizes the proliferation of weapons and the dynamics of the arms race is probably best. I fear that public weapons suppliers would be harder to limit or cut back than private ones, even pseudo-private ones. Much of the problem transcends economic issues, but at least the more technical conditions of public enterprise efficiency can be got right. The best estimates are that weapons costs are at least 20 percent higher than necessary because of sheer inefficiency —and this is apart from the buying of wholly unnecessary weapons. The design of specific new controls for such a situation offers some very high rewards. Whether or not it all adds up to "nationalization," we clearly need to have fewer subsidies and more controls.

Professional Services: Law, Medicine, Education

It is important to extend the discussion here to two major non-corporate areas: professions and prisons. Here public enterprise tactics can be quite crucial, and they provide important perspective on the industrial uses of public enterprise. Also, success in these sectors —in promoting equal opportunity and efficiency in these crucial services—would reduce the need for strict action toward the corporate sector. Indeed, corporations may bear only quite indirectly on the fundamental inequities in the system.

The allocation of professional services in law, medicine, and education critically affects both efficiency and equity in society. Equal access to them would be clearly fairer than the present system. It could also improve the aggregate productivity of the economy in many ways—some obvious, some indirect. The minimal public supply of these services tends either to be left to the most difficult and least lucrative cases, such as legally ignorant lower classes, chronically sick poor people, less clever and advantaged students. Or, where public provisions are liberal, they tend to be taken over by the middle class. Thus, the cleft stick is tight: either the programs are impoverished, ineffective, or else the middle classes crowd in on them.

One response is to take over and unify the whole system, as in a "national" health service. The opposite choice is to apply a means test, trying to keep out the hordes of unneedy users without humiliating and driving away the needy ones. Both tactics have certain costs and benefits; neither is ideal. But both have the serious defect that they do away with competition, one by monopolizing, the other by sealing off separate systems. They therefore run the risk of breeding the wrong levels of funding, inefficiency in operations, a lack of choice and innovation, and chronic unfairness which resists reform. In case after case, self-interested controls by the profession, and the basic inequities in society, are shielded from effective constraints and change.

These three cases—legal, medical, educational—show only too graphically what may happen. The bias in legal provisions favoring established groups is beyond dispute. Legal aid programs have at last begun to grow, but they are almost always inferior. They usually deal with superficial problems which clients initiate, rather than with the basic deprivations about which legally ignorant poor people are often unaware.

Medical care appears to be headed toward a universal virtual monopoly system under professional control. This runs the risk of the high total costs, inefficiency, and lack of innovating forces which Medicare and Medicaid already show. Finally, in higher education, competition is suppressed both among users and among suppliers. One partial result is that the net incidence of financing public universities is highly regressive.[25] That is, poorer families are paying to educate richer families' children. Another result is that innovation by colleges is inhibited. Indeed, many small colleges, which might be the freshest innovators, are literally dying as a side effect of subsidies to students on public campuses. Public enterprises in higher education—including my own employer—need drastic reform.

The balanced answer in these sectors seems to be programs focusing plentiful resources on deprived users, possibly under means tests, but always arranged so that the systems will have to contend and innovate. In law, for example, licensing and bar membership could require a minimum amount of work for poor clients (or an "alternative service") by all lawyers, young and old, as a matter of accreditation rather than of charity. This could be backed by a voucher scheme for all actual and potential users, in order to provide direct accountability and avoid abuses. In public schools, the level of funding probably should be inverse to neighborhood income levels;

i.e., the best schools would be in the worst neighborhoods. This scheme would be allied with absolutely free choice of schools and free busing. Such a strategy would quickly dissolve the present barriers and inequities which the public enterprises we call public schools presently breed. Perhaps, well-off citizens in our society simply won't let such a thing happen. But such possibilities are our proper concern. And in any event the need is for variety, experiments, and contention among ideas, rather than uniformity.

Penology

In the treatment of "deviant" behavior too there is more uniformity, unclear goals, and exclusion of competition than is optimum for a public enterprise activity.[26] The basic objective of "correction" is a large increment in "legitimate" productivity of inmates (including the probability that they will avoid illegal activity when released) per unit of resources. The resources include buildings, food, guards, space, and the time of the inmates. This function is just one element of society's entire effort to raise productivity in industry and schools. The efficient prison therefore operates as a training school, with incentives for inmates to learn and accumulate and for supervisors to generate an economic surplus via the rise in inmate production of goods. Prisons are, accordingly, public enterprises which could be operated far more efficiently.

This model is obviously not the old "factory prison," workhouse, or chaingang, but a unit which offers an alternative to "the street." Like the Army, correction and security units could be broadened into an alternative system to adjust behavior and provide training which schools or other groups have not supplied. This alternative should be freely available and, to a wide group of potential users, voluntary.

By contrast, many prisons presently are highly subsidized systems lacking sensitive public controls to avert damaging effects on inmates: a classic case of high costs and low controls. Worse, by fostering criminality, they create large external costs. At the least, inmate productivity could be developed and used to generate revenues to reduce the subsidies. Working conditions need not exploit. They could come under standard protections, and inmates could have a large degree of choice about their jobs and workloads. The products would presumably compete in normal markets as well as supply internal needs. If the inputs are properly compensated, this new competition would be fair and beneficial to all of society. Indeed, much work could be subcontracted from private firms. Prisons should mingle with the market place, as befits any healthy public enterprise. The basic lessons about public enterprise—clarify goals, cut subsidies, have effective controls, and experiment—may give high yields in this sector as much as in any other.

NEXT STEPS

In short, the scope of public enterprise is often far less important than how it is run. Subsidies should usually be minimized, but this depends on how regressive or progressive the subsidies are. Controls need to be effective, but there are many possible forms of control. All in all, public enterprise has not had a glorious track record, here or abroad. Much of the vast array of public enterprises in the U.S. seems clearly defective, regressive, with low net benefits to the public, and trapped in inefficient forms.

Still, the same can be said of all the other policies covered in this volume. Many new public enterprise experiments would be cheaper and less drastic than them. But "corporate power" is much too narrow a framework for judging this. If the aims are to spread welfare, power, and opportunity more widely, one must consider the alternatives beyond big business. Otherwise, policy choices and the allocation of political effort are sure to be narrow and unbalanced.

There are several directions for further scholarly and political effort on public enterprise. First, we need to develop our methods for evaluating costs and benefits. Second, we must take inventory on actual public enterprises in this and other countries and project possible new forms. Third, we need to evaluate these cases scientifically, both to test my hypotheses about worst and best forms, and to identify which specific cases need changing. Only then will it be possible to conduct a fair, rational debate about what ought to be done.

While we may never get these complete research results, we do have enough sensible hypotheses and data to begin trying to change the "worst" cases and experimenting with the "best" ones. If I am at all right, large public resources can be recouped from (or at least not extended to) a number of sectors. This alone could make new experiments more feasible. Moreover, I suspect that the regressive effect of much existing public enterprise, once candidly shown, will help to develop widely based public support both for pruning many present programs and for extending new projects with an equalizing impact. This approach differs drastically from the older strategy of a frontal assault to extend conventional public enterprise in many directions at once.

APPENDIX

A MODEST PROPOSAL:
THE PUBLIC DIRECTOR

ROBERT TOWNSEND*

If implemented properly, a public director could be the vehicle to make a real dent into corporate unaccountability. We must start with the law. Let us say that all manufacturing companies with over a billion dollars of assets should be required to have a public director. Although this would only cover 110 companies in the industrial sector, I would limit it to that. If we start out too ambitiously, we may lose the whole war. On the other hand, if the idea worked, it might well spread. Also, it is very hard to build a good case *against* public directors for these corporate giants.

Each public director should have a budget of a million dollars a year of the company's money—which comes out to something less than one cent a share. With it, he or she could pay himself a maximum of, say, fifty thousand dollars annually, spending the rest on scientists, engineers, lawyers, and accountants. They would not all be permanent staff, but would be on call to develop answers to questions that the company wasn't asking but should have been asking. He should have an office in the company headquarters and receive notice of all meetings conducted throughout the company, which should be open to attendance by him or one of his staff members. This is an important point, because one of the initial ploys of the company might be to hold four simultaneous meetings. Also, no doors or files should be closed to this public director or his staff. He, in turn, should be required to call at least two press conferences a year to report on the company's progress or lack of progress on issues of interest to the public. It will be argued that he will have to reveal company secrets. Let us pray he will. Secrecy is one of the most overrated and abused of corporate privileges.

John Kenneth Galbraith says that boards of directors don't really

* Former chairman of Avis Rent-A-Car and author of *Up the Organization!* (1970).

do anything—that all the real decisions are made further down the line. This is quite true. The average big-company director spends about forty hours a year in the boardroom. The meetings sound like those at the Augusta National Golf Club—discussion of recent trips, salmon fishing in Norway, some superficial discussion of the state of the economy, the goddamn unproductivity of labor. Then they adjourn with a few hundred-dollar bills or more in everyone's pocket. They don't really know what is going on, who the players are, or what attitudes, relationships, and problems govern the company's actions. How could the outside directors of Penn Central, for example, possibly know what was going on by spending a few hours a month in a room on the eighteenth floor of the Transportation Building in Philadelphia? They couldn't. And when the Penn Central went bust, it surprised them as much as it did anyone else.

Consider the plight of the twenty or so blacks who are currently on big-company boards of directors, without money and without staffs, yet expected to have a genuine impact on the company's behavior. Consider the difference between GM's Leon Sullivan, who has tremendous demands on his time, and a full-time public director, with an office in the headquarters building and a million-dollar budget. Consider the catalytic effect of having a dedicated, informed, and full-time outsider in the middle of what is now worthless ceremony. It would transform the board meetings completely. Out of sheer shame, the directors would be compelled to help him pursue the relevant questions, criticize the answers, and discuss important matters. It would give the nice country club types who now sit on boards an excuse to ask questions they may have long wanted to ask.

This proposal will not be well received by the top managements of the 110 companies. In fact, they may scream bloody murder. For who likes to be interrupted in the midst of his pleasure? And interruption it surely is, because they know they won't be able to keep on doing what they have been doing if a public representative is allowed to observe and report to the public. Some managements might even find it so distasteful that they would choose to spin off enough subsidiaries to get below the billion-dollar mark. Fine. Then they wouldn't have to have a public director. And to promote this healthy development, the tax laws, drawn to favor acquisitions, should be redrawn to favor de-conglomeration.

Other companies would attempt to corrupt the idea by choosing the directors or determining the kind of people chosen—a blob in every job. So the question becomes: Who would select, approve, and assign public directors? One possibility is to form an ad-hoc legislative committee of Representatives and Senators who have occupied at least vice-presidential offices in non-family businesses. Let them screen and approve candidates the way Supreme Court nominees are approved by the Senate. Once a pool of public directors is created, specific directors should be assigned to corporations by lot. They should also be rotated every four years to avoid corruption and co-option; and prior to reassignment they should be interrogated by the committee to see whether they have taken the shilling or lost their energy.

I would suggest that public directors should meet the following criteria: at least ten years' experience in a large corporation, some of it in line jobs as opposed to staff or expert jobs such as law or accounting; enough wealth so that he is unlikely to be bought, and uninterested enough in corporate power to be utterly incorruptible; energetic; and reasonable intelligence. I must say that within the space of a month I think I could come up with 110 people who might well qualify (and I'm not applying for a job—I'm completely disqualified on the criterion of energy). I'm sure that there are thousands more who would qualify.

One should be prepared for the next countermeasures taken by big companies. If they failed to take over the selection of public directors, they will try to swamp them by creating dead-end assignments and task forces, by deluging them with mountains of meaningless data. Their offices will soon be so full of computer printouts that they won't be able to get in to answer the telephone. The companies will try to plant phonies and ringers on the director's staff. They will try to transfer such business as has been conducted at executive committees, finance committees, and board meetings, to other anonymous committees.

If the public director turned out to be really experienced, intelligent, and energetic, he would be aware of these obstacles and able to overcome them. My guess is that he would get help from a lot of people in the company—people below the top-management level who are cool to what top management is doing or failing to do. He would find a lot of friends and a lot of sources of informal and valuable information if he were there all the time and especially if he gave out his home phone number to enough people.

It is no exaggeration to say that all the big-company managements I am familiar with are basically engaged (whether they are conscious of it or not) in screwing their stockholders, employees, customers, and the general public as well, while living off the fat of the land themselves. In my judgment, the government is not going to do anything about it; neither are the labor unions. Public directors could produce miracles of reform if they were selected properly and given an adequate bankroll. The stockholders, it must be conceded, would not know what to do even if they could somehow band together.

Professor Andrew Hacker has concluded that since economically and politically we are all on the *Titanic*, we may as well go first class. If we can make this public-director idea a matter of law for our supercorporations, and then get qualified people in the slots, I am not persuaded we will have to settle for a bad trip, first class or tourist.

NOTES

II. Governing the Giant Corporation (Dahl)

1. J. Vanek, *The General Theory of Labor-Managed Market Economies* 396–397 (1970).
2. *Ibid* at 393.
3. S. Melman, *Managerial Versus Cooperative Decision Making in Israel* pp. 57–8, Studies in Comparative International Development, Vol. VI, No. 3, Series 065, Rutgers University, 1970.
4. G. Bannock, *The Juggernauts* (1971); Snell, "Annual Style Changes in the Automobile Industry as an Unfair Method of Competition," 80 *Yale Law Journal* 567–613 (1971); J. Bain, *Barriers to New Competition* (1956); Comanor and Wilson, "Advertising the Advantages of Size," *American Economic Review*, May 1969, p. 91; F.M. Scherer, "Firm Size, Market Structure, Opportunity and the Output of Potential Inventions," *American Economic Review*, December 1964, pp. 1121–22; *Studies by the Staff of the Cabinet Committee on Price Stability* 81 (Government Printing Office, 1969).

III. The Politics of Corporate Power (Harris)

1. *Fortune*, May 1971, p. 144.
2. P. d'A. Jones, *The Consumer Society* 221 (1965).
3. R. Dahl, "Business and Politics: A Critical Appraisal of Political Science," *American Political Science Review*, March 1959, p. 13.
4. *Insurance Facts 1971*, pamphlet distributed by Insurance Information Institute, p. 64. From 1954 through 1970, more than ten thousand businesses failed per year, with the exception of 1968 and 1969, when failures were in excess of nine thousand. Failures have gone as high as 15,782.
5. Fred R. Harris, *Now Is The Time* 81 (1971).
6. *Ibid*.
7. M. Mintz and J. Cohen, *America, Inc.* 158 (1971).
8. Ralph Nader's Center for Auto Safety also sent out a rebuttal, in the form of a letter to the editor of each newspaper and magazine

that had published the Ford ad. Out of twenty-seven newspapers and magazines, two printed the Nader rebuttal—both long after the original ads were run.

9. Department of Transportation news release, Sept. 29, 1971, p. 1 (mimeo).

10. Transcript of sixty-second spot for Association of American Railroads. Script title "Circus," air date, June 10, 1971 (McCann-Erickson, Inc. mimeo).

11. Transcript of sixty-second spot for Association of American Railroads. Script title "Holdup," air date, May 18, 1971 (McCann-Erickson, Inc. mimeo).

12. Letter from Johnnie M. Walters to Fred R. Harris, November 30, 1971.

13. Mintz and Cohen, *supra* note 7, at 175–6, 195.

14. Charles R. Ross, statement before U.S. Senate Antitrust and Monopoly Subcommittee, Jan. 21, 1972, p. 3.

15. Ralph Nader, testimony before U.S. Senate Commerce Committee on S. 2404 (El Paso Bill), Oct. 22, 1971, p. 11.

16. Letter John Flynn to Senator Philip Hart, Oct. 18, 1971.

17. *Ibid.*

18. Mintz and Cohen, *supra* note 7, at 178.

19. Report of the Agribusiness Accountability Project, Congressional Record, December 2, 1971, pp. 20106–20108.

20. A. Hacker, *The Corporation Take-over* 7–8 (1964).

21. Lois G. Wark, "Consumer Report/Criticism of Advertising Prompts Agency Crackdown, Industry Self-Regulation," *National Journal*, August 7, 1971, p. 1638.

22. Ralph Nader and Mark Green elicited answers from 1972 Presidential Candidates to just such questions. See Congressional Record, March 22, 1972, p. s. 4489.

IV. The Corporation and the Community (Green)

1. *Standard Oil Company of California et al. v. United States,* 337 U.S. 243 (1948).

2. Mintz, "Sen. Hart Ponders: Do Conglomerates Destroy Individualism," *Washington Post*, Jan. 6, 1969.

3. Robert O. Schulze, "The Bifurcation of Power in a Satellite City," in M. Janowitz (ed.), *Community Political Systems* 43 (1961).

4. Cited in Davis and R. Blumstrom, *Business, Society and Environment: Social Power and Social Response* 268 (1971) (an April 1966 study conducted by the Opinion Research Corporation); *see also* Jones, "The Businessman and Small City Problems," 20 *Michigan Business Review* 18 (1968).

5. *Supra* note 3.

6. Robert A. Foster, "Our Merging Industries," #10, *Worcester Telegraph*, 1968.
7. Pellegrin and Coates, "Absentee-Owned Corporations and Community Power Structure," 61 *American Journal of Sociology* 413, 414 (1956).
8. "Small Business and Civic Welfare," Report of the Smaller War Plants Corporation to the Special Committee to Study Problems of American Small Business, U.S. Senate, 79th Cong., 2nd Sess., Doc. #135 (1946).
9. "Small Business and the Community—a Study in Central Valley of California on Effects of Scale of Farm Operations," Report of the Special Committee to Study Problems of American Small Business, U.S. Senate, 79th Cong., 2nd Sess., Comm. Print #13 (1946).
10. *See generally*, E. Kefauver and I. Till, *Monopoly Power in America* 160–185 (1965).
11. *See generally*, M. Green, B. Moore, B. Wasserstein, *The Closed Enterprise System*, 12–13 (1972).
12. *Supra* note 6, at #6.
13. Jon G. Udell, *Social and Economic Consequencies of the Merger Movement in Wisconsin*, sponsored jointly by the Department of Local Affairs and Development, Wisconsin, and Graduate School of Business, University of Wisconsin (May, 1969).
14. The Pullman material is described in M. Heald, *The Social Responsibilities of Business*, 8 (1970).
15. "Company Towns, 1956," *Time*, April 16, 1956, at 100.
16. J. Jenkins, "Barony in Carolina," *The Nation*, May 12, 1966, at 405.
17. The following material on St. Marys is taken from Shuck and Wellford, "Democracy and the Good Life in a Company Town," *Harper's*, May 1972.
18. This section is based on James Phelan's and Robert Pozen's *The Company State: Ralph Nader's Study Group Report of DuPont in Delaware* (1972).
19. *See generally*, J. Fallows, *The Water Lords* (1971).
20. *Ibid.* at 130 (Statement of R.L. Stockman, Washington State Department of Health, and Donald Anderson, University of British Columbia).
21. *Ibid.* at 95–96.
22. P. Greer, "The Town's Their Life—But It's Killing Them," *Washington Post*, May 22, 1972, at 1.
23. *New York Times*, May 17, 1972, at 49.
24. *Supra* note 19, at 172.
25. Austin and Kramer, "Fiscal Feud: Homeowners Challenge Business Tax Breaks in Some Communities," *Wall Street Journal*,

April 15, 1971; see also, Anderson, "Big Steel Firms Get Tax Breaks," *Washington Post*, June 18, 1972, at 87.

26. *Chicago Sun Times*, May 8, 1971, at 3.
27. *See generally*, letter from Ralph Nader to Senator Edmund Muskie, chairman of the Subcommittee on Intergovernmental Relations, August 9, 1970; also, Cong. Rec. October 29, 1971, E11508–E11523.
28. Special Tax and Investment Guides for Businessmen and Investors, quoting "The Prentice-Hall Guides to State Industrial Development Incentives" at 10.
29. Golden, "Holding the Line," *Saturday Review*, December 13, 1969, at 73.
30. Golden, "Doing What Has to be Done," *Saturday Review*, Feb. 14, 1970, at 79.
31. Baumol, "Enlightened Self-Interest and Corporate Philanthropy," in W. Baumol, *et al.*, *A New Rationale for Corporate Social Policy* 6 (1970).
32. R. Baker and W. Cary (3d ed.), *Cases and Materials on Corporations* 359 (1959).
33. *Supra* note 18.
34. *Supra* note 6.
35. Report of a Committee of the Rochester Chamber of Commerce on the Out-of-Town Acquisition of Rochester Companies (1959) (unpublished); cited in Kefauver and Till, *supra* note 10.
36. W. Shepherd, "Conglomerate Mergers in Perspective," 2 *Antitrust Law and Economic Review* 20–21 (Fall, 1968).
37. *Supra* note 18.
38. *Ibid.*
39. *Ibid.*
40. *Supra* note 35.
41. Udell, *supra* note 13.
42. D. Leinsdorf, Project Director, *Citibank: A Preliminary Report by the Nader Task Force on First National City Bank* 231–232 (1971).
43. *Ibid.*
44. *Ibid.* at 200.
45. *Wall Street Journal*, Feb. 28, 1972, at 1.
46. *Paper Trade Journal*, January 27, 1969.

V. The Case for Federal Chartering (Nader)

1. R. W. Boyden, "The Breakdown of Corporations" in *The Corporation Take-over* (1964) (A. Hacker, ed.).
2. Harbrecht and McCallin, "The Corporation and the State in Anglo-American Law and Politics," 10 *Journal of Public Law* 1 (1961).

3. H. Henn, *Corporations* 16 (1961).
4. *Ibid.*; E. Dodd and Baker, *Cases and Materials on Corporations* 18 (1951); H.W. Ballantine, *Ballantine on Corporations* 36 (1946).
5. Kempin, "The Public Interest in the Corporation," 64 *Dickinson L. Rev.* 357 (1960).
6. See generally, J. W. Hurst, *The Legitimacy of the Business Corporation* (1970).
7. Katz, "The Philosophy of Mid-Century Corporation Statutes," 23 *Law & Contemporary Problems* (1958); see also Latty, "Why Are Business Corporation Laws Largely 'Enabling'?", 50 *Cornell L. Rev.* 599 (1965).
8. Boyden, *supra* note 1, at 89; see also, *Liggett Gov. Lee.*, 288 U.S. 517 548 (Brandeis, J. dissenting) (1932).
9. R. C. Larcom, *The Delaware Corporation* 13–14 (1937).
10. "Little Delaware Makes a Bid for the Organization of Trusts," 33 *Am. L. Rev.* 418, 419 (1899).
11. Lindahl and Carter, *Corporate Concentration and Public Policy* (1959).
12. Flynn, "Why Corporations Leave Home," *Atlantic*, September, 1932, at 270.
13. See generally, "Law for Sale: A Study of the Delaware Corporation Law of 1967," 117 *U. of Pa. L. Rev.* 861 (1969).
14. Flynn, *supra* note 12, at 276.
15. *Supra* note 13.
16. *Ibid.*
17. Watkins, "Federalization of Corporations," 13 *Tenn. L. Rev.* 89 (1934).
18. A. Berle, "Economic Power and the Free Society," in *The Corporation Take-over* 87 (1964); Federal Trade Commission, Report on Utility Corporations, No. 69A, at 76, Sept. 15, 1934.
19. J. Davis, *Essays in the Earlier History of the American Corporation* (1917).
20. Quoted in G. Leinwand, *A History of the United States Federal Bureau of Corporations (1903–1914)* 1962 (doctoral dissertation, New York University).
21. *New York Times*, Feb. 13, 1903.
22. Leinwand, *supra* note 20 at 108.
23. FTC Report, *supra* note 19, at 56–57.
24. *Ibid.*, at 10.
25. Leinwand, *supra* note 20, at 161–2.
26. S. Rosenman (ed.), *The Public Papers and Addresses of Franklin D. Roosevelt* 202 (1938) ("A Recommendation to the Congress to Enact the National Industrial Recovery Act to Put People to Work, May 17, 1933.")
27. Watkins, "Federalization of Corporations," 13 *Tenn. L. Rev.* 89 (1934).

28. *See* Temporary National Economic Committee, Final Statement of Senator Joseph C. O'Mahoney, *The Preservation of Economic Freedom* 11 (March 1941).

29. J. O'Mahoney, "Federal Charters and Licenses for Corporations," 22 *J. of the National Education Association* 27 (1938).

30. *Supra* note 28.

31. Reuschlein, "Federalization—Design for Corporate Reform in a National Economy," 71 *U. of Pa. L. Rev.* 91 (1942).

32. *Hale v. Hendel*, 201 U.S. 43, 74–75 (1905).

33. 4 Wheaton 315 (1819).

34. *See N.L.R.B. v. Jones & Laughlin Steel Corp.*, 301 U.S. 1 (1934).

35. *Katzenbach v. McClung*, 379 U.S. 297 (1964); *Heart of Atlanta Motel v. United State*s, 379 U.S. 241 (1914).

36. *Santa Clara Co. v. Southern Pacific Railroads*, 118 U.S. 394 (1885); *Minneapolis Railway Co. v. Beckwith*, 129 U.S. 28 (1888); but see *Connecticut General Life Insurance Co. v. Johnson*, 308 U.S. 77, 83 (1938) (Black, J. dissenting).

37. *See. Gibbons v. Ogden*, 6 L. Ed. 23 (1824); *Willson v. Black Bird Creek Marsh Co.*, 7 L. Ed. 412 (1829), *Cooley v. Bd. of Wardens of the Port of Philadelphia*, 13 L. Ed. 996 (1851).

38. *Lottery Cases*, 188 U.S. 321 (1903).

39. *Ibid.*; *Hoke v. United States* 227 U.S. 308 (1913); *United States v. Darby*, 312 U.S. 100 (1940).

40. Flynn, *supra* note 12, at 272.

41. Wilgus, "Federal License of National Incorporation," 3 *Michigan L. Rev.* 264 (1905).

42. See Israels, "The Corporate Triangle—Some Comparative Aspects of the New Jersey, New York, and Delaware Statues," 23 *Rutgers L. Rev.* 615 (1969); Brown, "The Federal Corporation Licensing Bill: Corporate Regulation," 27 *Georg. L. Rev.* 1092 (1938).

43. E. Latham, "The Body Politic of the Corporation," in *The Corporation Take-Over* (A. Hacker, ed.) (1964).

44. W. Hamilton, *Politics of Industry* 7 (1957).

45. [If the Railway Labor Act confers an exclusive bargaining power on a union] . . . without any commensurate statutory duty toward its members, constitutional questions arise. For the representative is clothed with power not unlike that of a legislature which is subject to constitutional duty equally to protect those rights, *Steele v. Louisville & Nashville R.R.*, 323 US192, 198 (1944). Where a union has . . . attained a monopoly of the supply of labor by means of closed shop agreements and other forms of collective labor action, such a union occupies a quasi public position similar to that of a public service business and it has certain corresponding obligations. It may no longer claim the same freedom from legal restraint enjoyed by golf clubs or fraternal associations. Its as-

serted right to choose its own members does not merely relate to social relations; it affects the fundamental right to work for a living. *James v. Marinship Corp.*, 25 Cal, 2d 721, 731 (1944).

46. *Marsh v. Alabama*, 326 U.S. 501 (1946) (a private company town, when it functions like any public municipality, must extend First Amendment freedoms of press and religion to its citizens); *accord*, *Amalgamated Food Employees Union v. Logan Valley Plaza*, 391 U.S. 308 (1968) (peaceful picketing on private property, in a location generally open to the public, is protected by the First Amendment).

47. *Shelly v. Kraemer*, 334 U.S. 1 (1948) (the equal protection clause of the Fourteenth Amendment prohibits the judicial enforcement by state courts of restrictive covenants based on race, since such judicial enforcement is effectively "state action").

48. *Griggs v. Duke Power Co.*, 401 U.S. 424 (1970) (firms employing "objective" tests which require higher skills than are job related and weed out black applicants violate Title VII of the Civil Rights Act of 1964).

49. *See* Ingram, "White Collar Conscience: The Corporate Underground," *The Nation*, Sept. 13, 1971, at 206.

50. Ehrenseich and Ehrenseich, "Pugliese v. James & Laughlin: "Conscience of a Steelworker," *The Nation*, Sept. 27, 1971, at 268.

51. Branch, "Courage Without Esteem: Profiles in Whistle-blowing," *Washington Monthly*, May 1971, at 23.

52. *See* Latham, "The Commonwealth of the Corporation," 55 *Nw. L. Rev.* 25 (1960); Miller, "The Constitutional Law of the Security State," 10 *Stan. L. Rev.* 620 (1958); Friedman, "Corporate Power, Government by Private Groups, and the Law," 55 *Colum. L. Rev.* 155 (1957).

53. Kempin, "The Public Interest in the Corporation," 64 *Dickinson L. Rev.* 357 (1960); Revschlein, "Federation—Design for Corporate Reform in a National Economy," 91 *U. of Pa. L. Rev.* (1942).

54. R. Pound, "Visitatorial Jurisdiction over Corporations in Equity," 49 *Harv. L. Rev.* 369, 372 (1936).

55. Israels, *supra* note 42.

VI. Corporate Democracy:
Nice Work if You Can Get It (Flynn)

1. H. S. Maine, *Ancient Law* 154–55 (1861); O. W. Holmes, *The Common Law* (1881); S. Buchanan, "The Corporation and the Republic," in *The Corporation Take-over* 19 (A. Hacker, ed., 1964).

2. G. C. Means, "Collective Capitalism and Economic Theory," in *The Corporation Take-over* 67 (A. Hacker, ed., 1964); A. Berle and G. C. Means, *The Modern Corporation and Private Property* (Rev. Ed. 1968). *See also* Berle, *The 20th Century Capitalist Revolution* (1954); A. Berle, *Power Without Property* (1959); A. Berle, *The Three Faces of Power* (1967). For an incisive article surveying the current state of the corporate democracy debate *see* J. Hetherington, "Fact and Legal Theory: Shareholders, Managers and Corporate Social Responsibility," 21 *Stan. L. Rev.* 248 (1969). *See also*, P. Harbrecht, "The Modern Corporation Revisited," 64 *Colum. L. Rev.* 1410 (1964).

3. *See generally*, W. Hurst, *The Legitimacy of the Business Corporation* (1970). Arguments have long been advanced before the courts to analyze the rights and liabilities of corporations in terms of property rights. It reached full flower in the Supreme Court cases invalidating much of the earlier New Deal legislation and had a resurgence in the Steel Seizure Case, *Youngstown Sheet & Tube Co. v. Sawyer*, 343 U.S. 579 (1952). State courts still premise analysis of issues arising under corporation statutes largely upon concepts of property.

4. *Ancient Law, supra* note 1. *See also*, "The Corporation and the Republic," *supra* note 1, and *infra* note 7.

5. *Quoted in* S. Buchanan, "The Corporation and the Republic," in *The Corporation Take-over* 19, 35 (A. Hacker, ed., 1964).

6. *The Trustees of Darmouth College v. Woodward*, 17 U.S. (4 Wheat.) 518, 636 (1819).

7. B. Manning, "Shareholder's Appraisal Remedy," 72 *Yale L.J.* 223, 244 n. 37 (1962).

8. Ewing, "Who Wants Corporate Democracy?" 49 *Harv. Bus. Rev.* No. 5, p. 12, (Sept.–Oct. 1971); C. Israels, "Are Corporate Powers Still Held in Trust?," 64 *Colum. L. Rev.* 1446 (1964); J. Weiner, "The Berle–Dodd Dialogue on the Concept of the Corporation," 64 *Colum. L. Rev.* 1458 (1964).

9. L. O. Kelso, "Corporate Benevolence or Welfare Redistribution?" 15 *Bus. Law.* 259 (1960).

10. C. Reich, *New York Times*, October 21, 1970; *see also*, E. Latham, "The Commonwealth of the Corporation," 55 *Nw. U. L. Rev.* 25 (1960).

11. "Law for Sale: A Study of the Delaware Corporation Law of 1967," 117 *U. Pa. L. Rev.* 861 (1969).

12. The top five corporations on *Fortune* magazine's 500 list, "The 500 Largest U.S. Industrial Corporations," LXXXIII *Fortune* No. 5, 170–179 (May, 1971), had the following outstanding common stock and number of shareholders according to Moody's Industrials.

Rank	Company	Voting Stock	Shareholders
1	General Motors	287,586,000	1,333,707
2	Standard Oil (N.J.)	223,729,000	807,845
3	Ford Motor	72,714,000	374,043
4	General Electric	181,627,000	521,085
5	I.B.M.	114,587,000	586,786

The last five corporations in the top 200 had the following distribution of stock and stockholders:

Rank	Company	Voting Stock	Shareholders
196	Sterling Drug	37,095,000	50,585
197	Carrier	15,920,000	13,982
198	Corning Glass	6,949,000	14,643
199	Eli Lilly	33,830,000	16,800
200	Essex International	9,353,000	9,068

Some corporations in the top 200 are wholly owned subsidiaries of nonindustrial corporations like Western Electric, ranked number 10, with $5.86 billion in sales and 215,380 employees. Others are relatively closely held like Whirlpool, ranked number 100, with 11,873,-000 voting shares and 11,465 shareholders; Pullman, ranked number 170 with 2,380,000 voting shares and 3,081 shareholders; Anderson, Clayton, ranked 185, with 3,116,000 voting shares and 3,339 shareholders.

Any practical hope for effective shareholder control in large public issue corporations is effectively defeated by the vast increase of voting stock widely dispersed over thousands of shareholders. B. Manning, book review of J. Livingston, *The American Stockholder* (1958), 67 *Yale L. J.* 1477 (1958). One interesting suggestion for reversing this trend is to return to the early common law system of one shareholder–one vote, rather than one share–one vote. D. Ratner, "The Government of Business Corporations: Critical Reflections on the Rule of One Share, One Vote," 56 *Cornell L. Rev.* 1 (1970).

Some very large corporations have been rated as closely held. For example, Sun Oil, Gulf Oil, Jones & Laughlin, and National Steel. B. Hindley, "Separation of Ownership and Control in the Modern Corporation," 13 *J. of Law & Econ.* 185, 213 (1970). However, the widely held public corporation has become a political state. *See* A. Berle, "Property, Production and Revolution," 65 *Colum. L. Rev.* 1 (1965); M. Raskin, *Being & Doing* 340 (1971).

13. Ford Annual Report, p. 35 (1970). But see, J. Linter, "The Financing of Corporations," in *The Corporation in Modern Society* 166 (E. S. Mason, ed. 1959); *contra*, A. Berle, "*Property, Production and Revolution*," 65 *Colum. L. Rev.* 1 (1965); A.

Berle, "Modern Functions of the Corporate System," 62 *Colum. L. Rev.* 433 (1962). More refined research must be done on the question of whether management is freeing itself from capital markets. In truly large enterprises with widely held stock, however, even the shareholder purchasing it has no effective hope of realizing the rights of a contributor of "risk capital" or the purchase is by another corporation; *i.e.*, Institutional Investor Study. P. Harbrecht, "The Modern Corporation Revisited," 64 *Colum. L. Rev.* 1410 (1964). See also, A. Sametz, "Trends in the Volume and Composition of Equity Finance," 19 *J. of Finance* 450 (1964).

14. A. Berle, "Property, Production and Revolution," *supra* note 12 at 16.

15. *See generally* R. Kessler, "The Statutory Requirement of a Board of Directors: A Corporate Anachronism," 27 *U. Chi. L. Rev.* 696 (1960); M. L. Mace, *Directors: Myth and Reality* (1971).

16. R. Townsend, *Up The Organization!* 31–34 (1970). Townsend advises that it is best to "let sleeping directors lie."

17. *See generally* R. Pound, "The New Feudal System," 19 *Ky. L. J.* 1 (1930); M. Raskin, *Being and Doing* (1971); H. Morgenthau, "Modern Science and Political Power," 64 *Colum. L. rev.* 1386 (1964).

18. Institutional Investor Study of the SEC, Summary p. 102 (1971). P. Harbrecht, "The Modern Corporation Revisited," 64 *Colum. L. Rev.* 1410 (1964); M. Eisenberg, "The Legal Roles of Shareholders and Management in Modern Corporate Decisionmaking," 57 *Calif. L. Rev.* 1 (1969).

19. R. Lampman, *The Share of Top Wealth Holders in National Wealth*, 1922–56 (1962); F. Lundberg, *The Rich and the Super-Rich* (1968); L. Kelso & P. Hetter, *Two Factor Theory: The Economics of Reality* (1967); Haley, "Changes in the Distribution of Income," in *Perspectives on Poverty and Income Distribution* 17 (S. Colville, ed. 1971).

20. M. Mintz and J. Cohen, *America, Inc.* (1971). The recent spate of proxy campaigns like the Dow Campaign and Campaign GM have involved solicitations which are clearly designed upon a premise that large corporations are significant political institutions which should be subjected to broader public control. Several recent books have been written from this basic perspective: C. Reich, *The Greening of America* (1970); M. Raskin, *Being & Doing* (1971); R. Dahl, *After the Revolution?* (1970).

21. Professor Loss considers the disclosure required by the proxy rules the most important disclosure required by the Securities Acts. L. Loss, *Securities Regulation* 1027 (2d ed. 1961). See generally, D. Schwartz, "The Public-Interest Proxy Contest: Reflections on

Campaign GM," 69 *Mich. L. Rev.* 419 (1971); D. Schwartz, "Towards New Corporate Goals: Co-Existence With Society," 60 *Geo. L. J.* 57 (1971). *Medical Committee for Human Rights v. SEC*, 432 F. 2d 659 (U.S. App. D. C. 1970): D. Chisum, "Napalm, Proxy Proposals and the SEC," 12 *Ariz. L. Rev.* 463 (1970).

22. J. K. Galbraith, *The New Industrial State* (1967) (the technostructure); Drucker, *In the New Society* (Harpers 1949) (everybody); Donaldson, "Financial Goals: Management vs. Stockholders," 41 *Harv. Bus. Rev.* 116 (May–June 1963) (managers are trustees); W. O. Douglas, *Democracy and Finance* 53–55 (1940) (professional directors).

23. H. Schwartz, "Governmentally Appointed Directors in a Private Corporation—The Communications Satellite Act of 1962," 79 *Harv. L. Rev.* 350 (1965).

24. D. Vaghts, "Reforming the "Modern" Corporation: Perspectives From the German," 80 *Harv. L. Rev.* 23 (1966).

25. J. Kolaja, *Workers Councils: The Yugoslav Experience* (1966); Wooton, *Workers, Unions and the State* (1966); R. Dahl, *After the Revolution?* 130–133 (1970).

26. One obvious difficulty is that our society not only has a large number of "capital-less" citizens, our society also has a large number of citizens who are jobless or unemployable. Moreover, without economic deconcentration, the distribution of wealth by the Second Income Plan will not be equitable. Some will share in monopoly growth and profits; many will not. *See* also H. G. Manne, "Current Views on the "Modern Corporation," 38 *Det. L.J.* 559 (1961).

27. Liability may result from the signing of an inaccurate registration statement under Section 11 of the Securities Act of 1933, *Escott v. Barchris Construction Corporation*, 283 F. Supp. 643 (D.S.D. N.Y. 1968); the use of misleading proxies under Section 14(a) of the Securities Exchange Act of 1934, *J. I. Case Co. v. Borak*, 377 U.S. 426 (1964); the use of manipulative and deceptive devices in the purchase or sale of securities under Section 10(b) of the Securities Exchange Act of 1934, *Smolowe v. Delendo Corp.*, 136 F.2c 231 (2d Cir. 1943).

28. An increase of fear of exposure to individual liability by officers and directors has lead to considerable legislative activity with regard to indemnification, usually in the direction of broadening indemnification. See 4 Del. Code Annot. § 141 (Supp. 1970). There is also a growing business of selling liability insurance for officers and directors. See generally, D. Mace, "Directors and Officers Liability Insurance," 85 *Banking L.J.* 39 (1968); W. McCormack, "In-

demnification of Directors for Section 11 Liability," 48 *Tex. L. Rev.* 661 (1970); J. McKeown, "Comment, Corporate Indemnification of Officers and Directors—The Expanding Scope of the Statutes," 18 *Cath. U.L. Rev.* 195 (1968).

VII. Corporate Secrecy vs. Corporate Disclosure (Mueller)

1. Statement presented at Conference on Corporate Accountability, Washington, D.C., October 30, 1971. This statement draws heavily on a paper presented by the author at the Conference on Formulating Financial Standards, Northwestern University, October 18–19, 1971.
2. ITT annual report, 1968, p. 7.
3. Prepared statement of Willard F. Mueller in *United States vs. International Telephone and Telegraph Corp. and Grinnell Corp.*, United States District Court of Connecticut, p. 22 and Appendix 5.
4. For a discussion of the manner in which ITT allegedly mobilized its international connections in an attempt to secure "landing rights" for a proposed thirty-six-hundred-mile submarine cable, see M. Mintz and J. S. Cohen, *America, Inc.*, 330–338 (1971).
5. ITT, 1970 Annual Report, p. 34.
6. *Ibid.*, p. 3.
7. "ITT Denies Executives Who Sold Shares Before Justice Unit Pact Had Inside Tip," *Wall Street Journal*, August 13, 1971.
8. "Accountant Urges Better Reporting Practices," *New York Times*, July 24, 1971.
9. *Investigation of Conglomerate Mergers*, A Report of the Staff of the Antitrust Subcommittee, Committee on the Judiciary, House of Representatives, 92nd Cong. 1st Sess. 414 (June 1, 1971).
10. This information was required on its Forms S-1, S-7, and 10.
11. In response to a letter from Senator Philip Hart asking whether the SEC had authority to require fuller financial disclosure, Manuel F. Cohen, then chairman of the SEC, replied that "the Commission and its staff are vitally interested in seeing that full and fair disclosure is made to the investing public. . . ." He then forwarded to Senator Hart a memorandum prepared by the SEC staff. The memorandum explained at length that the Commission and staff had considered this problem "from time to time," and that "it is the opinion of the staff that the Commission presently has the authority to require more detailed disclosure in various respects, . . . if it deems it necessary for the protection of investors." The memorandum then listed six reasons why it had refrained from seeking fuller disclosure in the past, including

whether the value of such information would justify the cost. See exchange of letters between Senator Hart and Manuel Cohen reproduced in Hearings before the Subcommittee on Antitrust and Monopoly of the Committee on the Judiciary, U.S. Senate, 89th Cong. 1st Sess. 1069–1071 (March and April, 1965).

12. A. Rappaport and E. M. Lerner, *A Framework for Financial Reporting by Diversified Companies*, 45–55, National Association of Accountants, New York, 1969.

13. Prior to the promulgation of the SEC 10 percent rule, the staff of President Johnson's Cabinet Committee on Price Stability made an analysis of the proposed SEC rule which was submitted to Chairman Manuel Cohen. Chairman Cohen, commenting on the Cabinet Committee staff's analysis, replied in part,

> Although we await the recommendations of the staff upon the comments received with respect to these proposals, I am informed that over three hundred comments have been received and that substantially all of such letters which commented on the proposed reductions from 15 percent to 10 percent objected to such reduction. I am also informed that some suggestions were made that the Commission move in the other direction and perhaps use a 20 percent figure for this purpose. In any event, it is the 10 percent proposal which is presently before the Commission for review, and a further revision downward of these percentages would probably require public exposure of such a proposal.

Letter from Manuel F. Cohen, Chairman, Securities Exchange Commission to Willard F. Mueller, Executive Director, Cabinet Committee on Price Stability, December 27, 1969. For a discussion of the Cabinet Committee proposal see, "Industrial Structure and Competition Policy," *Studies by the Staff of the Cabinet Committee on Price Stability*, Washington, D.C., January 1969.

14. Letter accompanying the release of the statement explaining the SEC disclosure rules, August 14, 1969.

15. In H. C. Simons, *Economic Policy for a Free Society* 58 (1948) (emphasis in original).

16. *Ibid.*

17. See *Independent Offices Appropriations, 1965,* Hearings by Subcommittee of the Committee on Appropriations, U.S. Senate, 88th Cong. 2nd Sess. 1079–99, Part II.

18. *Economy in Government Procurement*, Committee print, Joint Economic Committee of the Congress, April 1968, p. 7.

19. See the discussion by Galbraith, Adams, Mueller, and Turner in *Planning Regulation and Competition*, hearings before the subcommittees of the Select Committee on Small Business, United States Senate, 90th Cong. 1st Sess. (June 29, 1967).

VIII. The Antitrust Alternative (Adams)

1. P. A. Samuelson, and R. M. Solow, "Analytical Aspects of Anti-Inflation Policy," *American Economic Review Proceedings*, 1960.
2. W. Adams, "The Role of Competition in the Regulated Industries," *American Economic Review Proceedings*, May 1958.
3. Hearings before the U.S. Senate Antitrust and Monopoly Subcommittee, *Economic Concentration*, Part 4, 89th Cong. 1st Sess. 1541–1551 (1965).
4. J. Galbraith, *The New Industrial State* 76 (1967).
5. J. Jewkes, D. Sawers, and R. Stillerman, *The Sources of Invention* (Chapter IV) (1959).
6. *Public Policies Toward Business* 258 (1966) (3d ed.).
7. *Business Week*, November 16, 1963, pp. 144–46.
8. W. Adams and J. B. Dirlam, "Big Steel, Invention, and Innovation," *Quarterly Journal of Economics*, May 1966.
9. J. K. Galbraith, *The Affluent Society* 253 (1952).
10. U.S. Senate Small Business Committee, "Report on the Role of Irregular Airlines in the United States Air Transportation Industry," *Senate Report No. 540*, 82d Cong. 1st Sess. (1951).
11. U.S. Select Committee on Small Business, House of Representatives, *Steel—Acquisitions, Mergers, and Expansion of 12 Major Companies, 1900–1950*, 81st Cong., 2nd Sess. (1950).
12. For a more complete discussion of the merger movement in the oil industry, see J. M. Blair, *Economic Concentration* 275–84 (1972).
13. See also *New Republic*, Nov. 6, 1971, and generally, M. Green et al., *The Closed Enterprise System* 210–310 (1972).
14. *United States v. Columbia Steel Co.*, 334 U.S. 495 (1948) (dissenting opinion).

IX. Corporate Social Responsibility: Shell Game for the Seventies? (Henning)

1. These figures are from "Annual Directory Issue," *Forbes* May 15, 1971.
2. M. Friedman, "The Social Responsibility of Business Is to Increase Profits," *New York Times, Sunday Magazine*, September 13, 1970, p. 32.
3. See the refutation of the Friedman thesis in D. Riley, "Taming GM . . . and Ford, Union Carbide, U.S. Steel, Dow Chemical," in *With Justice For Some* (B. Wasserstein and M. Green, eds.) (1971).
4. Quoted by G. Kolko, *The Triumph of Conservatism* 87 (1963).
5. G. W. Perkins, "Business: The Moral Question," quoted by A.

Seltzer, *Progressive Politics and the Idea of the Enlightened Businessman* (unpublished dissertation, University of Chicago, 1972).

6. *A Crossroads of Freedom: The 1912 Campaign Speeches of Woodrow Wilson*, edited by J. W. Davidson. 111, 493–4 (1956).

7. A. Berle, "For Whom Corporate Managers *Are* Trustees: A Note," 45 *Harvard Law Review* 1365, 1370 (1932). *See also*, A. Berle and G. Means, *The Modern Corporation and Private Property* (1932).

8. C. Kaysen, "The Social Significance of the Modern Corporation," *American Economic Review* 311, 313–14 (1957).

9. A. Berle, "Foreword," *The Corporation in Modern Society* viii, Mason (ed.), (1959).

10. D. Rockefeller, "The Social Responsibilities of Business to Urban America," address delivered to 37th Annual Conference, Financial Executives Institute (October 26, 1968).

11. B. R. Dorsey, quoted in *Business and Society*, August 25, 1970, p. 3.

12. Department of Defense, *100 Companies and Their Subsidiary Corporations Listed According to Net Value of Military Prime Contract Awards*, Fiscal Year 1969; Westinghouse *Annual Report*, (1970).

13. *Environmental Action*, April 17, 1971, pp. 3–5.

14. *Business Week*, November 20, 1971, p. 23.

15. *Wall Street Journal*, November 20, 1971.

16. *Wall Street Journal*, April 29, 1971.

17. J. Brown and S. Lusterman, *Business and the Development of Ghetto Enterprise* 55, (The Conference Board, 1971).

18. *New York Times*, May 7, 1970.

19. *Wall Street Journal*, September 1, 1971.

20. J. Cohn, *The Conscience of the Corporation* 10–13 (1971).

21. *Wall Street Journal*, May 19, 1970.

22. *Wall Street Journal*, January 11, 1971.

23. *Barron's*, May 18, 1970. In 1970, corporate charitable donations to education fell 9.3 percent, according to the *Wall Street Journal* of November 6, 1971.

24. *Social Responsibilities of Business Corporations*. Committee on Economic Development, 1971, pp. 17, 27, 65–6.

25. Quoted in Brief for Petitioner, *Medical Committee for Human Rights v. SEC*, No. 23, 105 U.S. Court of Appeals for the District of Columbia Circuit, p. 3 (1969).

26. Brown, "The Frawley Phenomenon," *Fortune*, February, 1966, p. 194.

27. *Wall Street Journal*, December 10, 1970, quoting a print shop foreman.

28. George Reedy, *The Twilight of the Presidency* 3 (1970).

29. Cohn, *supra* note 20, p. 16.
30. *Ibid.*, p. 1.
31. *Medical Committee for Human Rights v. SEC,* 432 F. 2d 659, 681 (U.S. App. D.C. 1970).
32. See sec. 14(a), Securities and Exchange Act of 1934, 48 Stat. 895, 15 U.S.C. sec 78n(a) (1964); Rule 14a-8 of the Proxy Rules of the Securities and Exchange Commission, 17 C.F.R. sec 240. 14 a-8.
33. *Supra*, note 31.
34. *Wall Street Journal,* October 25, 1971.
35. See generally transcripts of 1970–72 GM annual meetings.
36. Statement delivered on behalf of Campaign GM, May 22, 1970.
37. *Wall Street Journal*, May 21, 1971. The Dreyfus Leverage Fund nevertheless voted its GM shares in favor of the Campaign GM disclosure resolution. When the issue is abstract, fund holders will endorse the idea of investment in "progressive and socially responsible" companies. More than 80 percent of the Wellington Management Companies did so in a 1971 referendum.
38. Council on Economic Priorities, *Economic Priorities Report* 3 Vol. 2, No. 1 (April–May 1970).
39. *Wall Street Journal*, April 28, 1971.
40. Sec. 228, The Greyhound Corporation has availed itself of this option.
41. R. Townsend, *Up the Organization!* 42 (1970).
42. *Business Week*, May 22, 1971, p. 54.
43. See R. Dahl, Chapter I of this volume.
44. *New York Times*, May 30, 1971.

X. Citizen Counteraction? (Hacker)

1. *Quoted in* L. Hacker, *Major Documents ,in American Economic History 28* (1961).
2. As reported by *The Fortune Directory*, the five hundred largest firms in 1954 came to $137 billion, and by 1969 they stood at $445 billion—a 224 percent rise. According to *The Statistical Abstract,* the federal, state, and local governments collected $84 billion in taxes in 1954, and $223 billion in 1969—a rise of only 165 percent.
3. For an elaboration, see the discussion of corporate power in my *The End of the American Era* 43–52 (1970).
4. Figures on the numbers of inspectors come from *New York Times* articles of September 3, December 24, and December 27, 1971.
5. *New York Times*, December 9, 1971.
6. *See* M. Green, *et al., The Closed Enterprise System* (1972).
7. *New York Post*, October 25, 1971.

8. Reported, respectively, in the *Washington Post*, December 6, 1971, and the *New York Post*, March 29, 1971.

9. *See* Jenkins, *Power at the Top* (1959).

XI. Deterring Corporate Crime (Geis)

1. My views on prison reform are set out in *Saturday Review*, December 11, 1971, pp. 47–8, 56.

2. President's Commission on Law Enforcement and Administration of Justice, *Crime and Its Impact—An Assessment* 104 (Washington, D.C., Government Printing Office, 1967).

3. *New York Times*, December 27, 1971.

4. *Los Angeles Times*, May 11, 1971.

5. *Ibid*. Similarly, Nader has been quoted as saying, "If you want to talk about violence, don't talk of Black Panthers. Talk of General Motors." (*Quoted in* "White-Collar Crime," *Barron's*, March 30, 1970, p. 10.)

6. G. Christian Hill and Barbara Isenberg, "Documents Indicate 4 Beech Models Had Unsafe Fuel Tanks," *Wall Street Journal*, July 30, 1971, pp. 1, 6.

7. *Ibid. See also, Warnick v. Beech Aircraft Corp.*, Orange County Superior Ct., File #174046 (Calif. 1971).

8. Ralph Nader, "Foreword," to J. Esposito, *Vanishing Air* viii (1970).

9. Nicholas Johnson, quoted in Morton Mintz and Jerry S. Cohen, *America, Inc.* 81 (1971).

10. Brooks Atkinson, *Broadway* 315–316 (1970).

11. C. Wright Mills, *The Power Elite* 95 (1956).

12. James S. Turner, *The Chemical Feast* 63 (1970).

13. M. Green, *et al.*, *The Closed Enterprise System* 319 (mimeograph, 1971).

14. *Sharon* (Pa.) *Herald*, February 8, 1961.

15. *Supra* note 11, 343–344.

16. Gay Talese, *Honor Thy Father* 479 (1971). *Note also*:

Last year in Federal court in Manhattan . . . a partner in a stock brokerage firm pleaded guilty to an indictment charging him with $20 million in illegal trading with Swiss banks. He hired himself a prestigious lawyer, who described the offense in court as comparable to breaking a traffic law. Judge Irving Cooper gave the stockbroker a tongue lashing, a $30,000 fine and a suspended sentence.

A few days later the same judge heard the case of an unemployed Negro shipping clerk who pleaded guilty to stealing a television set worth $100 from an interstate shipment in a bus terminal. Judge Cooper sentenced him to one year in jail.

In fact, some judges don't think of white collar criminals as
criminals, legal experts say.

Glynn Mapes, "A Growing Disparity in Criminal Sentences Trou-
bles Legal Experts," *Wall Street Journal*, September 9, 1970.
17. Ronald Wraith and Edgar Simkins, *Corruption in Developing
Countries* 65–170 (1964).
18. Geoffrey Gorer, "Modification of National Character: The Role
of the Police in England," 11 *Journal of Social Issues* 24–32
(1955).
19. "The corruption of the robber baron days was more direct. Officials
made straight deals for big kickbacks and usually admitted they
were wrong when caught. Now the deals are comparatively small
and oblique, and all proclaim innocence at the end. The effect of
this hanky-panky on the restless and critical young generation in
America, however, is undoubtedly greater than the spectacular
official plunder of the past." James Reston, "Washington: The Supreme Court and the Universities," *New York Times*, May 18,
1969.
20. Barbara W. Tuchman, *Stillwell and the American Experience in
China, 1911–45* chap. 11 (1970).
21. G. Myrdal, *An American Dilemma* (1944).
22. Joint Commission on Correctional Manpower and Training, *The
Public Looks at Crime and Corrections*, February 1968, pp. 11–12.
23. "Changing Morality: The Two Americas," *Time*, June 6, 1969,
p. 26.
24. E. A. Ross, "The Criminaloid," in G. Geis (ed.), *White-Collar
Criminal* 36 (1968).
25. Quoted in Congressional Record, Vol. 111, Part 4 (March 10,
1965), p. 4631.
26. *See generally*, E. M. Schur, *Crimes Without Victims* (1965).
27. *See e.g.*, Bonnie and Whitebread "The Forbidden Fruit and the
Tree of Knowledge: An Inquiry Into the Legal History of Mari-
huana Prohibition," 56 *Virginia Law Review* 971 (1970).
28. E. H. Sutherland, *White Collar Crime* 222,225 (1949).
29. M. O. Cameron, *The Booster and the Snitch: Department Store
Shoplifting* 160–162 (1964).
30. *Ibid.*, p. 163.
31. G. Williams, *Criminal Law—The General Part* 865 (2nd ed.,
1961).
32. U.S. Senate, Committee on the Judiciary, Subcommittee on Antitrust and Monopoly, *Administered Prices*, 87th Cong., 2nd Sess.,
1961, Part 28, pp. 17223–17232, 17287–17288.
33. H. Salisbury, *The 900 Days: The Siege of Leningrad* 445 (1969).
34. F. S. Fitzgerald, *The Great Gatsby* 180–81 (1925).

35. M. Lowenthal, *The Federal Bureau of Investigation*, 12 (1950).
36. *Time*, February 17, 1961, p. 84.
37. Harold C. Wilkenfeld, "Comparative Study of Enforcement Policy in Israel, Italy, the Netherlands, the United Kingdom, and Other Countries," unpublished manuscript, Internal Revenue Service, October 7, 1965.
38. Paul R. Dixon, quoted in *New York Times*, February 10, 1966.
39. Joseph E. Finley, *Understanding the 1959 Labor Law* 24 (1960).
40. Crossland, "Confessions of a Business Dropout," *Wall Street Journal*, December 13, 1967.
41. U. S. Senate, *Administered Prices*, *supra* note 32, Part 27, p. 17067.
42. *Ibid.*, p. 16790.
43. *Ibid.*, p. 16694.
44. *New York Times*, February 7, 1961.
45. *New York Times*, February 11, 1961.
46. W. S. Porter, "The Chair of Philanthromathematics," in *The Gentle Grafter* 48 (1908).
47. *New York Times*, February 25, 1961.
48. Application of the State of California, 195 F. Supp. 39 E. D. Penn. 1961.
49. General Electric Company, *Notice of Annual Meeting of Share Owners*, March 17, 1961, pp. 17–27.
50. *Sharon* (Pa.) *Herald*, February 12, 1961.
51. Ralph J. Cordiner, "Comments on the Electrical Antitrust Cases," at 9th Annual Management Conference, Graduate School, University of Chicago, March 1, 1961, p. 9.

XII. Courts and Corporate Accountability (Miller)

1. Committee for Economic Development, *Social Responsibilities of Business Corporations* 21 (1971). See also C. C. Walton, *Corporate Social Responsibilities* (1965).
2. C. Horsky, *The Washington Lawyer* 68 (1952).
3. The early history is recounted in S. W. Bruchey, *The Roots of American Economic Growth, 1607–1861: An Essay in Social Causation* (1965).
4. 16 Wall. 36 (1873).
5. 94 U.S. 113 (1877).
6. *Santa Clara County v. Southern Pacific R.R.*, 118 U.S. 394 (1886).
7. J. R. Commons, *Legal Foundations of Capitalism* 7 (1924).
8. Quoted in L. Jaffe, *Judicial Control of Administrative Action* 12 (1965).
9. *Scenic Hudson Preservation Conference v. Federal Power Commission*, 354 F.2d 608 (2nd Cir. 1965); *Office of Communica-*

tion of the United Church of Christ v. Federal Communications Commission, 359 F.2d 994 (D.C. Cir. 1966).

10. *Phillips Petroleum Co. v. Federal Power Commission*, 347 U.S. 672 (1954).

11. *Cascade Natural Gas Co. v. El Paso Natural Gas Co.*, 386 U.S. 129 (1967).

12. The Alaskan case is *Wilderness Society v. Hickel*, reproduced in Reitze, *Environmental Law* 1–114 (1972); the DDT case is *Environmental Defense Fund v. Ruckelshaus*, 428 F.2d 1093 (D.C. Cir. 1970); *C.A.B. v. Moss*, 430 F.2d 891 (D.C. Cir. 1970).

13. *U.S. ex rel. Marcus v. Hess*, 317 U.S. 537, 541 (1943).

14. 2 *Environment Reporter*–Cases 1298 (S.D. Tex. 1971).

15. *Marsh v. Alabama*, 326 U.S. 501 (1946).

16. *Amalgamated Food Employees Union v. Logan Valley Plaza*, 391 U.S. 308 (1968).

17. *E.g., Smith v. Allwright*, 321 U.S. 649 (1944); *Terry v. Adams*, 345 U.S. 461 (1953).

18. *E.g., Garner v. Louisiana*, 368 U.S. 157 (1961); *Bell v. Maryland*, 378 U.S. 226 (1964).

19. *Burton v. Wilmington Parking Authority*, 365 U.S. 715 (1961).

20. *Ohio v. Wyandotte Chemical Corp.*, 401 U.S. 493 (1971).

21. F. Frankfurter, *Some Observations on Supreme Court Litigation and Legal Education* 17 (1954).

22. M. Massel, "Economic Analysis in Judicial Antitrust Decisions," 20 *A.B.A. Section of Antitrust Law* 46 (1962).

23. See Miller and Howell, "The Myth of Neutrality in Constitutional Adjudication," 27 *U. Chi. L. Rev.* 661 (1960).

24. L. Hand, "The Contribution of an Independent Judiciary to Civilization," in *The Spirit of Liberty: Papers and Addresses of Learned Hand* 118, 125 (Dilliard, ed., Vintage paperback 1959).

25. *Ibid.*, at 121.

26. See D. Truman, *The Governmental Process* (1951); T. Lowi, *The End of Liberalism* (1969).

27. Compare Miller, "Public Law and the Obsolescence of the Lawyer," 19 *U. Fla. L. Rev.* 514 (1967), with Donahue, "Lawyers, Economists, and the Regulated Industries," 70 *Michigan L. Rev.* 195 (1971).

XIII. Halfway up from Liberalism:
Regulation and Corporate Power (Lazarus)

1. A. M. Schlesinger, Jr., *The Vital Center* xii (1962).

2. Quoted in R. Hofstadter, *The Age of Reform* 247 (1955). Hofstadter viewed Theodore Roosevelt's statement as a forecast of

what would be accomplished by subsequent reform administrations.

3. Reformist officials were, however, in command of other regulatory agencies, at least for temporary periods, during the New Deal years. Examples are the FDA and the FCC. See Fainsod, Gordon, and Palamountain, *Government and the American Economy* 226–29 (3d. 1959).

4. Others on the list are the FCC, FDIC, FHLBB, FMC, NLRB, CCC, and the REA, all of which enjoyed the sponsorship of major organized interests. See W.A. Jordan, *Airline Regulation in America* (1970); J.R. Meyer, M.J. Peck, J. Stenason, C. Zwick, *The Economics of Competition in the Transportation Industries* (1959); Turner, "The Scope of Antitrust and other Economic Regulatory Policies," 82 *Harv. L. Rev.* 1207, 1232–41 (1969); M. Bernstein, *Regulating Business by Independent Commission* (1955).

5. *See*, in addition to sources cited in note 4 *supra*, M. Levine, "Is Air Regulation Necessary?" 74 *Yale L.J.* 1416 (1965); G. McConnell, Private Power and American Democracy (1966).

6. T.J. Lowi, *The End of Liberalism* 101–57 (1969); M. Freidman, *Capitalism and Freedom* 124–25 (1962).

7. R.H. Wiebe, *Businessmen and Reform: A Study of the Progressive Movement* 138–140 (1962).

8. R. Hofstadter, *supra* note 2, p. 252.

9. G. Kolko, *The Triumph of Conservatism* 228–47 (1963).

10. J.K. Galbraith, *American Capitalism: The Concept of Countervailing Power* 56 (1952).

11. H. Ickes, *The New Democracy* 77, 121 (1934).

12. W. Wilson, *The New Freedom* 120–22 (Prentice-Hall paperback ed., 1961).

13. The Antitrust Division of the Department of Justice may have slowed down somewhat since Thurman Arnold, but it remains an agency sufficiently devoted to its mission that its middle- and high-level civil service personnel are frequently *restrained* from taking a vigorous prosecutorial approach to their job by political appointees. See M. Green, *et al.*, *The Closed Enterprise System* (1972). The Securities and Exchange Commission is generally regarded as a successful enterprise whose basic orientation remains faithful to its mission. However, it is important to note that the SEC has compromised the public interest in serious respects, especially on the matter of fixed commission rates, in order to accomodate the interests of its regulatees. Furthermore, there are some indications that the SEC's capacity to retain a comparatively aggressive attitude toward fraud and deception in the marketing of securities rests on support from within the securities industry. Without public

confidence in the integrity of the securities markets, the stability
and profitability of Wall Street enterprises would no doubt be les-
sened, a fact presumably well understood by industry leaders.
When SEC initiatives are opposed actively by leading elements in
the securities industry, the Commission seems to have a difficult
time putting them across. *Cf.* W. Cary, *Politics and the Regulatory
Agencies* 90–122 (1967).

14. The President's Advisory Council on Executive Reorganization,
    *A New Regulatory Framework: Report on Selected Regulatory
    Agencies* 30 (1971). Hereafter cited as *Ash Council Report.*)

15. M. Bernstein, *supra* note 4. The following critique of the concept
    of Presidential control of regulation is based on sections of a re-
    port prepared by the Author and Joseph Onek for the Center for
    Law and Social Policy in May 1971 and submitted to the White
    House as a comment on the *Ash Council Report*. A revised ver-
    sion of that report appears in 57 *Va. L. Rev.* 1069 (1971).

In the discussion that follows, and in the rest of the present
essay, confusion may arise about my use of the term "the public
interest." In order to avoid that possibility I would like to refer to
two paragraphs from the text of the earlier report:

. . . It is necessary to distinguish two definitions of the ubiquitous
term "public interest." As former FTC Commissioner Philip
Elman has pointed out, the term is most often used in a strong or
substantive sense, frequently as an actual decisional standard in
regulatory statutes and decisions. When thus used, "public interest"
may be equated with "the public good" or "the national welfare,"
and refers to the result an agency ought to reach regarding the
merits of a controversy; it means the correct decision or the right
answer. There is, of course, no litmus test to determine whether a
particular agency decision promotes the public interest in this
sense of the term. The industry view of a particular issue may be in
the public interest as well as its own interest. Proponents of environmental beauty, for example, who wish to prohibit power companies from building new plants or stringing new lines above
ground, believe that their position represents the public interest;
but their triumph will mean higher utility rates, lower power
availability, and perhaps even more pollution for the urban public.
Under these circumstances, who can say which view is really in the
public interest?

Although the environmentalist view of such matters is not necessarily coincident with the public interest, in the substantive sense
of the term, environmentalists are frequently called "public interest
representatives" when they appear before administrative agencies.

Representative of consumer, minority, taxpayer, and other public groups often receive the same compliment. People who apply the public interest label in this manner are not wrong, but they are using the term "public interest" in a sense different from its strong or substantive meaning. They are using it to refer to important, but not necessarily correct, points of view which do not enjoy the sponsorship of an industry or other well-organized constituency, and which as a result are not frequently represented in the regulatory process. In this article, when referring to the need for agencies to be responsive to the public interest, we will be using the term in this second, weaker sense.

16. J. Landis, *Report on Regulatory Agencies to the President-elect* (1960).
17. P. Elman, "A Modest Proposal for Radical Reform," 56 *A.B.A.J.* 1045 (1970).
18. *Ash Council Report* at 30.
19. House Committee on Government Operations, *Deficiencies in Administration of Federal Insecticide, Fungicide, and Rodenticide Act* 13 (1969).
20. See the section of this essay entitled, "Can Regulation Ever Work?" *infra.*
21. The argument presented in the preceding two paragraphs is developed in similar terms in two articles for *The New Republic*, the first written for the September 26, 1970 issue and the second for the May 29, 1971 issue.
22. For a review of the efforts to establish federal incorporation during the Progressive Era, as well as references to other primary and secondary sources, see G. Kolko, *supra* note 9, especially at 132–38, 176–77; *cf.* W. Wilson, *supra* note 12, Chap. 9.
23. *See* sources cited in notes 4 and 5 *supra.*
24. W.G. Shepherd, "Communications: Regulation, Innovation, and the Changing Margin of Competition," in W. Capron, ed., *Technological Change in the Regulated Industries* (1971); P. Samuelson, *Economics* (8th ed. 1971).
25. See M. Green, *et al., supra* note 13, at 104–105 (mimeograph edition, 1971).
26. 359 F.2d 994, 1003–04 (D.C. Cir. 1966).
27. The Department of Consumer Affairs of the City of New York, where I served as General Counsel during 1969 and 1970, succeeded in obtaining from an extremely consumer-minded City Council a statute which may enable the Department to use unclaimed revenues collected in mass restitution lawsuits brought by the City. However, it was not contemplated at the time, nor has it turned out to be the case, that this authority could practicably

be turned into a source of funds to finance the agency's operations. See P. Schrag, "On Her Majesty's Secret Service: Protecting the Consumer In New York City," 80 *Yale L.J.* 1529 (1971).

28. Regrettably, the 1970 version of the Consumer Agency included this requirement, but it was dropped from the bill that passed the House (and will almost surely pass the Senate) in 1971 (perhaps to ensure its safe passage through Representative Holifield's House Committee on Government Operations).

XIV. Public Enterprise (Shepherd)

1. American economists have quietly let the whole topic fade, hardly mentioning it as a public policy toward business. See Richard E. Caves, "Industrial Organization and Public Policy," a chapter in the survey volume, Nancy Ruggles (ed.), *Economics*, Social Science Research Council, 1970; L.W. Weiss, *Case Studies in American Industry*, (2nd ed., 1971) last chapter; and F.M. Scherer, *Industrial Market Structure and Economic Performance* (1970). By contrast, public ownership is treated extensively, though not analytically, in successive editions of the late Clair Wilcox's *Public Policies Toward Business*, (4th ed., 1971). My own little book, *Economic Performance Under Public Enterprise: British Fuel and Power*, (1965), is virtually the only monograph in the area.

2. See C. Wilcox, *op. cit.*; W.A. Robson, *Nationalised Industry and Public Ownership* (1960); *Annals of Collective Economy*, annual surveys. These survey the old-style public enterprises and are therefore incomplete. Yet they are useful beginnings.

3. By "public control" I mean constraints responsive to the general public interest, as distinct from special-interest capture of specific programs. The distinction is critical, because programs are often captured and manipulated to benefit narrow, unneedy groups and with inefficient results.

4. Throughout I will assume that progressivity is socially preferable to regressivity. This seems a reasonable view in the present range of possible changes. I would be willing to defend it as a general proposition, also, against regressivity as a general goal.

5. I am presently developing these issues in depth in a monograph about policy choices toward market power. There are hints of them in Mark Green, *et al.*, *The Closed Enterprise System*, (1972).

6. See P.O. Steiner, *Public Expenditure Budgeting*, Brookings Institute, 1969, and references therein. This is much the same as "program planning and budgeting" (PPB) now common in the federal government but often poorly done.

7. The enormous scope and variety of such risk-guarantee programs in the U.S. is shown in "The Economics of Federal Subsidy Programs," Staff Study, Joint Economic Committee, U.S. Congress, January 1972.

8. See W.L. Hansen and B.A. Weisbrod, *Benefits, Costs and Finance of Public Higher Education* (1969); and W.J. Baumol and W. Bowen, *Performing Arts—The Economic Dilemma* (1966).

9. President's Commission on Law Enforcement and Administration of Justice, *Crime and Its Impact—An Assessment*, Task Force Report, U.S. Government Printing Office, 1967.

10. See Robson, *supra* note 2; M. Shanks (ed.), *Lessons of Public Enterprise* (1963); W.G. Shepherd, *supra* note 1.

11. W.G. Shepherd, "Alternatives for Public Expenditure," in R.E. Caves and Associates, *Britain's Economic Prospects*, Brookings Institute (1968).

12. See J. Hughes, chap. 7 in Shanks (ed.), *supra* note 1.

13. See, for example, Michael Harrington, "Whatever Happened to Socialism?" *Harper's*, February 1970, pp. 99–105.

14. W.G. Shepherd, "Residence Expansion in British Telephones," *Journal of Industrial Economics*, 1966, pp. 263–74.

15. *See* W.G. Shepherd and T.G. Gies (eds.), *Utility Regulation* (1966); A.E. Kahn, *The Economics of Regulation*, Vol. 2 (1971).

16. See Caves, (ed.), *supra* note 1, chap. 9 and references there, especially the Sainsbury Committee; Senate Subcommittee on Antitrust and Monopoly, *Report on Administered Prices, Drugs,* 87th Cong., 1st Sess., Report No. 448, U.S. Government Printing Office, 1961; M.J. Peck and F.M. Scherer, *The Weapons Acquisition Process* (1962).

17. One notable sector is utilities, where I would provisionally recommend a withdrawal of public resources, with regulation to be revised as follows: all franchises renewable (and cancellable) with five years notice, maximum opening of markets to entry, a graduated excess profits tax up to 90 percent, and floating (unregulated) "permitted" rates of return.

18. See *Electric Power and Government Policy* (1948) and Wilcox, *supra* note 1, chap. 21, 22.

19. M.V. Posner and S.J. Woolf, *Italian Public Enterprise* (1967); and annual reports of the Industrial Reorganization Corporation, London.

20. W.G. Shepherd, "The Elements of Market Structure," *Review of Economics and Statistics*, 1972, pp. 25–37, and "Estimated Yields from Reducing Market Power" (mimeograph), Ann Arbor, 1971.

21. The one contemporary analysis is W.C. Merrill and N. Schneider, "Government Firms in Oligopoly Industries," *Quarterly Journal of Economics*, 1966, pp. 400–12.

22. See C. Kaysen and D.F. Turner, *Antitrust Policy, A Legal and Economic Analysis* (1959); Shepherd, *supra* note 1.

23. See Wilcox, *supra* note 1, Shepherd and Gies (ed.), *supra* note 15; M.H. Bernstein, *Regulating Business by Independent Commission* (1955); Kahn, *supra* note 15.

24. On the discrimination coefficient and related issues, see G.S. Becker, *The Economics of Discrimination*, (1957); L. Thurow, *Poverty and Discrimination* (1968); W.S. Comanor, "Racial Discrimination in American Industry," Technical Report; and W.G. Shepherd and Sharon G. Levin, "Large Firm Employment Policies Toward Blacks and Women," (mimeograph), Ann Arbor, 1971. My own recent research generates a precise basis for setting such a tax scheme for hundreds of large firms, banks and utilities.

25. Hansen and Weisbrod, *supra* note 8.

26. See especially G.S. Becker, "Crime and Punishment: An Economic Approach," *Journal of Political Economy*, 1968, pp. 169–217; President's Commission on Law Enforcement and Administration of Justice, *Task Force Report: Corrections*, U.S. Government Printing Office, 1967; and references cited in both of those sources.

BIBLIOGRAPHY

I. On the Economic Image of Corporate Enterprise (Galbraith)

R. Barber, *The American Corporation* (1970).
A. Berle, *The Twentieth Century Capitalist Revolution* (1954).
A. Berle and G. Means, *The Modern Corporation and Private Property* (Rev. Ed. 1968).
P. Drucker, *The Concept of the Corporation* (1964).
M. Friedman, *Capitalism and Freedom* (1962).
J. K. Galbraith, *American Capitalism* (1956).
J. K. Galbraith, *The New Industrial State* (1967).
W. Hamilton, *The Politics of Industry* (1957).
F. V. Hayek, *The Road to Serfdom* (1944).
G. Means, *The Corporate Revolution in America* (1962).
The Public Interest, *Capitalism Today* (Fall, 1970).
M. Reagan, *The Managed Economy* (1963).
B. Rice, *The C5-A Scandal* (1971).
J. Schumpeter, *Capitalism, Socialism and Democracy* (1942).

II. Governing the Giant Corporation (Dahl)

G. Bannock, *The Juggernauts* (1971).
R. Barber, *The American Corporation* (1970).
P. Blumberg, *Industrial Democracy: The Sociology of Participation* (1969).
H. A. Clegg, *A New Approach to Industrial Democracy* (1960).
M. Derber, *The American Idea of Industrial Democracy, 1865–1965* (1970).
S. Melman, *Decision-Making and Productivity* (1958).
E. Rheman, *Industrial Democracy and Industrial Management* (1968).
A. Sturmthal, *Workers Councils* (1964).
R. Townsend, *Up the Organization!* (1970).
Y. Vanek, *The General Theory of Labor Managed Market Economies* (1970).
G. Wootton, *Workers, Unions and the State* (1966).

III. The Politics of Corporate Power (Harris)

E. Barfield, *Political Influence* (1961).

W. Carey, *Politics and the Regulatory Agencies* (1967).

J. Daughen and P. Binzen, *The Wreck of the Penn Central* (1971).

R. Engler, *The Politics of Oil* (1960).

E. Epstein, *The Corporation in American Politics* (1969).

J. Esposito and L. Silverman, *Vanishing Air* (1970).

M. Green, B. Moore, B. Wasserstein, *The Closed Enterprise System* (1972).

W. Hamilton, *The Politics of Industry* (1957).

R. Heilbroner, *et al.*, *In the Name of Profit* (1972).

H. S. Kariel, *The Decline of American Pluralism* (1961).

E. Latham, *The Group Basis of Politics: A Study in Bosing-Point Legislation* (1952).

F. Lundberg, *The Rich and the Superrich* (1968).

C. W. Mills, *The Power Elite* (1956).

M. Mintz and J. Cohen, *America, Inc.* (1971).

B. Nossiter, *The Mythmakers* (1964).

S. P. Sethi, *Up Against the Corporate Wall* (1971).

I. Tarbell, *The History of the Standard Oil Company* (1904).

J. Turner, *The Chemical Feast* (1970).

IV. The Corporation and the Community (Green)

I. Berg (ed.), *The Business of America* (1968).

R. Dahl, *Who Governs?* (1962).

D'Antonio and Ehrlich (eds.), *Power and Democracy in America* (1961).

J. Fallows, *The Water Lords* (1971).

R. Fellmeth, *Politics of Land* (1972).

M. Heald, *The Social Responsibilities of Business* (1970).

R. Heilbroner, *et al.*, *In the Name of Profit* (1972).

F. Hunter, *Community Power Structure* (1953).

Janowitz and Enlan (eds.), *Community Political Systems* (1961).

P. Jones, *The Consumer Society* (1965).

E. Kefauver and I. Till, *In a Few Hands* (1965).

D. Leinsdorf, *Citibank: The Nader Report on First National City Bank* (report) (1971).

R. Lynd and H. Lynd, *Middletown* (1929).

J. Newfield and J. Greenfield, *The Populist Manifesto* (1972).

J. Phelan and R. Posen, *The Company State* (1973).

San Francisco Bay Guardian, *The Ultimate Highrise—San Francisco's Mad Rush Toward the Sky* (1972).

"Small Business and Civic Welfare," Report of the Smaller War Plants

Corporation to the Special Committee to Study Problems of American Small Business, U.S. Senate, 79th Cong., 2nd Sess., Doc. #135 (1946).

"Small Business and the Community—A Study in Central Valley of California on Effects of Scale of Farm Operations," Report of the Special Committee to Study Problems of American Small Business, U.S. Senate, 79th Cong., 2nd Sess., Comm. Prout #13 (1946).

J. Udell, *Social and Economic Consequences of the Merger Movement in Wisconsin* (1969).

W. Whyte (ed.), *Capitalism and Freedom* (1962).

V. The Case for Federal Chartering (Nader)

J. Cadman, *The Corporation in New Jersey* (1949).

Daedalus, Journal of the America Academy of Arts and Sciences, *Perspectives on Business* (Winter, 1969).

M. Dodd, *American Business Corporations till 1860* (1954).

R. Eells, *The Government of Corporations* (1962).

Federal Trade Commission, *Report on Utility Corporations*, No. 69A (Sept. 15, 1934).

A. Hacker (ed.), *The Corporation Takeover* (1964).

H. Henn, *Corporations* (1961).

W. Hurst, *The Legitimacy of the Business Corporation* (1970).

R. C. Larcom, *The Delaware Corporation* (1937).

G. Leinwand, *A History of the United States Federal Bureau of Corporation (1903–1914)* (doctoral dissertation, New York University) (1962).

E. S. Mason (ed.), *The Corporation in Modern Society* (1959).

M. Mintz and J. Cohen, *America, Inc.* (1971).

R. Nader, P. Petkas, K. Blackwell, *Whistle Blowing* (1972).

C. Peters and T. Branch, *Blowing the Whistle* (1972).

J. Phelan and R. Pozen, *The Company State* (1972).

VI. Corporate Democracy:
Nice Work if You Can Get It (Flynn)

A. Berle, Jr., *Power Without Property* (1959).

A. Berle, Jr., *The Twentieth Century Capitalist Revolution* (1954).

A. Berle, Jr., and G. Means, *The Modern Corporation and Private Property* (rev. ed. 1968).

R. Dahl, *After the Revolution?* (1970).

A. Hacker (ed.), *The Corporation Take-Over* (1964).

W. Hurst, *The Legitimacy of the Business Corporation* (1970).

J. A. Livingston, *The American Stockholder* (1958).

J. Kolaja, *Workers Councils: The Yugoslav Experience* (1966).
E. S. Mason (ed.), *The Corporation in Modern Society* (1959).
M. Newcomer, *The Big Business Executive* (1955).
M. Rasken, *Being and Doing* (1971).
S.E.C., *Institutional Investor Study* (1971).
T.N.E.C. Monograph No. 11, *Bureaucracy and Trusteeship in Large Corporations* (1940).

VII. Corporate Secrecy vs. Corporate Disclosure (Mueller)

H. W. Bevis, *Corporate Financial Reporting in a Competitive Economy* (1965).
J. M. Blair, *Economic Concentration* (1972) (esp. chap. 22).
Concentration of Economic Power, Part 5, Concentration and Divisional Reporting, Hearings before the Subcommittee on Antitrust and Monopoly of the Committee on the Judiciary, U.S. Senate, 89th Cong., 2nd. Sess. (1966).
Economic Concentration, Part 8, The Conglomerate Merger Problem, Hearings before the Subcommittee on Antitrust and Monopoly of the Committee on the Judiciary, U.S. Senate (1969, 1970).
Federal Trade Commission, *Economic Report on Corporate Mergers* (1969).
Federal Trade Commission, *Economic Report: The Quality of Data as a Factor in Analyses of Structure Performance Relationships* (1971).
J. B. Imel, *Structure-Profit Relationships in the Food Processing Sector* (Ph.D. Dissertation, University of Wisconsin) (1971).
Investigation of Conglomerate Corporations, A Report by the Staff of the Antitrust Subcommittee of the Committee on the Judiciary, House of Representatives, 92d Cong., 1st Sess. (1971).
R. K. Mautz, *Financial Reporting by Diversified Companies* (1968).
Planning, Regulation and Competition: Automobile Industry—1968, Hearings before Subcommittee of the Select Committee on Small Business, U.S. Senate, 90th Cong., 2nd Sess. (1968).
A. Rappaport, P.A. Firman, and S.A. Zeff (ed.) *Public Reporting by Conglomerates* (1968).
A. Rappaport and E. Lerner, *A Framework for Financial Reporting by Diversified Companies.* National Association of Accountants (1969).
A. Rappaport and Levsine (ed.) *Corporate Financial Reporting* (1972).
Role of Giant Corporations in the American and World Economies, Parts I and Ia, Automobile Industry—1969, Hearings before the Subcommittee on Monopoly of the Select Committee on Small Business, U.S. Senate, 91st Cong., 1st Sess. (1969).
Role of Giant Corporations in the American and World Economies, Part 2, Corporate Secrecy—Overviews, Hearings before the Subcom-

mittee on Monopoly of the Select Committee on Small Business, United States Senate, 92 Cong., 1st Sess. (1971).

R. A. Smith, *Corporations in Crisis* (1963).

VIII. The Antitrust Alternative (Adams)

W. Adams (ed.), *The Structure of American Industry* (4th ed. 1971).

W. Adams and H. M. Gray, *Monopoly in America: The Government as Promoter* (1955).

J. M. Blair, *Economic Concentration* (1972).

R. Caves, *American Industry: Structure, Conduct, Performance* (1972).

J. B. Dirlam and A. E. Kahn, *The Law and Economics of Fair Competition: An Appraisal of Antitrust Policy* (1954).

C. Edward, *Maintaining Competition* (1964 Ed.).

M. Friedman, *Capitalism and Freedom* (1962).

J. K. Galbraith, *American Capitalism: The Concept of Countervailing Power* (1952).

J. K. Galbraith, *The New Industrial State* (1967).

M. Green, *et al., The Closed Enterprise System* (1972).

E. S. Mansfield, *Monopoly Power and Economic Performance* (1964).

F. M. Scherer, *Industrial Market Structure and Economic Performance* (1970).

W. G. Shepherd, *Market Power and Economic Welfare* (1970).

G. W. Stocking and M. W. Watkins, *Cartels in Action* (1946).

H. Thorelli, *The Federal Antitrust Policy* (1954).

IX. Corporate Social Responsibility: A Shell Game for the Seventies? (Henning)

R. J. Barber, *The American Corporation* (1970).

A. A. Berle, Jr., *Power Without Property* (1959).

A. A. Berle, Jr., and G. Means, *The Modern Corporation and Private Property* (1932).

J. K. Brown and S. Lusterman, *Business and the Development of Ghetto Enterprise* (1971).

J. Cohn, *The Conscience of the Corporations* (1971).

Committee on Economic Development, *Social Responsibilities of Business Corporations* (1971).

R. A. Dahl, *After the Revolution?* (1970).

O. Goddis, *Corporate Accountability: For What and to Whom Must the Manager Answer?* (1964).

G. Goyder, *The Responsible Company* (1961).

A. O. Hirschman, *Exit Voice & Loyalty: Responses to Decline in Firms, Organizations and States* (1970).

J. W. Hurst, *The Legitimacy of the Business Corporation, 1780–1970* (1970).

G. Kolko, *The Triumph of Conservatism: A Reinterpretation of American History, 1900–1916* (1963).

T. J. Lowi, *The End of Liberalism: Ideology, Policy, and the Crisis of Public Authority* (1969).

E. S. Mason (ed.), *The Corporation in Modern Society* (1959) (esp. Foreword, Introduction, Chaps. 2, 3, 4, 5, 10 and 11.)

G. McConnell, *Private Power and American Democracy* (1966).

J. Ridgeway, *The Closed Corporation: American Universities in Crisis* (1968).

J. Ridgeway, *The Politics of Ecology* (1970) (chaps. 3–6).

H. J. Spiro, *Responsibility in Government: Theory and Practice* (1969).

R. Townsend, *Up the Organization!* (1970).

X. Citizen Counteraction? (Hacker)

E. Epstein, *The Corporation in American Politics*, (1969).

D. Grunewald & H. Bass, *Public Policy and the Modern Corporation* (1966).

A. Hacker, *The End of the American Era* (1971).

K. Marx, *Capital. Vol. III: The Process of Capitalist Production* (1909).

G. McConnell, *Private Power and American Democracy* (1966).

R. Miliband, *The State in Capitalist Society* (1969).

M. Mintz and J. Cohen, *America, Inc.* (1971).

R. Nader and D. Ross, *Action for a Change: A Student's Manual for Public Interest Organizing* (1971).

M. Reagan, *The Managed Economy* (1963).

A. Shonfield, *Modern Capitalism* (1965).

XI. Deterring Corporate Crime (Geis)

F. Cook, *The Corrupted Land: The Social Morality of Modern America* (1966).

H. Edelhertz, *The Nature, Impact and Prosecution of White-Collar Crime*, Washington, D.C.: Law Enforcement Assistance Administration, U.S. Department of Justice. (1970).

J. Fuller, *The Gentleman Conspirators: The Story of Price-Fixers in the Electrical Industry* (1962).

G. Geis (ed.), *White-Collar Criminal: The Offender in Business and the Professions* (1968).

W. Goodman, *All Honorable Men: Corruption and Compromise in American Life* (1963).

P. Hadlick, *Criminal Prosecution Under the Sherman Antitrust Act* (1939).

J. Herling, *The Great Price Conspiracy: The Story of the Antitrust Violations in the Electrical Industry* (1962).

M. Josephson, *The Robber Barons: The Great American Capitalists, 1861–1901* (1934).

L. Leigh, *The Criminal Liability of Corporations in English Law* (1969).

M. Mintz and J. Cohen, *America, Inc.* (1971).

E. Ross, *Sin and Society: An Analysis of Latter-Day Iniquity* (1907).

E. H. Sutherland, *White Collar Crime* (1949).

D. Tompkins, *White-Collar Crime—A Bibliography* (1967).

C. Walton and F. Cleveland, Jr., *Corporations on Trial: The Electrical Cases* (1964).

W. Zirpins and Q. Terstegen, *Wirtschafts Kriminalität* (1963).

XII. Courts and Corporate Accountability (Miller)

E. R. Aranow, *Proxy Contests for Corporate Control* (1968).

D. V. Austin, *Proxy Contests and Corporate Reform* (1965).

J. Baum and N. B. Stiles, *Silent Partners: Institutional Investors and Corporate Control* (1965).

L. D. Brandeis, O. K. Fraenkel, (eds.), *Curse of Bigness; Miscellaneous Papers* (1965).

W. L. Cary, *Cases and Materials on Corporations*, 4th ed. (1969).

Z. Cavith, *Business Organizations* (1963).

J. S. Davis, *Essays in the Earlier History of American Corporations* (1917).

W. M. Fletcher, *Cyclopedia of the Law of Private Corporations* (1933–57).

P. O. Gaddis, *Corporate Accountability: For What and to Whom Must the Manager Answer?* (1964).

G. D. Hornstein, *Corporation Law and Practice* (1959).

N. D. Lattin and Richard W. Jennings, *Cases and Materials on Corporations*, 4th ed. (1968).

E. R. Latty and George T. Frampton, *Basic Business Associations: Cases, Text and Problems* (1963).

M. L. Lindahl and W. A. Carter, *Corporate Concentration and Public Policy*, 3d ed. (1959).

J. A. Livingston, *The American Stockholder* (1958).

L. Loss, *Securities Regulation* (1961).

A. Miller, *The Supreme Court and American Capitalism* (1968).

F. H. O'Neal, *Close Corporations: Law and Practice* (1958).

C. C. Walton and F. W. Cleveland, *Corporations on Trial: The Electric Cases* (1964).

D. Votaw, *Modern Corporations* (1965).

XIII. Halfway up from Liberalism: Government Regulation (Lazarus)

M. Bernstein, *Regulating Business by Independent Commission* (1955).

W. Capron, *Technological Change in Regulated Industries* (1971).

Fainsod, Gordon, and Palamountain, *Government and the American Economy* (3d. 1959).

R. Fellmeth, *The Interstate Commerce Omission* (1970).

M. Friedman, *Capitalism and Freedom* (1962).

J. K. Galbraith, *American Capitalism: The Concept of Countervailing Power* (1952).

R. Hofstadter, *The Age of Reform* (1955).

W. A. Jordan, *Airline Regulation in America* (1970).

A. Kahn, *The Economics of Regulation I and II* (1970 and 1971).

L. Kohlmeier, *The Regulators* (1970).

G. Kolko, *The Triumph of Conservatism* (1963).

G. Kolko, *Railroads and Regulation, 1877–1916* (1965).

J. Landis, *Report on Regulatory Agencies to the President-elect* (1960).

J. Larson (ed.), *The Regulated Businessman* (1966).

T. J. Lowi, *The End of Liberalism* (1969).

P. MacAvoy, *The Crisis of the Regulatory Commissions* (1970).

J. R. Meyer, M. J. Peck, J. Stenason, C. Zwick, *The Economics of Competition in the Transportation Industries* (1959).

R. Noll, *Reforming Regulation* (1972).

The President's Advisory Council on Executive Reorganization, *A New Regulatory Framework: Report on Selected Regulatory Agencies* 30 (1971).

A. M. Schlesinger, Jr., *The Vital Center* (1962).

J. L. Sharfman, *The Interstate Commerce Commission* (multivolume) (1931–1937).

R. H. Wiebe, Businessmen and Reform: *A Study of the Progressive Movement* (1962).

W. Wilson, *The New Freedom* (1961).

XIV. Public Enterprise (Shepherd)

M. Baratz, *The Economics of the Postal Service* (1957).

W. Baum, *The French Economy and the State* (1958) (esp. part III).

W. Baumol and W. Bowen, *Performing Arts—The Economic Dilemma* (1965).

R. Caves, *Britain's Economic Prospects* (1968) (esp. chap. 9).

C. Crosland, *The Future of Socialism* (1956).

D. Donnison, *The Government of Housing* (1967).

Einaudi, Mario, M. Bye, E. Rossi, *Nationalization in France and Italy* (1955).

C. Foster, *The Transport Problem* (1963).

L. Gordon, *The Public Corporation in Great Britain* (1938).

W. Haynes, *Nationalization in Practice: The British Coal Industry* (1953).

H. Klarman, *The Economics of Health* (1965).

A. Lerner, *The Economics of Control* (1944).

A. Lindsay, *Socialized Medicine in England and Wales* (1962).

I. Little, *The Price of Fuel* (1953).

A. Merrett and A. Sykes, *Housing, Development and Finance* (1965).

A. Mevitt, (ed.), *The Economic Problems of Housing* (1967).

M. Posner and S. Woolf, *Italian Public Enterprise* (1967)

President's Commission on Law Enforcement and Administration of Justice, *Task Force Reports on: The Courts; Corrections; and Assessment of Crime* (1967).

W. Robson, *Problems of Nationalized Industry* (1952).

Sainsbury Committee (Committee of Enquiry into the Relationship of the Pharmaceutical Industry with the National Health Service), *Report* (1967).

Select Committee on the Nationalised Industries, *Reports on Public Corporations* (National Coal Board, British Railways, Electricity Council, Gas Council, and others) (since 1955).

M. Shanks (ed.), *The Lessons of Public Enterprise* (1963).

W. Shepherd, *Economic Performance Under Public Ownership* (1965).

H. Somers and A. Somers, *Doctors, Patients and Health Insurance* (1961).

INDEX